CANADA'S

UFOS:

DECLASSIFIED

CANADA'S
UFOS:
DECLASSIFIED

CHRIS A. RUTKOWSKI

Foreword by MJ Banias

www.augustnightpress.com

For Donna, the best wife in the galaxy, and I should know.

ABOUT THE AUTHOR

~

Chris Rutkowski is a Canadian science writer and educator with degrees in astronomy and education. Since the mid-1970s, he's also been studying reports of UFOs and other unusual phenomena, writing about his investigations and research in various media.

He has nine published books on UFOs and related issues, including *Unnatural History* (1993), *Abductions and Aliens* (1999), *A World of UFOs* (2008), the children's book *I Saw It Too!* (2009), *The Big Book of UFOs* (2010) and is co-author of *When They Appeared* (2017), written with Stan Michalak.

He has appeared on numerous radio programs, podcasts and documentary TV series, including Unsolved Mysteries, UFO Hunters, Sightings, Eye2thesky, Night Time Podcast, Dark Poutine, The Paracast, Discovery's Close Encounters, NASA's Unexplained Mysteries, and A&E's The Unexplained.

He is past president of both the Winnipeg Science Fiction Society and the Winnipeg Centre of the Royal Astronomical Society of Canada.

He is administrator of several UFO-related Facebook groups, including UFO UpDates, a forum continuing the ground breaking work of famed journalist Errol Bruce-Knapp, which began in 1996.

He blogs about UFOs and related issues at: http://uforum.blogspot.com and he publishes an annual study of UFO reports in Canada at: http://canadianuforeport.com

CONTENTS

~

ACKNOWLEDGMENTS

~

The Warren Smith UFO photographs are published with the permission of the Board of Regents of the University of Colorado.

Special thanks to Patrick Osborne, Rights and Licensing Specialist, Copyright Services, Public Services Branch, Library and Archives Canada.

Library and Archives Canada has allowed the publication of many documents identified as part of the NRC UFO Files.

Thank you to Curt Collins for his comments, patience and insight when I kept asking him questions.

Thank you to Jan Aldrich for help in sourcing material.

Kudos and thanks to Matthew Hayes for his excellent doctoral thesis on the Canadian government's UFO files, and for his sharing of data.

Thanks to Ashley Kircher, my assistant extraordinaire, for her opinions and comments.

To my colleague and webmaster Geoff Dittman, whose analytics are invaluable.

To Sean "Danger" Moore, for matters of grammar and punctuation.

Thanks to Debra and Elwin Giesbrecht, for moral support. To Robbie Graham at August Night and Jonathan Beecher at White Crow for considering this book for publication and Robbie's effort in getting *Canada's UFOs: Declassified* into print. My appreciation also goes to MJ Banias for his kind words in the Foreword.

FOREWORD

~

For half a century, UFOs have not only traversed our skies but occupied our popular culture. They've graced our cinemas, TV screens, comic books, and even our lunch boxes. Moreover, UFOs have occupied our newspaper headlines and have been the subject of hot debate between believers and skeptics.

For those who study UFOs, often called "ufologists," the search for truth has been mired in a complicated mix of objective data points, subjective witness testimony, and a complex array of mythology that ranges from tales of dead aliens in deep bunkers, to deep-state conspiracy theories. This bizarre combination of factors took root in a conspiracy-rich post-war America, and ufologists have been attempting to unravel the fiction from the facts regarding UFOs ever since.

Canada, much like America, has its fair share of curious UFO myths. Some of these are discussed in this book. However, unlike America, the UFO topic in Canada is much less culturally potent. There is a social silence around the subject matter. Perhaps it is because Canadians are a little more reserved, or maybe we value the idea that certain subjects are discussed quietly outside the earshot of general public discourse. Even though Canadians are a little less likely to open up about their interests or experiences concerning UFOs, the country does have a significant part to play in the subject.

Rutkowski, whom I first met at a bar in Winnipeg's iconic Forks Market, is undoubtedly Canada's most exemplary researcher concerning UFOs. Unlike many of his contemporaries, he is not one to speculate or engage in frivolous fits of excitement concerning the latest fad in ufological discourse. In doing research for an article I wrote for Canada's national newspaper, *The Globe and Mail*, in August 2020, I dug deeply into Canadian UFO reports made by commercial and military pilots. As I tracked down various reports and the individuals who filed them, either at Transport Canada or at the Department of National Defence, many of them referred me to "a guy from Manitoba." There would then be a pause, followed by: "Chris... something. We send all this stuff to him."

When it comes to UFOs in Canada, oddly, all roads seem to lead to Chris Rutkowski.

Reflecting upon this, Rutkowski is genuinely the only person in Canada who could write this book. No one knows more about the strange and bizarre history the Canadian government has had with UFOs.

In my brief time researching UFOs in Canada, I have concluded that the government, apart from a tiny handful of Canadian politicians, wants no part of the UFO subject. For an authentic taste of the Canadian bureaucratic system, asking various government agencies about UFOs will place the petitioner into the slowest and most arduous version of "Hot Potato" ever conceived. Rutkowski has been playing this game for a long time, and he seems to have mastered it in his decades-long research into the subject. This book, *Canada's UFOs: Declassified*, is able to free the reader from the bureaucratic nonsense and allows us access to the most exciting and compelling UFO events in Canada's history.

These are all authentic reports that range from the mundane to the incredibly unusual. Many of these cases were investigated by law enforcement, the military, and even academic institutions. Some of these events were resolved with prosaic and straightforward explanations, but many remain mysteriously unexplained. In short, this book dives deeply into Canada's unusual and, at times, disquieting past with the UFO phenomenon.

UFOs may not be extraterrestrial spaceships, but, like ghosts, they do haunt Canada's history. Cabinets filled with old documents rest in federal government office basements across this nation that detail Canada's interactions with UFOs. Scores of rarely visited government websites, with a few simple keywords, open up an alien world of strange lights chasing commercial aircraft, air traffic control reports of anomalous radar tracks, and aviation incident reports that are eerie enough to make one rethink boarding an airplane.

UFOs will continue to be great mass media fodder to entertain audiences of terrible alien invasions. Many Canadians will continue to smirk when they read about UFOs on their favourite news website.

Ufologists will continue to debate over the merits of various cases, and believers and skeptics alike will continue their activism. However, in all that noise, this book points to Canada's silent UFO history. Rutkowski does not insult or berate. He does not try to convince his readers to believe, nor does he promote some crusade to force Canada to "disclose the truth" about UFOs. Instead, he brings his readers to those abandoned, locked filing cabinets and quiet corners of the internet, hands them a key, and says, "have fun."

—**MJ Banias**
Editor-in-Chief, *The Debrief*
Author, *The UFO People: A Curious Culture*

INTRODUCTION

~

Since 1947, the reality of flying saucers or UFOs has been hotly debated by fans, zealots, debunkers and scientists. Skeptics have been insistent that people who see UFOs are either mistaken or liars, whereas "true believers" are adamant that aliens are visiting Earth and interacting with its inhabitants.

While sightings of unidentified aerial objects had been reported long before 1947, that year marked what is considered the beginning of the UFO era. In June 1947, while piloting his small plane, Kenneth Arnold reported seeing several metallic disclike objects flying over mountains as they reflected the sun. He later described their flight as if they were saucers skimming or skipping across a lake, and media pounced on the visual image, labeling them "flying saucers."

Over the decades since then, millions of people around the world believe they have seen UFOs. Many of these have reported their sightings to civilian or government agencies of various countries, and several world governments have undertaken formal investigations of these reports. One motivation for such actions was an assumption that invasions actually may be occurring — not necessarily alien in nature, but at least by foreign powers of some kind.

In the USA, several military projects investigated UFO reports made by both enlisted and civilian witnesses. One prevailing theme among UFO fans is that some clandestine official or beyond-official body is controlling the release (or cover-up) of knowledge about alien visitation to denizens of Earth. This is usually called Disclosure (with a capital D), and many UFO experts, groups, and websites aver that any day now, the truth (or perhaps The Truth) about UFOs will be revealed to the public soon.

Adherents to Disclosure point to the release of UFO files by world governments such as the Ministry of Defence in Britain, the French space agency Centre National d'Études Spatiales (CNES), and even the Comité de Estudios de Fenómenos Aéreos Anómalos (CEFAA), a branch of the Chilean government. Recently, the US Navy itself sanctioned the release of some videos that appear to show jet pilots encountering UFOs off both the coasts of California and Florida, and the pilots themselves have been speaking openly about their encounters.

Also driving the belief in UFO cover-up was the revelation that the Pentagon had been conducting investigations into UFOs through the secret Advanced Aerospace Threat Identification Program (AATIP) between 2007 and 2012.[1] Further, it seems that a government-sponsored investigation into unidentified aerial phenomena (UAP) — the current and favoured term for UFOs — may be still underway in the USA. There's even a call today for a Congressional investigation or hearing into UFOs, although a similar a request was made by then-congressman Gerald Ford back in 1966, with no success.[2]

Despite all this hyperbole, UFO reports from military and official sources have been released or obtained for decades by diligent researchers poring through archives and filing Freedom of Information Act (FOIA) requests in the USA and Access to Information (AI) requests in Canada and other countries. It is likely that the slow uncovering of official UFO records is a matter of patient work by researchers and has little to do with a coordinated global effort by a secret group reminiscent of The Syndicate, the shadowy organization that was the foil of agents Mulder and Scully on the *X-Files*.

Canada has had its UFO projects as well, and files on these reports have been reviewed by researchers from time to time. I personally have viewed the physical records at Library and Archives Canada in Ottawa, and I have obtained UFO files it has made available to those interested in the subject. Over the years, these documents have been declassified from higher restrictions, sometimes even originally as high as Secret, but which are now available for perusal.

Some of the UFO cases within the files are downright mystifying. Most have obvious explanations. Others do not. A few are patently absurd.

Historically, these records are invaluable in demonstrating that many Canadians not only witnessed unusual objects in the sky (and on the ground) but that they were convinced their experiences were remarkable. So remarkable, in fact, that they willingly overcame their fear of ridicule and possible legal persecution from officials by reporting their sightings to the Canadian government.

If UFOs are not "real" and are only mistakes, hoaxes, or the result of wild imaginations, then these cases obviously document a human phenomenon that affects a large number of Canadians. In fact, polls have shown that about ten percent of all Canadians believe they have seen UFOs. That's enough on its own to suggest that the phenomenon deserves more scrutiny by the scientific community. If some UFO reports represent a real physical phenomenon such as charged electromagnetic fields, earthquake precursors, or physiological effects, then they deserve scientific attention too. If some reported UFOs are sightings of incursions into North American airspace by foreign manned or unmanned craft or devices, then that certainly would be extremely important to verify. And then there's that most commonly expressed proposal, having something to do with aliens...

I started going through the archived UFO files out of curiosity, wondering if there were any cases of interest. I knew that there were some detailed case reports on incidents such as the Falcon Lake case of 1967, about which I have recovered literally hundreds of pages of documents. Similarly, the Shag Harbour UFO crash, coincidentally also in 1967, is supported by official documents in the archives.

But what about the thousands of other UFO documents in the archives? Were there any other cases deserving of attention?

As it turned out, there were.

I invite you to journey with me on a tour of the UFO files contained within Library and Archives Canada (LAC) — at least, a small sampling of them. Barely scratching the surface of the mass of records, I have selected a collection of UFO reports that illustrate the kinds of objects seen by Canadians during about 1947 to 1980, the period covered by LAC's current digitization. Many more are expected to be available soon, not by a planned Disclosure but as funding and time allows.

I should note also that this overview of historical Canadian UFO cases is highly relevant to the current state of ufology. Some armchair ufologists could suggest that a study of "old" UFO cases isn't as important as research into those presently in the news or which occurred within the past few years. But since the nature of UFOs is still not well understood nor agreed upon with consensus, the mystery endures.

I would note that an examination of how UFO reports have been dealt with by a government is very relevant indeed, given that belief in Disclosure implies that in at least some way officialdom has been keeping its knowledge of UFOs secret or at least confidential. What has been found in Library and Archives Canada is no less than a treasure trove of UFO cases with better-than-average witnesses, and more-than-usual evidence of real events that occurred.

In addition to the UFO reports themselves, the documents in the archives give us insight into how the Canadian government went about studying UFOs, how it dealt with witnesses, and how it interacted with the public on the matter. Most amazing is how many of the UFO reports were made by military personnel, and how many of those did not have apparent explanations.

Actually, there are quite a few cases in this collection that defy simple explanation. They may not be proof that aliens have been visiting Canada, but they do show that the Great White North has seen its share of mysteries. I also acknowledge that alien visitation is only one popular explanation for UFO reports, and that the solution may be more psychological or sociological in nature.

My purpose for this book is neither to convince hardnosed skeptics that aliens are visiting Earth nor persuade dedicated believers that UFOs are not worth their time and talents. I simply wish to present a collection of actual documents detailing the sightings reported by Canadians as recorded in archival fonds. These cases were received and in many instances investigated in considerable detail by the official military or scientific bodies, and sometimes both.

In other words, these are not just anecdotes but matters of official record whereby civilian and enlisted individuals admitted seeing or encountering objects which defied their understanding. And I should add that I am including not just cases which are puzzling and seemingly without explanations, but also cases that can be or were explained, so that readers can get a better idea of the scope of UFO reports.

These, I suppose, are the real "X-Files" upon which much of pop culture versions of ufology are based. They are first-hand testimonies by people like you or I who appealed to authorities in the hope of receiving explanations. And there is also a documentation of how the cases were received, what was thought of the witnesses' stories, and who investigated them.

Here are Canada's UFOs: Declassified.

1

UFOS VS. THE CANADIAN
GOVERNMENT

~

A casual stroll through the digitized NRC UFO Files

Beginning in 1968, the National Research Council of Canada (NRC) acted as the investigating body of the Canadian government regarding UFO reports. It took over responsibility for these reports after much discussion within the Department of National Defence to relinquish the receipt and administration of them due to a view that flying saucers posed no danger to national security, thus echoing the position of the USA.

The general view of the NRC, in contrast, was that UFOs were probably a scientific matter rather than a military or security issue. This is not surprising, since the NRC is a scientific and ostensibly apolitical body. At the time, scientists within the NRC thought the public simply needed to be better educated that UFOs were not alien spacecraft. More importantly, since many flying saucer reports were explained as meteors and bolides, this presented meteor experts within the NRC's Herzberg Institute of Astrophysics with a unique opportunity. If enough

9

eyewitness reports of meteors could be obtained swiftly and efficiently, then it would be theoretically possible to triangulate their flight paths and locate meteorites on the ground—something valuable to science.

But to be able to get eyewitness accounts quickly and from across the vast expanse of Canada, the NRC needed many "feet on the ground." Fortunately, such resources already existed. The NRC formed a working arrangement with the Royal Canadian Mounted Police (RCMP) to investigate UFO reports on their behalf and send information on the reports to scientists at Herzberg in Ottawa. If enough UFO sightings were recorded for a specific meteor event, a meteorite could be recovered.

(This actually occurred, but only once. The combination of photographic tracking networks and the receipt of eyewitness reports combined for a significant meteorite find near Innisfree, Alberta on February 5, 1977.)

The trouble was that reported and received along with all the reports of meteors, fireballs, and bolides were incidents that were distinctly not astronomical in nature. Many cases involved detailed accounts of metallic disc-shaped objects seen or encountered at close range and behaving in ways that were very different from meteors and bolides. These cases became part of what became known as the "Non-Meteoric Sightings File" at the NRC.

All UFO reports initially went into this file, received from private citizens, civic police, the Department of National Defence, the Department of Transport, and the RCMP. At the end of each calendar year, the contents of the file was transferred to the Public Archives of Canada (which was renamed the National Archives of Canada in 1987 and in turn was merged with the National Library of Canada in 2004 to become Library and Archives Canada (LAC) in 2004).

Somewhat analogous to the image of a pop culture "UFO desk" of the USA depicted in the TV series *X-Files*, the Canadian version consisted of one dedicated administrative clerk in a small office in Herzberg, diligently taking teletypes off a printer, receiving and typing up UFO reports from phone calls and filing them in the top drawer of a single black filing cabinet. If a report did not seem to be a meteor, it was for the most part ignored. Very few cases were afforded any kind of significant investigations, especially those that involved close encounters with unusual crafts.

The prevailing view was that people reporting UFOs were in general unaware of astronomical objects or were otherwise poor and unreliable observers who could not tell a star from a saucer. Researchers at the NRC sometimes — but not often — took it upon themselves to patiently explain why witnesses had misidentified natural or conventional objects, often getting into lengthy exchanges of correspondence with them over weeks or months.

In 1995, due to budget restraint and the lack of continuing research in meteoritics at the NRC as a result of retirements, deaths and other staff changes (and a major shift in scientific direction following the creation of the Canadian Space Agency in 1990), the NRC announced it would no longer be accepting UFO reports as a matter of course. As a consequence, RCMP investigation into reports of UFOs and fireballs for the NRC summarily ceased.

However, also in 1995, I was at Herzberg in Ottawa and had been having a discussion with an NRC staff member when the subject of UFOs came up and the cessation of the Non-Meteoric Sightings File was mentioned. In conversation, I casually suggested that I could take over receipt of UFO reports if necessary. I had zero expectation that this would actually occur.

But my conversation in 1995 was the catalyst for when, in the year 2000, I began receiving UFO reports made to Canadian agencies. My group of associates, whom with me comprised Ufology Research of Manitoba, could now take a true yearly snapshot of UFO reports across Canada, with sources including civilian groups, cases directly reported to us, and the addition of sightings reported to official agencies. Our annual Canadian UFO Survey became even more comprehensive. We soon were renamed simply Ufology Research to reflect a broader national perspective.

Canadian UFO research was further bolstered in 2005 when more than 9,500 UFO reports and related documents that had been digitized by LAC were made available online. In 2019, Canadian studies scholar Matthew Hayes at Trent University completed his doctoral thesis on the Canadian government's investigations regarding UFOs. He included an excellent overview of the LAC digitization of the UFO files:

> In 2005, Library and Archives Canada released a virtual exhibition called "Canada's UFOs: The Search for the Unknown." The online exhibition allows users to search through a selection of the UFO documents, and offers a short timeline and map that feature some of the more sensational sightings described in the previous chapters. The exhibition was created as part of a broader initiative begun in the late 1990s that "utilised the

interactive technology of the Web, making digitised images more than just illustrations or pictures at an exhibition." The point was to make as many records as possible accessible to the public.[1]

Hayes further noted:

At LAC, during this wave of digitization, there was no special interest in the UFO material, other than that the public generally found it intriguing – it was a "hot topic" – and so it lent itself well to a virtual exhibition that might draw in more eyes.

This sudden availability of official UFO files had nothing to do with claims of "Disclosure" as advocated and promulgated by many UFO fans. It was simply a response to constant public interest in the subject, and was an appealing experiment to use new technology to offer a service as a gesture of public relations.

What do these UFO files actually look like? First of all, it's not just one set of records. As noted by Hayes:

"There is no single Canadian UFO archive. The approximately 15,000 pages of documentation... [are] from multiple archives and collections. Rather than a tidy archive, UFOs are a keyword search. The fact that Canada's UFO documents are spread across a number of different places is itself performative. It mirrors the individual actions that each department involved over the years took when confronted with UFO sighting reports."

The digitized 9,500 documents were about two-thirds of the estimated 15,000 that are part of the LAC collection on UFOs. They come from records including:

Department of Transport reports on UFO sightings, 1976-1978

RCMP reports of UFO sightings, 1959-1987

Department of National Defence intelligence sightings of unknown objects, 1947-1964

Department of National Defence files on target detection related to flying saucers, 1950-1967

Department of National Defence files on target detection related to flying saucers, 1968-1973

Department of Communications, air services, Project Second Story, 1952-1953

National Research Council, UFO sightings, 1965-1995

Even though the LAC collection includes other departmental UFO files beyond those of just the NRC, the digitized collection is often simply called the "NRC UFO files."

Several groups and individuals have downloaded this set of available digitized documents, some making them available online on their own hosted websites. However, for the most part, detailed analyses of this UFO data have not been done to any great degree. Hayes was one of the few to review the files and produce a database listing, and he even included the physical NRC files between 1981 and 1995 that have not yet been digitized.

Hayes listed 4,416 sighting reports as found in the LAC collection. Ufology Research went through the available digitized files and found 2,940 sighting reports between 1947 and 1981. (The difference between the two tabulations is largely due to the fact that the reports from 1981 to 1995 which have not yet been digitized are in the LAC collection in hard paper copy.)

A sampling of cases from this collection of 2,940 reports is reviewed in the following chapters. These cases will give you an idea of what the Canadian government considered when examining the UFO phenomenon. I'll let you judge if there was anything worthwhile discovered.

Politics, media and UFOs: Please tactfully say NO to CBC

Found within the LAC NRC UFO files is a series of memoranda regarding an inquiry by the Canadian Broadcasting Corporation (CBC) in Winnipeg of the Department of National Defence for assistance in preparing a television or radio documentary on UFOs. Dated Feb. 22, 1965, a confidential and formerly classified telex from the Canadian Air Training Command in Winnipeg to Canadian Forces Headquarters in Ottawa reads:

CBC Winnipeg want to do programme on UFO sightings. This office has been asked for background of any RCAF input or procedures that are followed. Advise current policy.

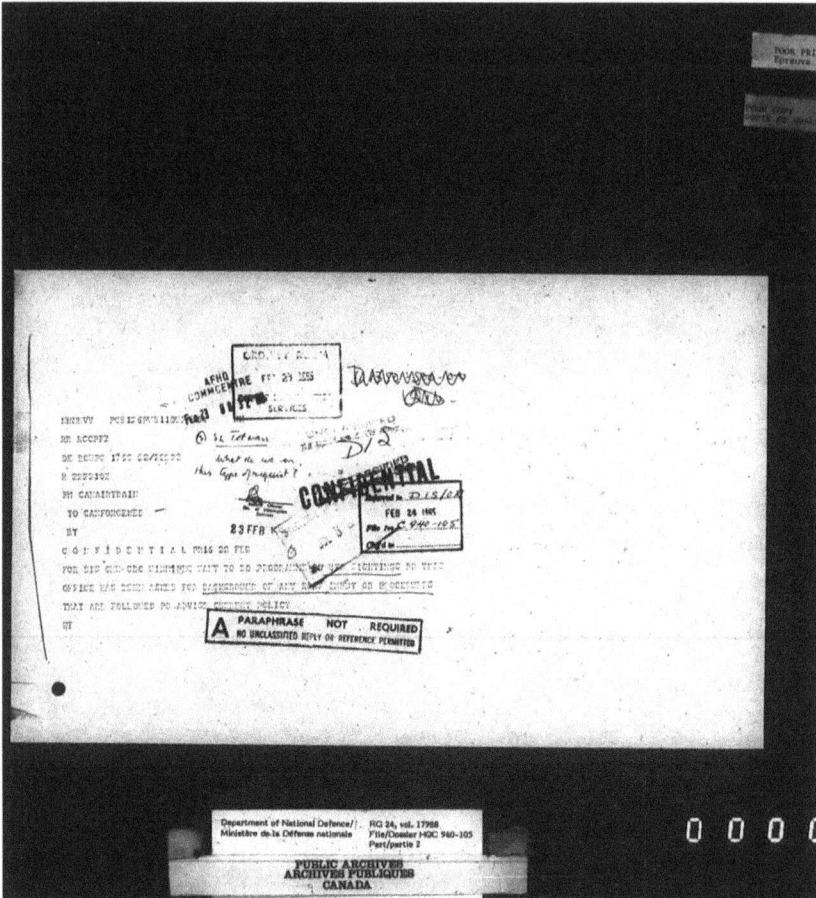

Document 1: "Response to CBC inquiry." Letter to the Office of Information at the Department of National Defence, 4 March 1965. © Government of Canada. Reproduced with the permission of Library and Archives Canada (2021). Source: Library and Archives Canada/Department of National Defence/vol. 17988 file HQC 940-105, part 2

A handwritten scribble on the memo reads: "SL (?) Tetreau (?): What [??] we on this type of request?"

That same day, a confidential DND Minute sheet was prepared by a military secretary named Totman for the Director of Information Services. It was sent to the Directorate of Air Intelligence, to the attention of "W/O Hardy(?)" It read:

> 1. Request your comments, please.
> 2. I suggest the policy would be to stay clear of this type of program except to answer this query with information contained in attached "form letter" that has been used by FFR (now DIS) for some time.

Unfortunately, there was no "form letter" in the file, so we are left to wonder what it might have been. Fortunately, there are some examples in the collection of documents of letters sent to individuals requesting information about UFOs. It's likely that some variant of these was considered.

Four days after the Minute Sheet was opened, on February 26, 1965, an annotation was made on the memo by "E.L. Bowey" of the office of the Director of Information Services. He simply noted: "Agree with your min (3) 100%," where the (3) referred to the first part of the Minute Sheet.

The following week, there was correspondence between Ottawa and the DND Office of Information in Winnipeg. On March 4, 1965, Colonel L.A. Bourgeois, Director of Information Services, gave his recommendations on the CBC request.

> UFO Reports – Policy
> CBC Programme Proposal
>
> 1. This HQ does not wish to become involved with such a program. It is policy to stay clear of this subject whenever possible.
> 2. Many inquiries are received on this subject. They are answered by a standard letter as per attached copy.
> 3. Please tactfully say "NO" to CBC.[2]

And so, the Canadian Forces set their bottom line in how to handle media when it came to UFOs. Even for "Canada's National Broadcaster."

One can wonder if this request and tactful response affected the way in which Canadian media handled the subject of UFOs in following years. If they were told that UFOs were nothing of interest by a high-ranking government official, that information alone could have attenuated their interest. Indeed, for decades later, the CBC was less than responsive and interested in covering UFO stories. What would they have done if the Minister of Defence had said that UFOs were real? Anyway, it looked like the Canadian military was not going to dally in the subject of UFOs, especially with the media.

At least, for a month or so.

Obviously, the request from the CBC must have sparked some discussion throughout DND, because within the DND files is a long, detailed four-page document titled: "Unidentified Flying Objects," dated April 20, 1965. It was written by J.C Arnell and was subtitled: "Suggested Statement by the Minister of National Defence."

UNIDENTIFIED FLYING OBJECTS

Suggested Statement by the Minister of National Defence

Abbreviated in rewriting by Parliamentary Returns

Stories of flying objects have existed throughout history and apparitions of strange objects in the sky have for centuries stirred popular emotion and at times caused crises and panics. Many interpretations have been placed on these reported sightings, ranging from visitations from outer space to the existence of terrestrial spirits, such as the "will o' the wisp". Before astronomers had discovered the planets of our solar system, the visitations were attributed to the gods; in more recent times, the gods have been displaced by the beings from other planets.

While some writers have interpreted archaeological drawings and carvings as reflections of extraterrestrial visitations in prehistoric times, the earliest recorded account of a sighting of an unidentified flying object is probably that of the prophet Ezekiel in the Old Testament. In the first chapter of this book, a description is given of a sight. In the Chebar River in the land of Chaldea and machine which landed near the Chebar River in the land of Chaldea and included therein are expressions similar to those often included in modern sighting reports, particularly with respect to bright and flashing lights. Ezekiel could only describe his sighting in terms of the life he knew on earth, and the war chariot and the plough represented the "advanced technology" of the time. Hence, wheels figure very prominently in his account.

The forms of the unidentified flying objects which have been reported over the millenia have changed as civilization has developed on earth. The Greeks and the Romans saw horses drawing chariots across the sky; the seafaring people of the middle ages saw full-rigged sailing ships; today, the spheres and cylinders of space craft tend to be reported. Thus, the present sighting reports must be considered against this historical background.

Until man learned to fly early in this present century, there were very few man-made objects in the sky to contribute to the aerial sightings. There were, of course, kites and a few balloons; but kites were tied to the ground and had little movement, while only the occasional balloon was released. Thus, most of the sightings recorded in history must have been due to natural phenomena or inaccurate reporting. The development of high performance jet aircraft and the placing of many satellites in orbit around the earth have added many new objects in the sky, which have shapes strange to the uninformed.

The sighting of strange objects tends to be seasonable and usually begins in the spring, dies away, only to develop a second peak during the period when large numbers of people are on holiday and out of doors for a large percentage of the time. The degree to which the reports in a given season come to the notice of the general public depends entirely

.../2

- 2 -

on the play being given by the news media. Once there has been a certain amount of publicity, there are enough pranksters in North America to create the circumstances for a few well documented sightings by the use of hot air balloons, gas-filled balloons with flares dangling from them, etc., or even just good stories planted in the right quarters.

As a result of rather complete coverage of sightings by the various types of news media this year, a situation comparable to the general level of interest in early 1950's exists with respect to the subject among the public today. In order to satisfy a concerned public in both Canada and the United States some fifteen years ago, scientific committees were set up under defence auspices in both countries to investigate the existing reports of unidentified flying objects. After several years of study, both committees were able to explain all but a very small percentage of the many thousands of sighting reports in terms of natural phenomena and man-made objects. Among those which could not be explained were those where the descriptions were too vague for careful analysis and where the reporter was of doubtful reliability. Of the relatively few sightings of good reliability which remained unaccountable, the American committee concluded that the evidence presented on Unidentified Flying Objects shows no indication that these phenomena constitute a direct physical threat to national security" and recommended "that the national security agencies take immediate steps to strip the Unidentified Flying Objects of the special status they have been given and the aura of mystery they have unfortunately acquired." Although it was not so formally stated, the Canadian committee reached the same conclusions and ceased to function about ten years ago. Since that time, such reports as were referred to the Department of National Defence have been studied by interested staffs, and, where warranted, investigations have been made.

About five years ago, in an attempt to further the study of optical effect in the upper atmosphere, such as fireballs (shooting stars), and to assist in the recovery of fallen meteorites for scientific study, the National Research Council established a scientific committee, on which the Department of National Defence is represented, to coordinate all Canadian activity. One of the prime contributions of this committee has been the improvement of the reporting of fireballs on an organised basis. This is largely through the efforts of members of the Royal Astronomical Society of Canada and other interested amateur astronomers. However, the RCAF has cooperated in this endeavour through the collection of sighting reports made by pilots on night manoeuvres, etc. This method of reporting has been augmented by similar systems operated through the Department of Transport and the Royal Canadian Mounted Police. Although the reports coming through defence channels are primarily for the use of the National Research Council Meteor Centre in maintaining records of fireballs, the individual messages are examined routinely within the Department for any unusual reports. In this way, the Department of National Defence has maintained a partial record of unusual sightings across the country.

.../3

- 3 -

There is no doubt that there are many things to be seen in the sky which can lead to reports of unidentifiable objects. Over the years the introduction of each new higher performance aircraft has tended to produce such reports until its existence has become commonplace. For example, in April 1952, there was a scare in Toronto when a dark cylindrical object was sighted over the city airport. The current RCAF MUSTANG fighters attempted to chase this object, but were quickly outdistanced. It was subsequently learned that the object was a British CANBERRA jet aircraft on its way to the United States, flying at 40,000 ft. with a good tail wind. The U-2 aircraft was responsible for similar reports a few years ago. At night, even ordinary aircraft are often not recognized, particularly when the presence of other noise or a strong wind prevents the observer from hearing any sound in association with the sighting.

Balloons of many types have in their turn been a cause of concern. In the early 1950's, very large, very high altitude balloons were released for scientific purposes and these were often seen after dark still shining in the sunlight. More commonly, small meteorological balloons, carrying a trailing light for optical tracking, have been released at night and are often reported. As these are subject to the vagaries of the wind, their tracks may be strange and varied. Large satellites, such as the two ECHO's, are fairly regularly reported, particularly during the summer months, traversing the sky in 5-10 minutes.

A seemingly more frightening type of man-produced aerial phenomenon is that of lights reflected off low lying cloud. Occasionally such a cloud lying near an airport will act as the screen against which the rotating aircraft beacon will track at great speed. Unless the observer continues to watch, he may see only a single path. Similarly, the large modern shopping centre, with its myriad of lights can produce any variety of glows off cloud formations, with the shape of the glow being dependent on the clouds themselves. If such light sources include many flashing signs, it is possible that the observer will see flashing coloured lights against a background of yellow or white. Perhaps one of the more remarkable recent sightings, which was photographed, was that of a small flight of geese flying over a well-lighted city at night. The reflection of the lights off the white bellies of the birds produced the effect of a strange delta-shaped object, which was only recognizable to the careful observer.

There are, of course, a variety of well recognized natural phenomena which are strange to the average viewer. Among the meteorological effects are the many forms of halos which can be seen around the sun and moon and occasionally bright stars which may be complete or partial or fluctuating if there is marked cloud movement. This type of phenomenon formed a large percentage of the sightings reported fifteen years or so ago. In addition, terrestrial effects resulting from the luminescence of marsh gas and the various forms of electrical discharge, such as ball lightning and St. Elmo's fire have been responsible for many reports.

.../4

- 4 -

In attempting to analyze reports of unidentified flying objects, the investigator is faced with the known unreliability of untrained observers. The police files are full of contradictory evidence of witnesses to such commonplace events as automobile accidents. It is not surprising therefore to find doubtful information included in observations of aerial phenomena strange to the viewer. For this reason, the Department of National Defence has been prepared to accept the occasional inexplicable report as due to inaccurate reporting, recognizing that the great majority of all sighting reports can be readily explained as due to natural or man-made occurrences and at the same time recognizing that inexplicable sightings have been reported throughout history without any evidence that the cause was other than natural phenomena. As a result, the earlier conclusion that the unexplained sightings do not pose a threat to the security of Canada is still considered to be completely valid.

J.C. Arnell, Dr./2-5947

APR 28 1965

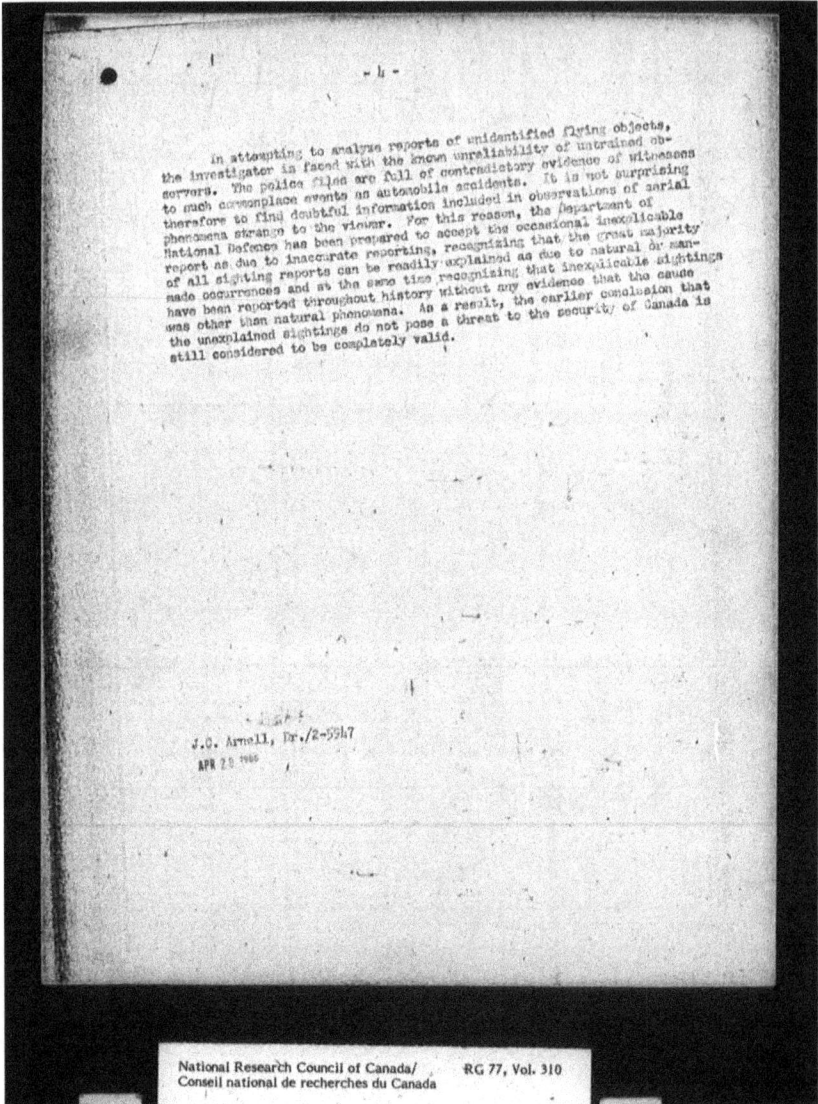

Documents 2 - 5: "Statement on UFOs prepared for the Minister of National Defence, 1965." Unidentified Flying Objects: Suggested Statement by the Minister of National Defence, April 20, 1965, © Government of Canada. Reproduced with the permission of Library and Archives Canada (2021). Source: Library and Archives Canada/Department of National Defence/e002799662 to e002799665

This wasn't a form letter. It was a very specific discussion about UFOs prepared for the highest executive in the Air Force and Canadian Forces. If this wasn't written for the CBC, which presumably would have been a good public relations move, then why was it prepared at all? It's also not just a briefing statement for the Minister. It was prepared for him to present in some context. Also, there's no indication that this statement was classified in any way, although it had never been discussed in public.[3]

It's also interesting to note who was the author. In 1965, John Carstairs Arnell was Scientific Advisor to the Chief of Air Staff and the Chief of Naval Staff. He was also somewhat of a genius. According to National Defence Archives, at the age of twelve Arnell enrolled at Ridley College in Ontario and later attended Dalhousie and McGill universities. In 1924, at the age of only 24, he received his PhD in physical chemistry. In 1942, he did chemical warfare research for the Canadian Army and after the war joined the Defence Research Board in Ottawa. Essentially, Arnell set national defence policy for Canada in the 1960s. What's more, it appears he was greatly involved in the decision to unify the Canadian Forces, a move that occurred in 1966-67 under the man who was Minister of National Defence at that time, the Hon. Paul Hellyer.

Arnell's 1965 report on UFOs reiterated the American stance that "the evidence presented on Unidentified Flying Objects shows no indication that the phenomena constitute a direct physical threat to national security." He also revealed the existence of a Canadian committee to study UFOs "some fifteen years ago" (i.e., 1950) which "ceased to function about ten years ago" (i.e., 1955). This could have been Project Magnet, run by Wilbert Smith, which was formally shut down in 1954 but which Smith continued to operate unsanctioned until his death in 1962. It could also have referred to Project Second Story, which ran concurrently with Project Magnet but was involved in the collection of flying saucer reports, whereas Magnet considered the physics of flying saucers.[4]

Arnell noted:

> Since that time, such reports as were referred to the Department of National Defence have been studied by interested staffs, and, where warranted, investigations have been made.

However, in the end, Arnell noted that most UFO sightings were explained as meteors, aircraft, balloons and meteorological effects:

After several years of study, both committees [American and Canadian] were able to explain all but a very small percentage of the many thousands of sighting reports in terms of natural phenomena and man-made objects. Among those which could not be explained were those where the descriptions were too vague for careful analysis and where the reporter was of doubtful reliability. Of the relatively few sightings of good reliability which remained unaccountable, the American committee concluded "that the evidence presented on Unidentified Flying Objects shows no indication that these phenomena constitute a direct physical threat to national security" and recommended "that the national security agencies take immediate steps to strip the Unidentified Flying Objects of the special status they have been given and the aura of mystery they have unfortunately acquired."

It's been noted here and elsewhere by historians and researchers that the "very small percentage" claimed as the American results was actually of the order of about 20 per cent, so the statement is misleading if not simply incorrect.[5]

Arnell's final argument in the minister's statement is essentially a collective shrug of shoulders:

In attempting to analyze reports of unidentified flying objects, the investigator is faced with the known unreliability of untrained observers. The police files are full of contradictory evidence of witnesses to such commonplace events as automobile accidents. It is not surprising therefore to find doubtful information included in observations of aerial phenomena strange to the viewer. For this reason, the Department of National Defence has been prepared to accept the occasional inexplicable report as due to inaccurate reporting, recognizing that the great majority of all sighting reports can be readily explained as due to natural or manmade occurrences and at the same time recognizing that inexplicable sightings have been reported throughout history without any evidence that the cause was other than natural phenomena. As a result, the earlier conclusion that the unexplained sightings do not pose a threat to the security of Canada is still considered to be completely valid.

Arnell's reasoning was simple: UFO witnesses are generally unreliable and reports are inaccurate, so even if some cases are unexplained, it's no big deal. But what if some unexplained sightings were by reliable witnesses and the reports were accurate? The NRC files have many examples with excellent descriptions and testimony by trained observers.

The other point of note here is that Arnell's prepared statement was for Paul Hellyer, a person who many years later would be very vocal about the reality of UFOs and aliens on Earth. In 2013 at the Citizens' Hearings on Disclosure, Hellyer told the audience:

> At least four species of alien have been visiting Earth for thousands of years... some of the aliens hail from the 'Zeta Reticuli, the Pleiades, Orion, Andromeda, and Altair star systems' and 'may have different agendas'... and 'there are live ETs on Earth at this present time, and at least two of them are working with the United States government.[6]

Yet back in 1965, Hellyer reviewed the prepared statement for his presentation that stated UFOs were nothing of interest or importance. Forty years later, after his retirement from public office, he told an audience at the University of Toronto in 2005 something very different. In a 180-degree turn from the official standpoint during his term as Minister of National Defence, he said that, "UFO's are as real as the airplanes flying overhead."

Hellyer revealed at the Disclosure Hearings in 2013 that:

> Although as Minister of National Defence I had sighting reports of UFOs, I was too busy to be concerned about them because I was trying to unify the Army, Navy and Air Force into a single Canadian Defence Force.[7]

So, when he was in a position to study UFO reports, he didn't see them as particularly worth bothering with. But before he recently passed away in 2021, he stated that UFOs are ostensibly the most important issue on the planet and believed working with the aliens to save the Earth is essential to the survival of humanity. Hellyer's testimony at the Hearings ranged from warning of an international cover-up to an all-out "Bilderberg Conspiracy" in which a clandestine group is suppressing the truth about UFOs.

Arnell's prepared statement for Hellyer shows that something changed between 1965 and today, long after Hellyer's security clearance as Minister of National Defence had lapsed. Furthermore, only two years later, in 1967, the Robertson Briefing painted a very different picture of UFOs in Canada.

The Robertson Briefing: An inside look at how the Canadian government viewed UFOs

In going through the UFO files within the Canadian National Archives, there is a curious briefing document that had been prepared in November 1967 to give an overview of the status of the UFO phenomenon in Canada. It had been created, with accompanying slides, by Wing Commander D.F. (Douglas Furg) Robertson of the Canadian Forces, for General Jean-Victor Allard, Chief of the Defence Staff (CDS). Allard directly advised the Minister of National Defence, who was then Hon. Leo Cadieux as Pall Hellyer had just left the position a few months earlier. It would have made sense that Allard wanted to know the current view on the UFO issue as there had been a great deal of attention in media about the topic and there had been pressure on the ministry for its involvement.

The *CDS Briefing on Unidentified Flying Objects* was undoubtedly prepared to help alleviate the burden of dealing with UFOs within the Canadian Department of National Defence (DND) by summarizing its current extent of knowledge. The *Robertson Briefing* reviewed facts and procedures, and also described cases that had been handled within the ministry. This was the cornerstone of Canadian military studies on UFOs. It is worthwhile to examine this *Briefing* in detail because of the highlighted UFO cases and its discussion of policy and the viewpoint of the Department of National Defence towards UFOs at that time.[8]

For the reader's benefit, the entire 28-page document is reproduced in the following pages, and certain details noted.

DOPS 4

CDS BRIEFING

ON

UNIDENTIFIED FLYING OBJECTS

Prepared by: W/C D.F. Robertson, D Ops 4

Dated: 15 November, 1967.

INTRODUCTION

SLIDE 1

ON

Gentlemen:

1. The purpose of this briefing is to provide a short resumé on unidentified flying object (UFO) reports and the procedures adopted by this Headquarters to action these reports.

2. The Department of National Defence is the recognised agency charged with the responsibility for investigating UFO reports which are referred to governmental agencies.

3. UFO reports are received through many sources, such as private citizens, police offices, governmental departments and RCAF bases throughout the country. A UFO is an unusual aerial sighting which the observer is unable to identify or explain.

.../2

222

National Research Council of Canada/   RG 77, Vol. 311
Conseil national de recherches du Canada

25

- 2 -

4. In accordance with instructions contained in the Canadian Forces Administrative Orders (CFAO) 71-1, Fireball and Meteorite Observations; and CFAO 71-6, UFO reports; the Director of Operations is tasked with the responsibility

SLIDE 1 OFF for investigating unusual aerial sighting reports.

BACKGROUND ON UFOs

5. UFO sightings are not unique to this modern age. In fact, records show that UFOs have been reported throughout history. However, it would appear that more sightings are reported during the summer months as compared to winter months. This may be expected as the general public spends more time outdoors during the summer months.

6. In the early 1950s, scientific committees were established in both Canada and the United States, under defence auspices, for the purpose of investigating UFOs. Following several years of study, both committees were able to explain all but a very few of the many thousands of sightings which were investigated. The American Committee concluded its investigations by stating "that the evidence

...../3

26

- 3 -

presented on UFOs show no indication that these phenomena
constitute a direct physical threat to the security of the
U.S.", and recommended that, "the national security agencies
take immediate steps to strip the UFOs of the special status
they had been given and the aura of mystery they have unfortunately acquired". Although the Canadian Scientific
Committee arrived at the same conclusions it was not
formally stated.

7.   Approximately seven years ago, the National Research
Council (NRC) established a scientific committee, on which
DND is represented, to co-ordinate Canadian activity on the
study of optical effect in the upper atmosphere, such as
fireballs and meteorites. This committee receives reports
on fireballs and meteorites from such sources as, DND,
government departments, police forces and the general public.
It is important to note that this committee is primarily
interested in optical observations pertaining to fireball
and meteorite activity and is not engaged in the scientific
evaluation of unusual aerial sightings.

...../4

- 4 -

8.   UFO reports which have been referred to DND for investigation have followed a varied career; at one time, UFO reports were forwarded to Air Defence Command for investigation. At this time, ADC, in co-operation with North American Air Defence (NORAD) was most interested in aerial objects which could not be properly identified. However, as investigations failed to disclose any evidence which would suggest that UFOs posed a threat to national security, and as UFO activity neither directly nor indirectly interfered with the defensive capability of the Command, the responsibility for investigating UFOs was transferred to CFHQ. At that time, the Director of Intelligence co-ordinated DND action on UFO reports. Correspondence held on CFHQ UFO files indicates that Dr. J.C. Arnell, who was at that time the Scientific Deputy Chief of Technical Services, was an active and interested participant in dealing with UFO matters. In the spring of 1966 the responsibility for investigating UFO reports was transferred to the Director of Operations.

.../5

- 5 -

USAF PARTICIPATION IN UFOS

9.   In 1948, the USAF established the "Blue Book" program for the purpose of investigating UFOs. The objects of the program are to determine whether UFOs pose a threat to the security of the U.S. and to determine whether UFOs exhibit any unique scientific information or advanced technology which could contribute to scientific or technical research. UFO sightings referred to the USAF are objectively and scientifically analysed, and if necessary, all the scientific facilities available to the USAF can be used to assist in arriving at an identification or explanation. Recently, and probably due to the increasing concern of the general public, the USAF has selected the University of Colorado to conduct an independent investigation into UFO reports. Under this research agreement, the University expects to call on the services of more than one hundred scientists around the country to assist in this research study. A full report is expected to be submitted to the USAF in 1968.

...../6

- 6 -

OTHER INTERESTED AGENCIES

10. There are a number of civilian organizations in both
the U.S. and Canada which have been established for the sole
purpose of investigating UFOs. In addition, there are many
distinguished and prominent citizens, many of them exceptionally well qualified who have either joined these civilian
organizations, or, are carrying out their own individual
research into UFOs.

11. Probably one of the most active participants who is
endeavouring to create an international scientific interest
in UFOs is Professor James E. McDonald of the University of
Arizona. Professor McDonald strongly supports the views that
the United Nations must make a serious and determined effort
to study and evaluate the large number of credible reports of
low-level, close-range sightings of machine-like objects
that have been recorded from all over the world. On the
7th of June, 1967, Professor McDonald submitted a statement on
the international scientific aspects of the problem of UFOs

.../7

- 7 -

to the Outer Space Affairs Group of the United Nations. This statement received the support of the Secretary General of the United Nations. Professor McDonald has grouped past and current information into seven broad categories comprising the following spectrum of UFO hypothesis:

SLIDE 2 ON

    a. hoaxes, fabrications and frauds;

    b. hallucinations, mass hysteria, rumour phenomena;

    c. lay misinterpretation of well-known physical phenomena such as, meteorological, astronomical, optical, etc;

    d. advanced technologies such as, test vechicles, satellites and re-entry efforts;

    e. poorly understood physical phenomena such as, rare atmospheric-electrical effects, cloud phenomena, plasmas of natural or technological origin, etc;

SLIDE 2 OFF

    f. poorly understood psychological phenomena.

    g. unusual aerial sightings which the observer is unable to identify or explain, namely, UFOs.

.../8

- 8 -

12.   A recent press item contained in a Toronto paper indicated that the University of Toronto will undertake a serious academic review with the object of determining whether UFOs are amenable to scientific study. The current journals of the American Association for Advancement of Science have recently contained letters suggesting that some serious thought be given to the scientific evaluation of UFOs. It has become quite evident that a number of scientific agencies are begining to show an interest in UFOs and are accepting the view that the investigation of UFOs is primarily a scientific responsibility and, to a lesser degree, one which concerns the military.

CFHQ INVESTIGATION OF UFOs

SLIDE 1 ON 13.   On receiving a UFO report at CFHQ, the Operations Staff first endeavour to classify the information into one of two categories, namely:

   a. Category One - Information which suggests the type of phenomena associated with fireballs and meteorites, or,

...../9

- 9 -

b. Category Two - Information that does not conform

to the physical patterns usually associated with

fireball or meteorite activity.

SLIDE 3 OFF

14. A "fireball" may be described as a bright meteor with

a luminosity which equals or exceeds that of the brightest

planet and which moves rapidly across the sky. At times, the

fireball may leave a trail of glowing particles, in addition,

the fireball may explode with a burst of light and a loud sound;

this course of events may be repeated several times during a

single fall.

15. The Director of Scientific Co-ordination (DSC) assists

the Operational Staff to differentiate between fireballs,

meteorites and UFOs. Fireball and meteorite reports are for-

warded to the National Research Council (NRC) Meteorite Centre

and to a representative from the province in which the sighting

was made for study and evaluation.

SLIDE 4 ON

16. Reports which are classified under category "two" are

re-classified into one of three classes based on the importance

of the information provided, namely:

.../10

- 10 -

a. Class "A" - Information provided warrants a

    formal investigation, or;

b. Class "B" - Information provided is of an

    interesting nature but does not

    warrant a formal investigation, or;

c. Class "C" - Information provided is of little

    practical value, no investigation

    or further action required.

SLIDE 4 OFF

SLIDE 5 ON   17.   Prior to 1966, DND received approximately forty (40)

UFO reports a year, however, in the last two years the number

has increased appreciably. As an example, between the period

1 Jan 67 to mid-November 67 *[31 DEC 67]*, a total of 195 *[167]* reports (these do

not include reports which have been identified as fireballs

and meteorites) have been referred to this Headquarters. Of

these 195 *[167]* reports, 9 *[8]* contained sufficient information to

warrant a formal investigation and were classified under

Class "A"; 25 *[21]* contained information of an interesting nature

and classified under Class "B", and the remainder classified

under Class "C".

...../11

- 11 -

18.   A formal investigation may take the form of a simple interview between the party making the report and the investigating officer, or it may develop into a detailed investigation in which such agencies as the RCMP, NRC, DRB, National Health and Welfare are requested to provide assistance.

SLIDE 5 OFF

SLIDE 6 ON

19.   UFO sightings reported to this Headquarters from the 1 January 1967 to the 30 November 1967 have been plotted on a map of Canada. An unsuccessful attempt was made to draw a relationship between such factors as place of sighting, time, description, manoeuvres and other relating factors. It may be noted from the sighting plots on the map that it is not possible to draw any fixed relationship or pattern between the various sightings. The plots recorded were reported from various places on different dates and times. Only in the very broadest of terms is there a small relationship in the

SLIDE 6 OFF   size of the UFO contained in a number of reports.

....../12

- 12 -

29

20.　　Of the 32 UFO reports received at this Headquarters during the last year and reclassified under Class "A" or Class "B", the following sightings may be of interest:

　　a.　UFO Sighting - Falcon Lake Area

　　　　(1)　A Mr. Steven Michalak of Winnipeg, Manitoba, reported that he had come into physical contact with a UFO during a prospecting trip in the Falcon Lake Area, some 90 miles east of Winnipeg on the 20th May 67. Mr. Michalak stated that he was examining a rock formation when two UFOs appeared before him. One of the UFOs remained airborne in the immediate area for a few moments, then flew off at great speed. The second UFO landed a few hundred feet away from his position. As he approached the UFO, a side door opened and voices were heard coming from within. Mr. Michalak states he approached the object but was unable to see inside due to a bright yellow - bluish light which blocked his vision. He

...../13

- 13 -

endeavoured to communicate with the personnel

inside the object but without result. As he

approached within a few feet of the object, the

door closed, he heard a whining noise and the

object commenced to rotate anti-clock wise and

raised off the ground. He reached out his left

gloved hand and touched the object as it began

Circulate the
two photographs

(a) body burns

(b) clothing burns

(c) clothing burns

(d) sketch drawn by
Mr. Michalak.

its lift off; the glove burned immediately he

touched the object. As the object left the

ground the exhaust gases burned his cap,

outer and inner garments and he sustained

rather severe stomach and chest burns.

As a result of these burns he was hospitalized

for a number of days. The doctors who

attended and interviewed Mr. Michalak were

unable to obtain any information which could

account for the burns to his body. The

personal items of clothing which were alleged

to have been burnt by the UFO were subjected

to an extensive analysis at the RCMP crime

...../14

- 14 -

laboratory. The analysis was unable to reach
any conclusion as to what may have caused the
burn damage. Soil samples taken from the immediate area occupied by the UFO by Mr.
Michalak were analysed and found to be radioactive to a degree that the samples had to be
safely disposed. An examination of soil samples
from the alleged UFO landing area was carried
out by a radiologist from the Department of
Health and Welfare and a small area was found to
be radio-active. The Radiologist was unable
to provide an explanation as to what caused
this area to become contaminated.

(2) Neither the DND nor the RCMP investigation
teams were able to provide evidence which could
dispute Mr. Michalak's story. Although the
investigation has been completed, a satisfactory
explanation or conclusion is still lacking.

...../15

- 15 -

b. UFO Sighting - Mr. Warren Smith

(1) Another interesting UFO report was made by

Mr. Warren Smith of Calgary, Alberta, on the

3rd July, 1967. Mr. Smith and two companions

were prospecting in an area 30 miles west of

Nanton, Alberta, when a UFO suddenly appeared

above an area of trees a few hundred feet from

the observers. Mr. Smith was able to take

two coloured photographs of the object and

the two prints were developed and submitted

Circulate the two photographs of the UFO

to RND for study. The two prints were sub-

jected to a detailed analysis by the Photo

Intelligence Interpretation Centre. The

Centre concluded its investigation by

stating, assuming the photograph to be

genuine, the UFO fitted the description of the

object reported by Mr. Smith.

...../16

- 16 -

c. UFO Sighting - Mr. B. Greene

  (1) Mr. Greene and members of a family from Clear
      Water Bay, Shoal Lake, Ontario (4935N 9507W)
      were returning to their home by boat on the
      evening of the 18 June when they observed a UFO.

  (2) The object was first observed hovering approximately
      50 feet above tree tops approximately a mile away.
      As Mr. Greene was unable to identify the object
      he decided to carry out an investigation. As he
      approached the hovering object, it suddenly descended
      towards his boat at great speed. Mr. Greene
      immediately retreated using maximum power to the
      opposite shore where the occupants left the boat.
      The object broke off its flight and returned to its
      original position. Mr. Greene and party decided to
      make a second attempt to investigate the object by
      boat. However, as he approached the object, it again
      descended at great speed towards his boat; and once
      again he was forced to retreat at full speed to the
      opposite shore. Immediately on reaching shore the
      ..../17

- 17 -

party ran to the home of a Mr. B. Greene and awoke
the entire household who in turn observed the object
for approximately 15 minutes before it rapidly disappeared in a west, northwest direction towards Falcon
Lake. (The scene of another UFO sighting of interest
reported by Mr. Michalak.)

(3) The object was described as oval in shape with a
slight rise on top, (much like a canopy). When first
observed it was described as metalic or glassy in
colour. No lights were visible, however as the object
descended towards the boat the tops of the trees
appeared to glow white. The object was clearly visible
and was estimated as being 25 to 30 feet across and
approximately 10 to 15 feet in height. As the object
approached the boat it took on an orange tinge and no
noise was heard by any of the observers. However, a
neighbour in the area who was questioned during the
investigation distinctly remembers listening to his
radio at the time that the UFO was sighted and received
so much static on the radio that he was forced to turn

...../18

- 18 -

it off. The incident was remembered for after
turning the radio off he went to the window
expecting to see a build up of thunderstorms and
was surprised to note that the sky was clear.

(4) A detailed investigation conducted by DND in
co-operation with the RCMP found Mr. Greene to be a
reliable, competent and sincere witness with no
indulgence tendencies. The investigation confirmed
that no alcoholic beverages was consumed by any
members of the party during the evening in question.
Mr. Greene's eye sight is rated excellent and he does
not wear glasses.

(5) Wilted leaves from a tree in the immediate area of
the UFO sighting have been analysed by the University
of Manitoba and one set of samples showed evidence of
fungus which caused the wilting, but the other
remaining samples showed no evidence of fungus or
blight. The Department of Forestry have examined a
number of trees in the UFO sighting area and reported
that they are unable to explain the reason for wilting

...../19

- 19 -

of leaves on a number of trees. Several trees were affected with no set pattern evident except the wilting occured at the top of the trees. The Forestry Department stated that the wilting may have been caused by heat although no other evidence is available to support this possibility.

(6) The investigation has been concluded without any fixed conclusions or findings being made.

d. UFO Sighting - Cpl. Werricky (RCMP)

(1) A Cpl. Werricky of the RCMP and six other witnesses reported a UFO sighting at Barrington Passage on the 5 October 1967.

(2) The object was described as dark, in excess of 60 feet, 4 white lights spaced horizontally approximately 15 feet apart. When first sighted the object was moving in an easterly direction at a low altitude over the water. Suddenly the object descended rapidly to the water making a high whistling noise. It made contact with the water with a bright splash which resulted in a single light floating on the water. As the RCMP

.../20

- 20 -

official approached the white light by boat it sank. The area was carefully searched by the Canadian Coast Guard lifeboat and a number of small boats without success.

(3) An investigation conducted by RND which included an underwater search failed to locate any evidence which could be associated with a UFO. The investigation was concluded without arriving at any fixed findings.

e. Unidentified Radar Returns by DOT

(1) At 0100 hrs G.M.T. on the 7 July 1967 DOT reported that an unidentified radar target was tracked through seven sweeps of their radar and witnessed by three controllers and two technicians some 70 miles east of Winnipeg. The radar plot showed that the target increased from a speed of 720 Knots to 3600 Knots in one minute and ten seconds. The three controllers and the two technicians who witnessed this feat are certain it was a radar target and not something associated with mechanical, electronic or equipment faults.

.../21

- 21 -

(2) Kenora radar reported an unidentified radar object
at 0324 hrs G.M.T. on the 7 July. The unknown
object was under positive radar contact and followed
for some 29 minutes. The object followed Air Canada
Flight 405 for a period then disappeared from the
scope. It reappeared and followed Air Canada Flight
927 for a period of time. DOT are unable to explain
these radar returns.

(3) An investigation by DND has failed to account for
these positive radar returns reported on the 7 July
by Winnipeg and Kenora radar controllers.

f. UFO Sighting - Mr. R. Patrige

(1) A Mr. R. Patrige of Camrose, Alberta made a report to
DND on the 8 August 67 concerning several deep
impressions which were made by an unknown object in
a pasture located near Camrose, Alberta.

(2) An investigation conducted by DND substantiated that
an unknown object or objects had left six, six inch
width, 31 to 36 diameter circles in the soil as stated

....../22

- 22 -

and the impressions indicated distinct pressure.
There was no physical evidence of any damage to
trees or shrubs in the field and no evidence to suggest
a deliberate interference or involvement by any
person. A survey by Dr. Jones from the DRB Experi-
mental Station at Suffield, with a geiger counter
failed to show any radiation contamination.

(3) The investigation was concluded without arriving at
any fixed conclusions as to what made the marks in the
soil.

- 23 -

REPRESENTATION TO NRC TO UNDERTAKE
THE RESPONSIBILITY FOR INVESTIGATING UFOs

21.   Information obtained from certain UFO investigations would suggest that these UFOs exhibit some scientific or technical features which could possibly contribute to scientific or technical research. On the basis of this finding, formal representation has been made to the National Research Council (NRC) with the view of this scientific government agency accepting the responsibility for investigating UFOs.

With reference to a letter from the Minister of Industry, C.M. Drury, addressed to the Minister of National Defence dated 12 December 1967 arrangements have been made for Dr. R.G. Rettie, Chief of the Space Research Facilities Branch, NRC to visit Dr. H. Sheffer, Scientific Assistant to the VCDS to discuss effective reporting procedures to be developed so that careful decisions can be made as to the need for further investigations of specific selected UFO cases.

- 24 -

DND POLICY - RELEASE OF UFO INFORMATION
HELD BY DND

22.   In view of the increased interest in UFOs by the general

public, it is imperative that DND adopt a firm policy designed

to release DND held UFO information to recognised persons and

organisations whose purpose is to provide a public service and

to further the scientific and objective research into UFOs.

It is important that due caution be exercised to avoid creating

an impression that DND is "hiding or concealing something".

23.   Classified material such as police investigations

which may be included as part of the DND report would be

protected from release. However, unless otherwise specifically

stated, the release of other than classified material would be

made in the interest of the general public.

SUMMARY

24.   The administrative work load required to action UFO

reports referred to this Headquarters has increased appreciably

during the last twelve months. The marked increase in the Air

..../25

48

- 25 -

Section administrative work load which is directed towards

actioning UFO reports is reaching a stage which is considered

detrimental to the primary operational responsibilities and

duties of the section. Correspondingly, Field Units have also

indicated that the administrative work load increase associated

with UFOs is causing some concern and disruption to their normal

duties.

25.   It is also important to stress at this point, that the

Director of Operations has neither the qualified technical

staff, the established strength, nor the necessary scientific

assistance required to conduct an objective type investigation

into UFO reports.

26.   It is evident from investigations conducted by DND,

and from the findings made by a number of prominent and highly

qualified personnel, that the primary interest of UFOs lies in

the field of science, and to a lesser degree, to one that is

associated with national security. It is, however recognised,

that should NRC accept the responsibility for investigating UFOs,

...../26

- 26 -

the Department of National Defence must be willing to assist

in such areas as field investigations. It will also be necessary

to ensure that NRC advise DND on any information, findings or

conclusions which may, or could possibly affect national security.

27.   It is the opinion of the Operations Staff, that NRC should

make a serious effort to ensure that a scientific research effort

is properly co-ordinated with other scientific agencies undertaking

UFO studies in order to avoid a needless duplication of effort. It

would indeed be unfortunate should such agencies as NRC, University

of Toronto, University of Colorado and other scientific groups

investigating UFOs were to carry out their own private and independent

studies without due liaison and co-operation with each other.

RECOMMENDATIONS

28.   The following recommendations are made:

addition →   a. The National Research Council accept the responsibility

for co-ordinating a scientific and objective investigation

into UFO reports.

b. The Director of Operations shall be the DND co-ordinating

agency between NRC and DND units providing a field

.../27

- 27 -

investigation service.

c. For other than classified material the Director of Information Services (DIS) shall be responsible for releasing DND held UFO information to the general public. The Director of Operations shall be responsible for acting on matters concerning UFOs which are not normally a function of DIS.

National Research Council of Canada/ Conseil national de recherches du Canada   RG 77, Vol. 311

Documents 6 – 32: "Robertson Briefing, 1967, pages 1-28." Herzberg Institute of Astrophysics – Reports on non-meteoric sightings, unidentified flying objects, UFO's 7/7/1967 © Government of Canada. Reproduced with the permission of Library and Archives Canada (2021). Source: Library and Archives Canada/National Research Council of Canada fonds/e002749793 to e002749819 [Robertson Briefing]

On the first page of the document, Robertson defined a UFO as "an unusual aerial sighting which the observer is unable to identify or explain." This definition is at odds with more refined versions that place some responsibility on the investigator rather than the observer. But if someone saw something he or she couldn't explain, it was a UFO, at least to the Canadian Forces.

At the top of page 2 it was noted there was an actual Administrative Order, CFAO 71-6, which specifically instructed the Director of Operations (DOps) to investigate UFO reports. In fact, DOps was "tasked with the responsibility to investigate unusual aerial sighting reports." It's interesting that while the Briefing title used the term UFO, here the phrase used was unusual aerial sighting (UAS). As there is today an apparent shift from the term UFO to unidentified (or unusual) aerial phenomena (UAP), according to a present-day program within the United States military branches, this use of yet another term suggests that the actual description of the objects of concern could have been arbitrary.

On page 3 is a reiteration that the USAF UFO investigation group found no evidence that UFOs "constitute a direct physical threat to the security of the USA." Further, it was recommended that UFOs should be "stripped" of their mystery. Robertson noted that in about 1960, the National Research Council of Canada (NRC) established a scientific committee to study fireballs and meteors, but carefully explained that the committee was interested in optical observations of astronomical events and not "the scientific evaluation of unusual aerial sightings." So, the NRC may have been receiving UFO (or UAS) reports, but its mandate was in the scientific assessment of meteors.

The *Briefing* explains that UFO reports referred to the Department of National Defence (DND) were forwarded to Air Defence Command (ADC) for investigation. Furthermore, ADC and its partner North American Air Defense (NORAD) were "most interested in aerial objects which could not be properly identified." But as most UFO reports were explainable and were not considered threats to the nation, responsibility for UFO investigations was transferred to Canadian Forces Headquarters (CFHQ). At that point, the Director of Intelligence coordinated UFO investigations.

Robertson identified Dr. J.C. Arnell, the Scientific Deputy Chief of Technical Services, as someone who "was an active and interested participant in dealing with UFO matters." Then, in the spring of 1966, UFO investigations became the duty of the Director of Operations (DOps).

Page 5 in the *Briefing* was a description of the USAF Project Blue Book and the Colorado Committee, based at the University of Colorado, that produced the infamous Condon Report which eventually would state that UFOs were not worthy of scientific study.[9]

On page 6, Robertson told his internal audience that some civilians are investigating UFOs and that "distinguished and prominent citizens," many of whom are "exceptionally well qualified," are studying UFO reports. He mentioned Dr. James McDonald specifically, noting his evaluations of "credible reports of low-level, close-range sightings of machine-like objects." McDonald was a noted physicist and a celebrated figure in ufology for his outspokenness about UFOs and criticism of the scientific community for ignoring evidence that suggested some cases could not be explained.[10]

Page 7 laid out the seven categories of UFOs as classified by the Department of National Defence: hoaxes, hallucinations, misidentifications, military vehicles, natural electromagnetic phenomena, psychological phenomena, ... and UFOs! This indicates that even DND held that UFOs were not ordinary objects mistaken for something unusual, or anything produced by the military. In other words, UFOs were "something else."

Page 8 noted that "the University of Toronto will undertake a serious scientific review" of UFOs. This study was based out of the U of T Institute for Aerospace Studies (UITAS), which had a subcommittee of UFOs that met regularly in the 1960s and early 1970s. UTIAS reports on UFOs were at one time searchable online. Some UTIAS reports have been uncovered in archives, and there is a summary report from UTIAS on its UFO operations that was published. However, UTIAS essentially came to the conclusion similar to the Condon Report: that UFOs were not of any significance to science.[11]

This is important because recently, Dr. Avi Loeb, a Harvard astrophysicist, made international news when he suggested an odd interstellar object might have been an extraterrestrial probe. He further offered that the subject of UFOs be studied as evidence of alien visitation through the dedicated work of "a dozen physicists" who would approach the problem scientifically.[12]

UTIAS was such a conglomeration of scientists, and did not conclude UFOs were of scientific value.

Also on this page, Robertson detailed the CFHQ procedure for investigating UFO reports. As a first step, Operations Staff had to decide whether the report was of a fireball or meteor, or something else.

Fireball reports were to be sent to the NRC Meteor Centre and to a provincial NRC representative. But as for the second category, the "non-meteors," these were pigeonholed into three classes: Class A cases warranted a formal investigation; Class B were "interesting," but didn't need investigation; and Class C were of "little practical value," so no investigation was required. A logical question that arises is: if Class B cases were interesting, why wouldn't they be investigated? Did they already have explanations?

And this is where the *Briefing* gets more curious.

On page 10, Robertson noted that prior to 1966, DND was getting about 40 UFO reports each year. But in 1967, the number jumped to 167. In fact, an even higher number was crossed out: 193 reports as of mid-November 1967. That would mean a five-fold increase from 1966 to 1967. It is not clear why the numbers were revised lower for the briefing document.

Robertson noted that the 167 (or 193) did not include reports explained as meteors or fireballs. That means the 167 (or 193) were already minus the misidentified IFOs and reports that were otherwise explained; yet these were not the Class C cases.

Robertson wrote that there were 8 (or 9) Class A cases in 1967, and 21 (or 23) Class B cases. He noted: "the remainder classified under Class 'C.'" So, therefore, sightings of fireballs were not part of the UFO report collection. These were cases that could not be explained as conventional objects and could be considered "true" unknowns.

On page 11, the nature of the department's UFO investigation was given in more detail. Formal investigations could have been as simple as an interview of a witness by an investigator, or as complex as involving other agencies such as the RCMP, NRC, Defence Research Board (DRB) or the Department of National Health and Welfare. The last agency is a bit puzzling. What aspects of a UFO report would require investigation by an agency interested in health?

Robertson attempted to plot the UFOs reported in 1967 on a map of Canada to see if there was some kind of obvious geographical distribution. There apparently wasn't, and his attempts to draw relationships or see patterns between location, time, description, movement and other factors all failed as well, except one: "a small relationship in the size of the UFO contained in a number of reports." But what this means is anyone's guess. Unfortunately, the map he produced did not accompany the *Briefing* in the digital archives for examination.

On page 12 was the beginning of the most interesting part of Robertson's document. He had noted that of the 29 (or 32) cases in 1967 that were either Class A or Class B, six were worthy of discussion in the *Briefing.* The first was the Falcon Lake case, involving the physical effects of a UFO on Stefan Michalak on May 20, 1967.

Robertson's review of the Falcon Lake case included the note that the RCMP Crime Laboratory was "unable to reach any conclusion as to what may have caused the burn damage" to Michalak's clothing. (More on this case in Chapter 5.)

Soil samples from the site "were analysed and found to be radioactive to a degree that the samples had to be safely disposed." Here is a confirmed instance of a UFO case where radiation was associated with a UFO landing. Furthermore, the radiation level was so high, the samples were deemed dangerous! A radiologist from the Department of Health and Welfare (this is perhaps why that department had been named earlier) "was unable to provide an explanation as to what caused the area to become contaminated."

Finally, the kicker: "Neither the DND nor the RCMP investigation teams were able to provide evidence which could dispute Mr. Michalak's story. Although the investigation has been completed, a satisfactory explanation or conclusion is still lacking."

Military and police investigators could not explain the case, despite very thorough investigation. This does not mean that what Michalak encountered was an alien spacecraft, but it does say that a real event of some kind seemed to have occurred.

The second case included in the briefing was the "Warren Smith photos" from July 3, 1967 (see Chapter 6). While hiking with companions, Smith took two photos of a saucer-shaped object flying over some trees while in the Rocky Mountain foothills 30 miles west of Calgary, Alberta. The Canadian Forces' Photo Intelligence Interpretation Centre concluded: "...assuming the photograph to be genuine, the UFO fitted the description of the object reported by Mr. Smith." That weaselly statement didn't say it was unexplained, only that the object in the photo *looked* like a UFO.

Next up was a strange sighting that took place on June 18, 1967, at Clearwater Bay on Shoal Lake in Ontario. What isn't obvious to the casual reader is that Clearwater Bay is barely 30 kilometres (less than 20 miles) from where Stefan Michalak was burned by a UFO not even a month earlier. What's more, this case also involved physical evidence.

At about 10:30 pm that evening, Mr. Greene and his family were in a boat on Shoal Lake when they saw a domed, disc-shaped object moving above the trees on shore about a mile away (although the original report on file said ¼ mile away). Greene decided to turn the boat towards the craft to get a better view. The object seemed metallic, about 25 to 30 feet across and about 10 to 15 feet thick. (In other words, almost exactly the same dimensions and appearance as the Falcon Lake object.) But as Greene approached, the object suddenly dropped down and approached their boat at high speed. Greene and his passengers were scared, so he turned around and headed to the opposite shore where they got out of the boat.

The playful object moved back to its original position, so they got *back* into the boat and tried to get near it again. It came towards them once more so they beat a hasty retreat. They woke up some neighbours (who were relatives and also named Greene), and they all watched the object as it hovered for 15 minutes in the west before it flew away in that direction.

As for physical effects, another Greene relative who lived ¼ mile from where the object had hovered was listening to his transistor radio at the time and found it was overwhelmed by static. An investigation carried out by RCMP and DND found a freshly fallen tree near where the craft was said to have hovered, as well as a strange wilting of leaves in the treetops. Leaves from the affected area were analysed and showed "no evidence of fungus or blight."

The investigation of the Clearwater Bay case was "concluded without any fixed conclusions or findings being made."

The fourth case was the noted Shag Harbour UFO "crash" of October 5, 1967. The case was given only a very brief treatment by Robertson, describing it as a dark object, 60 feet wide with four white lights, moving low over the water before it descended rapidly to the water making a whistling noise. His description noted the object made "a bright splash" when it hit the ocean, and a single light floated for a while, then went out. RCMP Corporal Wercicky was said to be one witness. (However, investigation actually discovered that no one saw the object enter the water; this was only an assumption that has been recounted in most versions of the story.)

Robertson noted: "An investigation conducted by DND which included an underwater search failed to locate any evidence which could be associated with a UFO. The investigation was concluded without arriving at any fixed findings."

What does that mean? No evidence that could be "associated" with a UFO? Like what? And there were no "fixed findings?" Does that mean it was unexplained?

On page 20 of the *Briefing*, Robertson lists something rather remarkable: a radar case, a category relatively rare in ufology. On July 6, 1967, at about 7:00 pm, three air traffic controllers and two radar technicians all witnessed "an unidentified radar target" that was tracked through seven sweeps. And where did this take place? According to Robertson, it was "some 70 miles east of Winnipeg." That's fairly close to Falcon Lake. Again. And very close to Clearwater Bay, too.

In 1967, there was a USAF radar base in Canada near Milner Ridge, Manitoba, about 50 kilometres (30 miles) northeast of Winnipeg. Something certainly seems to have been going on in an area along the Manitoba/Ontario border that year.

At any rate, the object tracked on radar sped up from 720 knots to 3,600 knots in 70 seconds, an amazing acceleration. Robertson noted the witnesses were "certain it was a radar target and not something associated with mechanical, electronic or equipment faults."

Not to be outdone, page 21 of Robertson's *Briefing* listed a *second* radar case that occurred only a few hours later. At 9:24 pm on July 6, 1967, radar operators at Kenora airport, just inside the Ontario border and only 65 kilometres (40 miles) from Falcon Lake, tracked an unknown object for at least 29 minutes, deeming it a "positive radar contact." The object followed Air Canada airlines Flight 405 for a while then disappeared from the scope. It reappeared and followed another Air Canada plane, Flight 927, for a while. Robertson noted: "DOT (Department of Transport) are unable to explain these radar returns." (More on this radar case in Chapter 6)

Finally, Robertson's sixth case was practically mentioned only as an afterthought, even though it represented a new phenomenon: crop circles. Yes, the first crop formations were not found in Britain as is usually believed, but in Canada, on August 6, 1967, near Camrose, Alberta.

As Robertson noted:

> An investigation conducted by DND substantiated that an unknown object or objects had left six, six-inch width, 31 to 36 diameter circles in the soil... and the impressions indicated distinct pressure. There was no physical evidence of any damage to trees or shrubs in the field and no evidence to suggest a deliberate interference or involvement by any person.

The first "crop circles" found in North America were actually investigated by the Canadian Armed Forces. There was no associated sighting of a UFO, yet this was included in a briefing on UFOs for the Canadian Minister of National Defence. [More on this case in Chapter 9.]

On page 23, largely because the Department of National Defence was not prepared for the significant requirement of man-hours and expenses to conduct thorough UFO investigations on all cases, Robertson made a case for shuffling the UFO problem from DND off to the NRC. It made sense, because the NRC was the main scientific body in Canada, and UFOs seemed to be a scientific issue and not a military threat.

Page 24 addressed the topic of secrecy and classification of material related to UFOs. This was because the public was demanding information about UFOs, and "...it is important that due caution be exercised to avoid creating the impression that DND is 'hiding or concealing something.'" Robertson noted that certain documents would be protected from release, but "the release of other than classified material would be in the interest of the general public."

Robertson realized that being forthcoming and cooperative with the public (*i.e.*, media) about UFOs would be a good public relations tactic. The advantage of such a policy was that it would "provide a public service and to further the scientific and objective research into UFOs."

(If only other governments (or even current versions of the government) would adopt such a policy.)

Robertson's recommendations were based on practical considerations regarding UFO sightings. He noted: "The marked increase in the Air Section (RCAF) administrative workload which is directed towards actioning UFO reports is reaching a stage which is considered detrimental to the primary operational responsibilities and duties of the section."

In other words, those pesky flying things (PFTs, my own acronym) were interfering with the more important day-to-day operations of the Air Force:

> It is important to stress at this point, that the Director of Operations has neither the qualified technical staff, the established strength, nor the necessary scientific assistance required to conduct an objective type investigation into UFO reports.

UFOs, therefore, were viewed as a scientific problem unrelated to terrestrial military activity. However: "... the primary interest of UFOs lies in the field of science, and to a lesser degree, to one that is associated with national security."

So, while the Air Force had an interest in UFOs because of a potential security threat, the subject was placed directly into the lap of the scientific establishment (which didn't want it either). Although the problem of dealing with UFOs was bounced to the NRC, Robertson conceded that DND "must be willing to assist in such areas as field investigations." That "back door" ensured that should anything involving actual national security was discovered, DND would still have jurisdiction.

The Robertson *Briefing* was presented in 1967 as a way to move responsibility for UFO reports away from the Canadian military and into Canada's scientific establishment. One can surmise that a similar discussion took place within the American military at one point as well.

What is most interesting about the *Robertson Briefing* is that it contained details of a handful of fascinating UFO cases that occurred during a few months in 1967, all of which involved physical evidence and were unexplained by DND. In fact, several took place within a radius of only about 100 kilometres, centred on Falcon Lake, Manitoba. It is probably justified to muse that in 1967, that area was Canada's "UFO Hotspot."

The unexplained cases mentioned in the *Briefing* involved physical evidence, reputable and highly trained witnesses, and even military and police investigations. They were definitely the kind of cases that would have challenged the scientific community and demanded further attention.

Furthermore, these cases were presented to the highest-ranking military officer in Canada for his consideration. It is very likely that he conveyed this information to the Minister of Defence, since we know that the issue of UFOs was raised in the House of Commons on several occasions and questions were answered publicly by the Minister as a matter of record.[13, 14]

A plague of UFOs upon you

One almost has to feel sorry for the RCMP officers who had to investigate UFOs on behalf of the NRC. The paperwork alone, especially during a local UFO flap, must have been challenging. This would have been particularly the case with UFO reports that even after a cursory investigation turned out to be stars or planets.

One such case was N76/061 which occurred on August 11, 1976, starting at about 10:50 pm. It involved a stationary light that flashed colours of red, white and blue as it sat over Bras d'Or Lake in Nova Scotia for at least half an hour. It had all the earmarks of an astronomical explanation, but there were few other details and no indication of where in the sky it was situated.

NCR DEE OTT

COMM SQN OTT
PUZ 020/12
P R 121721Z AUG 76
FM CFS SYDNEY
TO RCCWC/NDHQ OTTAWA
INFO RCCPUCX/NATIONAL RESEARCH COUNCIL FOR RADIO AND ELECTRICAL
ENGINEERING DIVISION
BT
UNCLAS CADO 179
NDHQ FOR CFOC
SUBJ: UFO SIGHTINGS
REF: A. CFAO 71-1
1. THE LATEST AMENDMENT ON REF A WAS AL 16/68
2. THIS STATION IS PERIODICALLY PLAGUED WITH INFO ON UFO SIGHTINGS.
WHEN THIS OCCURS DUTY PERSONNEL MUST BE AROUSED TO PREPARE PRIORITY
MSGS ETC
3. REQUEST DIRECTION TO CEASE SENDING THESE MESSAGES OR AUTHORITY
TO SEND DAY AFTER IF CALL RECEIVED AT NIGHT. ADVISE
BT

RADIO RECORDS N-50

PUZ 021/12
P R 121720Z AUG 76
FM CFS SYDNEY
TO RCCWC/NDHQ OTTAWA
INFO RCCPUCX/NATIONAL RESEARCH COUNCIL FOR RADIO AND ELECTRICAL
ENGINEERING DIVISION
BT
UNCLAS CADO 178
NDHQ FOR CFOC
SUBJ: UFO SIGHTING
A. 120250Z AUG 76
B. CLEAR
C. MRS CYRIL HILL
D. NORTH SYDNEY ON GEORGES RIVER
E. MR CYRIL HILL
F. MILL HILL, MISS HILL
G. STATIONARY OVER BRAS DOR LAKES RED WHITE BLUE
H. 30 MINS PLUS
J. SEVERAL OBSERVED FOLLOWING ORIGINAL SIGHTING
BT
WA F. MISS HILL.
NCR DEE OTT

COMM SQN OTT

N77/43 see N76/061

Document 33: "National Defence memo complaining about 'plague' of requests regarding UFOs." Herzberg Institute of Astrophysics – Reports on non-meteoric sightings, unidentified flying objects, UFO's 3/7/1977 © Government of Canada. Reproduced with the permission of Library and Archives Canada (2021). Source: Library and Archives Canada/National Research Council of Canada fonds/e002747542 [plague]

CANADAS UFOS: DECLASSIFIED

But the exact same teletype was repeated as NRC Case N77/43, with an additional message from CFS Sydney to National Defence Headquarters in Ottawa. It was tucked away between N77/042, a bright flash in the sky seen in Penticton, BC, on March 7, 1977, and N77/044, about a group of red flashing lights seen over Edmonton on March 20, 1977.

Something spurred someone in March 1977 within the NRC to copy the 1976 case and its extra note into the 1977 batch of cases. The extra note read:

Ref: A. CFAO 71-1
1. The latest amendment on Ref A was AL 16/68.
2. This station is periodically plagued with info on UFO sightings. When this occurs duty personnel must be aroused to prepare priority msgs etc.
3. Request direction to cease sending these messages or authority to send day after if call received at night. Advise.

In other words, to paraphrase: "Can we please stop responding to UFO reports as regulations currently dictate?" Up until then, they had to send details of the UFO reports to the NRC as soon as possible. This was because the original reason RCMP detachments were investigating UFOs on behalf of the NRC was so that if a meteor was observed and it was seen to fall to Earth, the reports of observations were needed so that scientists could locate the fallen meteorite quickly. Delaying the report (or not receiving it at all) would negate the reason for the directive.

Because RCMP continued to investigate UFO sightings for many more years, it seems this request was turned down. However, one can only imagine that an attitude that UFOs were not all that important would carry over into the way in which RCMP handled citizens' reports in general.

2

FROM THE FAR NORTH TO SHIPS AT SEA

~

Some cases of interest

What kinds of UFO reports are in the NRC UFO Files? Everything you can imagine, from simple lights in the sky to landed spacecraft, crashed saucers, occupants and creatures, mystical experiences reported by witnesses, and even some truly confounding and puzzling accounts. Some reports are barely a few lines in length, while other cases are literally hundreds of pages of documentation detailing specific incidents, including transcripts of investigators' pointed interrogations of witnesses and authentic witness testimony.

Some of the documents are really fascinating, either in their descriptions of the objects seen, or in the context of the documentation itself. To get a taste of what is contained in the UFO files, here is a small sampling of some of the more curious and interesting cases, barely scratching the surface of the huge number of reports in the archives.

Most readers will be aware of the most-lauded UFO event near Roswell, New Mexico, in 1947. On either July 2 or July 4, 1947 (researchers disagree on the precise date), a bright object was seen falling in the area of Roswell that night. Around the same time, rancher Mac Brazel came upon some debris scattered across the desert near his ranch and took it to show the local sheriff on July 6, 1947. The assumption was that a craft of some kind had crashed, possibly even after it had been struck by lightning. That started the chain reaction of events and media interest that followed, bringing a "crashed flying saucer" to public attention.

Around the same time, unbeknownst to most people, Canadians had been reporting sightings of flying saucers too. One of the earliest cases in the NRC UFO files is from Prince Edward Island on July 3, 1947, when a resident living near Augustine Cove reported seeing an object "the size of an apple" in the east traveling south at high speed during daylight hours. The "flying saucer" was at an estimated altitude of 10,000 feet and left a vapour trail as it "dived earthward." There were two other people who saw the same or similar object about the same time, at 5:45 pm, and the object was observed for 1½ to 2 minutes, a long time for a fireball or bolide, but still within the realm of possibility. This case may have had a simple explanation, but shows that Canadians were keeping an eye out for the saucers, just like Americans.

On February 26, 1950, at 2:45 pm, three witnesses observed a more "classic" UFO that looked like "two wide-edged cigarette ash trays placed face to face." The bronze object flew over the city of Vancouver, BC, slowing down as it passed overhead and "oscillating" or wobbling as it flew, with sunlight flashing off its surface. One witness admitted he had been a skeptic and had thought flying saucers were merely caused by mass hysteria, but was forced to change his mind after witnessing the remarkable craft, reporting it to the air force only after "deliberate consideration."

On July 10, 1952, a flying saucer was seen by a pilot flying 50 miles northwest of the hamlet of Wrigley in the Northwest Territories at 12:25 pm, just past noon. The same pilot was flying near Stewart Lake on July 19, 1952, at about 10:00 pm and saw two objects, this time in the company of a survey crew member. And on August 9, 1952, at 1:55 pm, two employees of the Hudson Bay post at Hay Lakes in the NWT watched a silver oval object with "a projecting tail" moving in the daytime sky. It "manoeuvred horizontally, vertically, spiralled and also hovered directly over the post." The silent object was "larger than a Lancaster, with speed beyond estimate," and flying at approximately 6,000 feet in altitude.

On April 16, 1953, a commercial airline pilot and his co-pilot were flying over Chatham, New Brunswick, at 3:45 pm in the afternoon. They watched in amazement as a metallic disc-shaped object approached their plane and then passed underneath them as they flew at 9,000 feet. They were both adamant that the object was not a balloon.

The investigating officer noted the witnesses were "very reliable" and commented that they had been interrogated by a captain in the United States Air Force as part of the American study of UFOs. This would have been Project Blue Book, which has been featured on two different television series, depicting the USAF investigations into unidentified flying objects. This Canadian case, however, was never part of the TV shows, which is too bad, because it involved pilots seeing a physical object during the day, and which was clearly not an illusion or hoax.

Just a week later, on April 23, 1953, at about 3:00 pm in the afternoon, a disc the size of a car was seen by two witnesses at their home at Iberville, Quebec. A man was having dinner with his mother-in-law:

> ...when suddenly in front of me through the window glass, [to the southwest], I saw something coming at me, very bright and speedy, small when I first saw it coming... getting bigger and bigger, then suddenly stopped.

Confounded by what he was seeing, he got up from the table and went over to the window where his mother-in-law was standing, turning her around to see the object. She, too, was surprised by what she saw—a saucer-shaped object flying towards them.

The man then ran outside the house and got a better look at the object for about 15 seconds. The silent object seemed to have taken up a position about 250 feet above the river near their home, approximately 3,000 to 3,500 feet away. It looked to be about the same size as the Iberville water tank, which was about 25 feet in diameter. According to the man's detailed sketches, it was disc-shaped, but had a slight bump or dome on its upper surface.

> I realized that it was spinning, always staying at the same place, then suddenly, [as if I had] seen it long enough... always spinning, it [flew] backward approximately southwest position very fast and disappeared.

The man said he was most surprised at the speed at which the object could fly in any direction, and was constantly spinning counter-clockwise. He noted: "It reminded me of a hummingbird [or as he called it in French *oiseau mouche*], flying very fast forward or backward."

He also was amazed at how near it came to the house:

CANADAS UFOS: DECLASSIFIED

CONFIDENTIAL OFFICIAL USE ONLY

940-105

PROJECT SECOND STOREY

Sighting Report

(A Separate form is to be used for each observer) UNCLASSIFIED

A. Details of observer.

1. Name of observer:

   Surname.. ████ ....Initials...

   DIRECTORATE OF OPERATIONS
   JUL 3 1953

2. Address of observer:

   C/o Maratime Central Airways   Moncton
   Number   Street   City

   New Brunswick
   Province

3. Occupation and previous relevant experience:

   ████ is a Government Inspector flying with
   Maratime Central. He is an experienced 'bush' and
   RCAF transport pilot.

4. Age Group:..................... Unknown

5. Has observer seen "flying objects" before, and if so, briefly,
   when, where, and circumstances:

   Unknown

6. Was observer wearing glasses?

   Unknown

B. Details of Observation

7. Date and local time: 16 April 53   1834 AST

8. Position of observer as accurately as possible:

   Pilot of aircraft flying at 9000' over Chatham.
   Speed 170 knots - heading 009.

9. General description of sighting:

   ████ sighted the object some 3 to 5 miles
   ahead at an estimated altitude of 7500'. Object
   approached at approximately 150 knots and passed beneath
   and behind the observers aircraft.

Department of National Defence/   RG 24, vol. 17988
Ministère de la Défense nationale   File/Dossier HGC 940-105
                                       Part/partie 1

PUBLIC ARCHIVES
ARCHIVES PUBLIQUES
CANADA

Document 34: "On April 16, 1953, a metallic sphere flew underneath a plane over New Brunswick." Project Second Storey, Sighting Report, New Brunswick, 16 April 1953 © Government of Canada. Reproduced with the permission of Library and Archives Canada (2021). Source: Library and Archives Canada/Department of National Defence/e002750789 [Chatham]

Believe me, it was big enough in diameter and so close to me, that I could easily have a picture of it with a camera.

Within a minute, the object had flown away back to the southwest, as mysteriously as it had come. The man noted: "I was glad when it disappeared, because for a moment it made me worry."

It's obvious that today we would ascribe the object to something like a drone or remotely operated device, but in 1953, this was out of the question, especially with the observed maneuverability.

The witnesses were understandably reluctant to come forward with their sighting, and it wasn't until December of that year—eight months later—that a report was filed. But when it was filed, it was very detailed and covered several pages, with drawings, sketches, personal comments and frank admissions.

The man noted in his submission:

> I hope all these details [although] long and complicated will meet with your approval. But you can believe in my sincerity in all these facts, which are rather strange and quite difficult to put down on paper. I have done everything I could to give you all possible details. I have put much time on this report, however, I know it is for research, and as I like that type of thing myself, I feel it was for a worthy cause.

The case made a big impression within the Royal Canadian Air Force (RCAF) office that handled such cases. On March 16, 1954, Squadron Leader G.C. Campbell, on behalf of the Air Defence Command, wrote a letter to the man who had sent the report, praising him for his detailed account.

> Dear [redacted],
>
> This is to advise you that your exceptional report concerning a strange flying object has aroused a great deal of interest among officials of the RCAF who are responsible for this type of research.
>
> Your detailed report, one of the best received to this date, is undoubtedly the result of considerable work and interest on your part. The information you have given us has proved very valuable, particularly when compared with other information possessed by the RCAF.

> Please be assured, sir, that your earnest and complete cooperation in this project is greatly appreciated.
>
> It has been a pleasure to work with you and we hope to be able to repeat the opportunity to cooperate with such a gentleman.

The letter addressed one of the ongoing issues within ufology: that of the ultimate value of individual UFO sighting reports. While some believe UFO reports don't offer much of anything to present-day studies of the phenomenon, Campbell's letter notes that the Iberville case was "very valuable," especially in the context of "other information possessed by the RCAF."

Of course, we don't know what this "other information" might have been, but if the Iberville case represented the observation of an actual flying saucer, it may have been essential to the RCAF's understanding of the phenomenon as a whole.

This ability of a UFO to change direction effortlessly was also noted by two conservation officers almost a year later at about 4:25 pm on March 18, 1954, on Hecla Island, Manitoba. They had been driving their Bombardier across frozen Lake Winnipeg when their attention had been drawn to a silver "match-like" object, estimated to be 100 feet long and only eight feet thick. Over the next 20 minutes, they watched the object as it changed orientation from vertical to horizontal and back again, moving at an estimated 15,000 feet in altitude and about 10 miles away.

The Flight Lieutenant who interviewed them was impressed. One of the witnesses, he noted in his report, was:

> A genial alert individual whose many years of outdoor life are reflected in his faculty of observation. He was astounded at what he saw and originally would not consider reporting his sighting until he thought of its possible significance. He is definitely not perpetrating a hoax nor seeking publicity. The interrogator is certain that the observer reported exactly what he had seen and although unable to correlate his sighting with any known object or behavior pattern, did his best to truthfully convey the details.

One of the most remarkable UFO cases in the NRC files is not Canadian at all, and was witnessed by an American man. On June 24, 1953, at 11:30 am local time in Simiutak (now Simiutaq) Greenland, a weather observer stationed at the remote base on an uninhabited island had launched a weather balloon and was tracking it with a small telescope called a theodolite. The technician, who had 3 ½ years' experience performing his job, watched in amazement as a rotating red object flew from the southeast to the northwest, approaching the balloon that was at 18,000 feet in altitude.

As he watched the either triangular or circular object (he couldn't tell which), three times the size of the balloon, it collided, resulting in a "disintegrating balloon." The weather technician continued watching through the theodolite and reported: "Object hovered after collision in circular motion for fifteen seconds and then rapidly departed into wind." He observed it for five more minutes until it was lost to sight.

As with most UFO reports, many cases in the NRC UFO Files have explanations, some a bit more complicated than others. At 2:15 pm on January 27, 1968, two groups of people on shore at Queen Charlotte City in BC each reported something that seemed truly mysterious. In NRC case file N68/008, an observed object was described as looking like a "black whale," kind of like a "helicopter without rotors." For three minutes, the object silently approached from the west at about 500 feet, hovered in place briefly, then returned back to the west.

However, after investigation by the RCMP, it was found that the strange object had actually been a homemade paper balloon about the size of a ten-gallon drum. It was made from tissue paper with a lighted candle inside that heated the air and allowed the balloon to float over the ocean. In the 1960s, such pranks were relatively common in the USA, and it was not surprising that a copycat case would turn up in Canada.

In the wee hours of July 18, 1968, an RCMP Constable and three other people had two separate UFO sightings that highlight the difficulty that UFO investigators have in understanding how witnesses describe what they see.

According to NRC Case file N68/060, at 1:05 am that day, Cst. W.J. Whyte was with his wife at their home in Truro, Nova Scotia, when they saw a yellow circular object at high altitude moving west to east across the sky. The object appeared to travel "at speed of NORAD flights but at higher altitude" and appeared "several times larger and brighter than brightest star." It was seen for two or three minutes, and the witnesses judged it to be like a satellite but turned reddish before disappearing into the distance.

Five minutes later, a couple near Onslow Mountain, about eight kilometres north of Truro, saw a "large circular twinkling rosy red light" in the southwest, just above the trees. For about 15 minutes, they watched the stationary light, approximately twice the size of the brightest star, before it began to move and accelerated out of sight. Star charts show there was no bright planet in that location at the time of observation.

Despite the proximity of the witnesses to each other and their similar time frame, it doesn't sound like they saw the same object. But this case file illustrates some important factors in UFO case investigation.

First of all, one of the witnesses was a member of the RCMP. In the NRC UFO files, I would say that at least one-third to half of the cases involved RCMP, provincial or city police, or military witnesses. This is partially because the RCMP as a division had partnered with the NRC to investigate UFOs, and RCMP officers were most often called out to respond to witnesses' reports of UFOs. Since the NRC UFO investigations were part of a government program, it was an official body to which law enforcement officials felt confident about reporting their observations. Therefore, the quality of the UFO witnesses was what I would describe as very high.

Secondly, one interesting result from an analysis of the annual Canadian UFO Survey is that many UFO cases have more than one witness. The average number of witnesses in the Canadian UFO Survey has always been greater than one, and in some years was close to two. This means that in most cases there was immediate corroboration of the UFO observation, and more than one person saw the object or objects in the sky. In the Truro cases, each had two witnesses, bearing out this trend.

Third, the description of the UFO in case N68/060 was "circular," which presents a serious problem for investigators after the fact. What does "circular" really mean? Does it mean the witness judged the object to be round? A disc? A sphere? In fact, many cases filed even today have witnesses who say the object they saw was circular, but upon investigation and further questioning, it turns out they meant it was like a pancake or disc shaped.

Also, in practical terms, the actual shape of an object at an altitude of tens of thousands of feet simply cannot be determined unless its size is known accurately. Therefore, "circular" is just a guess or an assumption made by an observer. Both a square object and a sphere that are each about six feet across cannot be told apart by an average person looking at them from a distance of five miles. And then there's another issue: illumination. If an F-16 is flying at an altitude of five miles, you would not see it in the sky unless it was illuminated by lights, and the lights themselves are often not round or circular. What shape are lights that are that far away?

This concern is shown to be even more significant in NRC case N68/149, from Wanup, Ontario. There's not much to the report, other than that an object looking "approximately like a star" was seen on October 16, 1968, at 0040Z (1940 ET or 7:40 pm) for about 20 minutes. However, the report notes that the object was "green and red" and was "oval," but also that it appeared "circular." Yet in the witness' judgment, the UFO was "in outer space about 100 miles out." Was it starlike? Spherical? Disc-shaped? And more to the point, none of that would have been possible to see if it was actually 100 miles away.

With only the few details recorded by the RCMP or RCAF personnel about what the witnesses' reported, it's literally impossible to determine what actually was seen. At the very least, we can see that UFO reports by themselves don't prove much at all, least of all that UFOs might be alien spacecraft as some believe. UFO investigation isn't always easy.

As well, you never know where or when a UFO will be encountered. Imagine the surprise that two telephone linemen had when they saw a strange metallic cylinder while working atop a pole near the town of Lebel-sur-Quevillon in Northern Quebec on February 19, 1969. The case is recorded as NRC Case N69/066. It was just after lunch, at about 12:30 pm when a grey cigar-shaped object with "four fins" at its end moved slowly west to east over the trees and about 150 feet above the ground. The object was 100 feet long and only 15 feet in diameter with no visible windows, portholes, or cockpit. The men watched it for a few minutes as it glided slowly out of sight, bewildered by what they were seeing.

Although most cases in the NRC UFO files were simply textual reports, there were some copies of photographs taken by witnesses. Some of the most curious were those accompanying N72/025, concerning a disc-shaped object seen hovering over Willow Point, BC, on Vancouver Island.

The report simply says that: "The observer is apparently a reputable Campbell River businessman who does not want his identity divulged." The rest of the file is a typewritten version of an article in the *Inner Islander News*, detailing what was seen but again not revealing the name of the photographer.

The photos were taken on April 24, 1972, and the film was given to the newspaper for developing and publication then forwarded to the nearby Canadian Forces base at Comox for analysis. The photographer explained: "I'd like you to do it because I don't want people to think I'm some kind of kook. I know what I saw, and what I photographed, but I don't really expect anyone to believe me."

What he had seen was a "discus-shaped" object hovering stationary in the sky off the coast and apparently over Quadra Island, and the photos show this saucer in the sky among clouds. It had been spinning "like a top."

The object had a dull sheen, like "dirty chrome," and had "no markings, no wings, and not rotors," leading the witness to insist it was not any kind of helicopter or aircraft. It had lights flashing "on and off around its rim in what seemed to be a totally random sequence."

The saucer wobbled, titled, and shuddered, then shot straight upward about a thousand feet. It took off to the north on a zig-zag course and was lost to sight.

Only one of the photos was usable, and even it was blurry, showing the disc but not much else. The file did not include any additional photographic analysis, and the Comox radar was not of any use that day, either.

Some cases in the NRC UFO files are remarkable simply for where they occurred. For example, case N72/107, took place on Christmas Eve in 1972 at 9:40 a.m. Its location was given simply as: "PIN 1, Clinton Point."

This site is in the far north in what is now Nunavut but at that time was the Northwest Territories, on the shore of the Beaufort Sea. In 1972, it was little more than a military installation, in fact part of the Distant Early Warning (DEW) Line that stretched across the Canadian Arctic as part of NORAD's defence against over-the-pole enemy incursions.

L.J. Reeves was stationed at the site and reported seeing an object that: "Looked like a star, but brighter than a star." It moved west to east, stopped, then continued on and faded into the distance after five minutes.

This could very well have been simply a satellite that was passing overhead and possibly tumbling or re-orienting to the sun, losing some of its brilliance. But it was duly reported as a UFO, even from Canada's far north, from a cold military installation, during the long Arctic almost-24-hour night at that latitude.

Another interesting case in the NRC UFO files that didn't occur in Canada involved a Canadian navy ship, a destroyer-class submarine hunter, the *HMS Mackenzie*. According to case N68/100, on August 21, 1968, the *Mackenzie* was on a mission about 1,500 kilometres west of California in the Pacific Ocean. At 1258Z (almost 7 am local time), four of the ship's crew, including Major W.J. Draper, saw a group of starlike lights approaching from the northeast, initially only about ten degrees above the ocean horizon. The lights were all in a row and all appeared to be similar to the brightness of satellites, although one in the middle of the line seemed larger than the rest and seemed to have "a white glow" around it.

Within five minutes, the procession of lights progressed towards the ship until they passed almost directly overhead, and it then could be seen that there were 20 of them, all now heading towards the west. They kept their course steady and true until they were lost to sight in the west 13 minutes later.

A check of known satellite re-entries did not show anything recorded on that day. It was also a bit too long to have been a meteor train. What this well-witnessed group of lights was, is a mystery.

If this was a recent case, it might have been possible to explain it as a Starlink satellite constellation, one of hundreds of refrigerator-sized instruments launched into space during the last few years by SpaceX as a way to get low-cost Internet service to isolated parts of the world. But this was 1968, long before such things were even dreamt of.

Curiously, the location of this sighting in the Pacific was barely a hop, skip and jump from where the infamous "Tic Tac" UFO was encountered by pilots from the US navy ship *Nimitz* in 2004 off the coast of California. The case has become famous because of some leaked video purporting to show an advanced unknown vehicle maneuvering and moving at impossible speed while being chased by jet pilots.[1]

Coincidence?

Probably.

UFOs over Ottawa

Near midnight on July 19, 1952, air traffic controllers at Washington National Airport in Washington, D.C. observed several unusual objects on radar that did not seem to match any known aircraft in the area. Visually, a strange light was seen over the city that then flew away at high speed. At the same time, radar operators at Andrews Air Force

Base were seeing on their scopes odd groups of returns that moved slowly then moving away at incredible speeds—faster than 5,000 mph.

From Andrews, too, a bright light was seen, and pilots in the area also saw fast moving lights zipping through the sky. Concerned that enemy aircraft were in the air over the White House, F-94 jets were scrambled, but when they were vectored to where the radar returns were on screen, the objects vanished. This series of sightings is often characterized as the night that UFOs buzzed Washington—a brazen alien invasion of America's capital.[2]

Seventeen years later, in Canada, the official reaction to a similar event was somewhat more subdued. On March 4, 1969, at about 10:00 pm, RCMP Constable R.J. Shannahan was on routine foot patrol near the Prime Minister's residence in Ottawa. He happened to look up and saw "two rather bright flashing red lights in the sky," glowing sources of light but with no definite shape.

From his report, filed as N69/078:

> These lights were first seen directly overhead at a point slightly inside the gates to Government House, and were very bright red. The lights were very clear with no obstructions to hinder visibility. No definite shape could be distinguished nor was any type of trail behind these lights visible.

ROYAL CANADIAN MOUNTED POLICE · GENDARMERIE ROYALE DU CANADA

OTHER FILE REFERENCES	DIVISION	DATE	RCMP FILE REFERENCES
	"A"	5 MAR 69	69-400-5.
	SUB-DIVISION - SOUS-DIVISION		
	Protective		
	Section #1. (Gov't Hse)		

Unidentified Flying Objects -
Ottawa, Ontario - March 4th 1969.

4-3-69

1.   At approximately 10:00 P.M. this date, while on foot patrol from the Police Lodge at Government House to the Prime Minister's residence, I noticed two (2) rather bright flashing red lights in the sky. At first glance I assumed that they were aircraft, but could hear no sound of engines. At this time the sky was very clear.

2.   One of these lights proceeded east and was lost from view within a minute or less, while the other one travelled in a westerly direction. The light travelling west was visible for approximately 5 to 6 minutes. These lights were first seen directly overhead at a point slightly inside the gates to Government House, and were very bright red. The lights were very clear with no obstructions to hinder visibility. No definite shape could be distinguished nor was any type of trail behind these lights.visible.

3.   The forgoing information was passed to the Police Lodge via radio and Cpl. MARH reported same to the "A" Div. Desk NCO., Sgt. SMITH. A close watch was maintained for the next hour, while at the Prime Minister's residence, but no further sighting was made.

CONCLUDED HERE:

                                3/Cst.
                        (R.J. Shannahan) #26671.

CC Prot Subdiv RCMP
            Forwarded 6-3-69. 3/Cst. SHANNAHAN was unable
to give any estimation of the altitude of these objects.
CONCLUDED HERE.

                        S/Sgt.
                (A. MORRIS) Reg. No. 16184,
                1/c Section 1.

MAR 13.90*   5

Document 35: "On March 4, 1969, UFOs were seen by RCMP over the Prime Minister's residence." National research - Radio and Electrical Engineering Division - Unidentified flying objects, sighting of 3/4/1969 © Government of Canada. Reproduced with the permission of Library and Archives Canada (2021). Source: Library and Archives Canada/ Department of National Defence/e003000643

Shannahan wrote: "At first glance I assumed that they were aircraft but could hear no sound of engines."

As he watched, one light flew east and was lost to view within a minute, while the other went west "towards Parliament Hill" and was in sight for five to six minutes. For the next hour, RCMP officers maintained "a close watch" for anything else in the sky over the Prime Minister's residence, but nothing further was seen. No jets were scrambled, and there was no indication that nearby radar installations were asked about unidentified blips.

This is Canada, after all.

However, a little over a month later, on April 22, 1969, something more unusual was lurking near the nation's capital. At about 8 pm that night, according to case N69/091, three witnesses were traveling near Hammond, about 25 miles east of Ottawa, driving in heavy rain, when they topped a hill and saw an object that looked like: "a huge drinking cup turned upside down. It had two bright lights that were directed more horizontal than down and appeared to have a row of portholes."

Pink light was coming from inside the craft through the portholes, while white lights lit up the surrounding field. The 20-foot-long object was judged to be about 200 feet away and about five feet above the ground. Despite the rain, the witnesses rolled down the car windows for a better look and heard: "a whirling or whining sound, something like the noise of a generator."

They watched it for about 15 minutes before the object turned and zoomed over the nearby power transmission lines, over the trees, then out of sight. Drawings by the witnesses don't seem to be of anything conventional, and agree in their depiction of a saucer-shaped craft.

3

UFOS TAKE FLIGHT

~

Travelers near and far

It was late at night on August 15, 1968, and three people were traveling back home to Hamilton, Ontario, after a vacation in the Maritimes. They had left Truro, Nova Scotia, and were about 20 minutes east of Springhill on the Trans-Canada Highway when their car was "buzzed" by UFOs.

At around midnight, Dick Skewes was driving with his wife Anne Marie and their babysitter Gail Yemm. He drove up a hill and around a bend and saw what he thought was a group of aircraft hovering over the trees on his left. His wife thought the objects looked like water bombers putting out a fire, because they were flying so low.

Yemm recalls that there were five or six craft which she thought were planes hovering only about 50 feet above the trees, and: "...all I can remember is that there were a lot of lights. The only one I can remember is a yellow one, it appeared to be at the front and bigger than the rest." Mr. Skewes said that another craft was approaching at high speed to join the others.

All three were interviewed separately by RCMP, with slightly varying testimony. One thing they all agreed on was that as they watched the group of "unconventional" aircraft, one of the objects left the cluster and approached their car.

According to Mr. Skewes:

> ... as I came nearer the center of this activity, one of the forementioned craft broke away from the group, moved over the hwy. in front of me and began a slow descent of about 60°. I was sure we would be on a collision course. I slowed to a crawl but feared to stop. I turned the radio off and put my head out the window [but] could not hear a sound... a distinct outline of this vehicle was obscured by the series of rapidly & brilliantly flashing lights on the craft... the lights were extremely unconventional; unlike any I had ever seen. When the closing craft was 40-50 ft. away at, I would say at 35-40 ft. high, it suddenly veered up and disappeared into the distance behind me.

Mrs. Skewes had a stronger reaction when the object came towards them:

> I was positive it was going to land and collide with us. Dick slowed the car right down but there seemed to be no way of missing a collision. I prayed hard!!! I think was too frightened to even scream! It reared up just in time, passed right over the car and back over the trees to our right.

When the danger had passed, Mrs. Skewes was able to get a good look at what had buzzed their car:

> I watched it out the window and for the first time saw an outline other than the mass of lights. It was dark in colour with what looked like white dots all over it. It reminded me of the World War II plane on display in front of the CNE grounds.

Yemm had a decidedly less visceral reaction to what had been happening:

> We slowed down and one passed in front of us and this is the one I thought would hit us. We did not stop nor could I hear any sounds from these objects. As I thought these were airplanes, I did not pay much attention to them. It was just the yellow light I could remember best. When I glanced at it first I thought of a flying saucer then after

I thought I could see wings without lights so I thought nothing more about it.

Mr. Skewes continued on down the highway and his wife noted: "After we reached the end of that straight stretch of highway and rounded the corner, we lost sight of the crafts because they were so low. My last impression was of a light in the sky."

Now, one would think that being dive-bombed by a UFO would throw you off your game for a bit and rethink your continued travels. But once the UFOs had disappeared into the distance, Mr. Skewes kept driving—all the way to Toronto! In fact, it wasn't until *two days later*, on Saturday, August 17, as they were driving near Toronto that Mrs. Skewes asked Yemm what she thought of the objects they had seen two nights earlier.

"This was the first time the subject had been brought up," Yemm stated.

It was two additional days later, on Monday, August 19, 1968, that the Skewes reported their experience to the RCMP and the Canadian Forces. RCMP noted that Skewes explained: "He did not discuss this event with the other occupants of the car as he did not want to upset them." This, even though he admitted he was himself frightened by the near miss. Also, he didn't want to report what they had seen because he didn't want people to think he was unbalanced.

The RCMP report notes that Mr. Skewes was honourably discharged from the Royal Canadian Navy in 1964 and that while enlisted, he was a lookout on ships so he knew what aircraft looked like.

But if they weren't aircraft, what were they?

A little over a year later and a few provinces over, the setting was again perfect for a close encounter with a UFO. It was after 8:00 pm on October 3, 1969, with a light rain and a mist hanging in the air over the forest in eastern Manitoba.

It was into this eerie atmosphere that RCMP Constable S.B. Barrie and his wife Vivian drove their practically new 1968 Ford Falcon as they set off on the beginning of their vacation, heading for Quebec. Barrie was from the Pine Falls Detachment and they had already traveled for more than an hour along a very poor highway that was under construction. The condition of the road and the weather were so bad, he was barely doing 20 mph. And at a point about five miles west of the town of Rennie, he had to stop to clean mud off his headlights.

When he got out of the car, Barrie took advantage of the opportunity to get a better look at a light he had been watching in the sky ahead of them. He thought it might have been a reflection on the windshield, but could now see the light more plainly as it hung just off the highway and over the trees.

He got back in the car and continued driving, and soon could see the light resolved into "an inverted saucer," hovering and moving "back and forth in short, jerky movements," and even a "rocking motion." The object was "light pink" and shone with an intensity that reminded Barrie of white-hot stainless steel.

After about 15 minutes of driving, the puzzled couple found themselves getting much closer to the saucer, or rather, it to them. It was now only about 500 feet away, about 50 to 100 feet above the forest. It seemed to be about 20 feet in diameter with a flat bottom, and they could both see a strange white "tail" that snaked from the object towards the ground.

Suddenly, the car's windshield wipers stopped working. Soon the headlights went out and the engine stalled as well. Barrie was unable to get the ignition to fire so he got out of the car again. When he did, the UFO zoomed to the southwest over the trees without making a sound and was lost to sight. Barrie said that after the object left, he could sense the air had "a heaviness about it, and a strange odour." After the UFO was gone, he was able to get the car started again, and the electrical system was working as before.

It should be emphasized that Barrie was an RCMP constable whose veracity and observation skills were considered much above average. He undoubtedly risked his career by making a formal UFO report to the NRC through his own police detachment office.

This object as described was definitely not a star or planet, as the cloud cover precludes that possibility. It did not appear to be a helicopter or aircraft and the explanation of a reflection is ruled out because it was seen even after Barrie exited the car.

In fact, the biggest problem with the case is that there is no supportive evidence other than the eye witness testimony of two people. There might have been a chance that the car itself might have yielded some clues, if the electrical system had been inspected immediately by investigators.

But that never happened, because after the UFO left and the car started, the Barries kept driving on their trip eastward. Constable Barrie dutifully reported their experience, but not until October 29th when they returned home 26 days later, and it became NRC Case N69/167.

Why let a UFO spoil a vacation, anyway?

Along the same lines, on November 5, 1974, Harold Verge was driving from Mahone Bay to Bridgewater, Nova Scotia, at about 8:30 pm, when he saw three bright amber lights appear in his rear-view mirror. It was a scene right out of the movie *Close Encounters of the Third Kind*, when Ron Neary saw some lights come up behind him and he assumed they were on a car, when in fact they were on a UFO.

Similar to what would be depicted in the movie a few years later, Verge assumed the three lights behind him were on a truck about to pass him—until they moved around the *right* side of his vehicle and paced him as he drove.

NRC Case N74/100 goes on: "The lights paralleled the car in this position for about 30 seconds and then abruptly disappeared."

This all happened while Verge was driving in the pouring rain at 50-60 mph and the lights remained at eye level throughout the encounter. It was all over in a minute and a half, and Verge was left wondering what had just happened. It unnerved him so much that he was compelled to report it even though he must have known he might not be believed.

Case N69/122 in the NRC files seemed rather bland compared with some of the other cases in the collection. In the wee hours of July 13, 1969, a round, white object was seen by Edgar Paquette and Mrs. Leo Edwards as they were driving near Petawawa, Ontario. The object was at an altitude of 1,500 feet and was rising as it slowly headed southeast.

That was essentially all that was in the teletype report, other than that a third witness was an Ontario Provincial police officer named McKay, from nearby Pembroke, Ontario.

But there was something else appended to the report: a newspaper clipping from the *Ottawa Journal*, dated July 14, 1969. It told a somewhat different story.

The newspaper article contained an interview with Paquette, who was described as being a civilian employee of the Department of National Defence. He had indeed been driving with "a female companion" at about 3:30 am when she pointed out the object to him.

"It was no falling star, and it was following us," he said, noting that the Petawawa River which paralleled the road was "lit up like day" by the bright object.

Convinced the object had seen them and was targeting their vehicle, Paquette shut off the car's headlights so they couldn't be seen anymore. This tactic seemed to work because the UFO "appeared to hesitate."

Of course, the best plans tend to fall apart. Paquette thought he would get out and have a better look at the object, so when he opened the door, the interior light turned on, illuminating him and the car.

The newspaper account noted: "That was when the UFO descended to within 60 feet of the ground."

Naturally, Paquette got out of the car and started signalling the UFO with a flashlight, "and this rig started to come for us."

At its closest point, the object seemed to be eight feet in diameter and Paquette was able to see it had two "legs" beneath it.

Completely unnerved, Paquette got back into the car with his companion, who was similarly hysterical. They drove to the nearest farmhouse and she ran to the door, pleading with the occupants to call the police.

Spurring to action, Paquette reported: "I finally got her in the car to drive her home after telling her that if we were going to get it, we were going to get it."

His lack of reassurance notwithstanding, they drove to their home where they woke their teenage children to watch the UFO and then drove with them back to the highway where the object "came down at us again."

The newspaper account noted ten other witnesses, including OPP Constable Jack McKay and Grant Chaplin, who said they followed the UFO for 38 minutes as it traveled southeast "at high altitude."

Questioned by a reporter on whether the UFO was just a bright star, McKay retorted: "This was really bright, mister...There wasn't another thing in the sky at the time, and it was daylight before it disappeared."

He said they lost sight of it when it passed behind some trees, and this immediately made me think the UFO was in fact a star or planet after all. Star charts show that Venus was low in the northeast and Saturn was low almost directly east on that date and time. That suggests the object seen by police was a planet, although since both planets were visible, that doesn't jive with McKay's view that there wasn't anything else up there. It also doesn't go well with Paquette's close encounter, although what we can read about him suggests he may have been an excitable guy and possibly could have imagined the UFO was getting close.

Or—it was something else.

Something else—like the object that paced some travelers in 1970. In an incredible scene right out of a movie, a UFO was said to have got much too close for comfort to a couple driving along the Trans-Canada Highway in Saskatchewan.

Case N70/076 tells how on November 1, 1970, at about 10:30 pm, Mr. and Mrs. Stewart Wilkinson were traveling west and were just past the town of Pense, Saskatchewan, when they saw an odd light not far from them near the highway. It seemed to be "mainly flat" and about three to four feet long, like a disc or oval.

The NRC report explains what happened next:

> Object followed Mr. Wilkinson's car at approximately 20 feet to the right at an altitude of 10 to 15 feet. At one point the object moved ahead of the car and hovered over a truck parked approximately a half mile away. As Mr. Wilkinson came abreast of the truck, the object moved to the left side of his car approx. 30 feet away and almost on the ground. It remained at this distance for the rest of the period of observation.

What's highly significant is that the UFO was initially to the Wilkinsons' right side and then moved to their left. This eliminates the possibility that they were mistaking a star or planet for a saucer since the highway at that point in Saskatchewan is almost poker straight, without any curves that would make a light in the sky seem to change its orientation. It's also remarkable that the object looked like it was so close to the car. At night, it is very hard to judge distance, but a matter of only a car length or so away would have been pretty much to dismiss as anything easily explainable.

The NRC report continued:

> Mr. Wilkinson reduced his speed and came to a gradual stop, the object slowed to a stop and hovered beside the car for approx. 10-15 seconds, then moved ahead towards Moose Jaw, remained visible for 20 seconds, and gradually disappeared or fused into the lights of that city.

One would have expected, if the UFO had actually been a star or planet, that it would naturally have stopped when Wilkinson stopped his car, but then when it started moving again and disappeared into the distance, that rules a few possibilities out.

In total, the object followed the Wilkinsons' car for about 12 minutes over a distance of about ten miles, and their speeds varied between 70 mph and a dead stop. When stopped beside the car, Wilkinson rolled his window down to listen for a noise from the UFO, but there was only silence.

The NRC report notes their other tidbits of information about the object:

The object moved with a wobbling motion similar to a small boat in choppy water. A beam of light was observed extending from the bottom of the object and was beamed towards the ground. The object was brighter when on the right side of the car than when on the left side.

Although there is nothing else in the NRC file to show that the case was followed up to any extent, there was at least some checking done. The last line in the file simply notes that: "There was no reported aircraft in the area during the period of this sighting."

So, what was it that flew alongside the Wilkinsons that night?

Less than a year later, on September 19, 1971, three other witnesses were followed by a UFO as they drove along a highway just outside of Winnipeg. Case N71/075 has a lengthy account by Arthur Honke of what he, his brother Alec, and their friend Gordon Campbell saw at about 3:30 am that morning.

The three men were heading for their favourite location to do some wild chicken hunting. As Alec was driving northward, he saw a bright flash as something passed quickly ahead of them in front of the car. They both saw a light that had now appeared just off the right side of the road not far ahead. Alec pulled abreast of it, stopped the car and turned off the ignition. They rolled down the windows to see if they could hear anything and heard a low-pitched humming noise coming from the object that was only about 50 to 75 yards away.

From the report:

The object was shaped like two saucers, one on top of the other and there was a red light on the left side in the middle, and a green light right in the very centre of it and a white light to the right of it still in the middle. The lights appeared to be stationary and just blinked on and off while the rest of it was spinning. The red and green lights were both flashing together while the white one stayed on...

They judged the object to be about "a car length long" and "a car width wide." The UFO remained stationary for about 30 seconds, although once during that time the side farthest from the witnesses seemed to dip down and backward slightly then righted itself again. The object then slowly started moving at about 15 mph back southwards towards Winnipeg. The three men debated whether they should turn around and follow it, but it was decided to keep going and report their experience to the RCMP at the next town.

As they drove north, they realized the object was following them at a distance. It kept pace with them for about 45 minutes then seemed to cross back over the highway and disappeared.

The men had second thoughts about reporting their experience. Alec Honke admitted: "We were going to report it to the RCMP but we didn't, 'cause Gordon thought we'd be locked up or something."

Despite these reservations, they did eventually report it to the RCMP, whose primary questions were whether any of them had been drinking to excess that night. (They hadn't.)

All three gave detailed statements to police, and all were consistent. Even their sketches showed a football-shaped object with lights.

But why would aliens bother chasing humans in cars?

Speed Bird and friends

According to NRC Case N70/032, "Speed Bird" saw a UFO on June 15, 1970. The report in the NRC file itself was brief, with meagre information, and I puzzled over the odd phrase for some time.

The report noted that at 1259Z (GMT), Speed Bird 591 was about 400 kilometres east of the northern tip of Newfoundland, over the North Atlantic Ocean. The object seen was described as triangular and resembled a "partially inflated balloon." It was at an altitude of 34,000 feet and was traveling west, in view for about five minutes.

Eventually, I discovered a reference that explained "Speed Bird" was pilot jargon for British Airways jetliners, and this made sense because in the report it was noted that the crew of a second aircraft, Air India 101, had also witnessed the UFO.

N 70 /032

JUN 16 70

NRC REED OTT

COMM SQN OTT
00R024
P R 151538Z JUN 70
FM CANDEFRAD SENNETERRE
TO RCCWC/CANFORCEHED
INFO RCCPC/DEFRES OTTAWA
RCCSLW/22NRHQ NORTH BAY
BT
UNCLAS OPS 101
FOR CFQC AND NRC UFO REPORT
(A) 1259Z
(B) CLEAR
(C) SPEED BIRD 591
(D) 52N - 50W
(E) AIR INDIA 101
(F) TRIANGULAR SHAPE, 34000 FEET, WEST BOUND, PARTIALLY INFLATED
BALLOON
(G) APPROXIMATELY 5 MINS
(H) NIL
(I) PASS INFORMATION TO NORAD
BT
NRC REED OTT

COMM SQN OTT

RECEIVED
16 JUN 1970
RADIO REGISTRY
National Research Council

National Research Council of Canada/   RG 77, Vol. 306
Conseil national de recherches du Canada

Document 36: "On June 15, 1970, a UFO was reported by
pilots over the North Atlantic." Herzberg Institute
of Astrophysics - Reports on non-meteoric sightings,
unidentified flying objects, UFO's 6/15/1970 © Government
of Canada. Reproduced with the permission of Library
and Archives Canada (2021). Source: Library and Archives
Canada/National Research Council of Canada fonds/e002745441

Whatever the UFO was in the clear sky that morning, it was seen by crews of two different commercial aircraft. And it made a sufficient impression on the pilots that it was requested in their report to the NRC: "Pass information to NORAD."

More than a year later and thousands of miles west on September 28, 1971, at 10:52 pm, the pilot and crew of an Air Canada airliner reported to the Canadian Forces base in Winnipeg that they were flying at 31,000 feet when they saw a "flashing white light heading SSE at moderate speed." Its altitude was estimated to be higher than 50,000 feet. The NRC Case file N71/074 notes: "The white light was of the intensity of a navigation light, not a strobe light." It was seen for about a minute and was lost to sight.

And about a year later still, over Quebec, a pilot and co-pilot were: "In fighter aircraft 35,000 ft. 060 degrees 70 miles of Val D'Or" when they saw: "One object, white oval, small red tail." According to NRC Case 072/042, this happened at 9:00 pm on July 3, 1972. They watched the object for two minutes, during which time it traveled an estimated 40 miles. According to the experienced airmen, the object was: "at approx. 100,000 ft., traveling south very fast."

On July 25, 1973, the flight crew of a passenger airliner reported a UFO, the statement becoming NRC case N73/071. It was 1735 GMT when Empress 381 (a Canadian Pacific DC-8), on its way from Amsterdam to Vancouver, had passed over Greenland and was just over the eastern coast of Baffin Island.

Unbeknownst to the passengers on board, the pilot had just seen a strange object uncomfortably near to his aircraft. He radioed air traffic control and told them there was a "large balloon in close proximity." When the ATC centre asked what it looked like, at 1739 GMT, the pilot replied that the balloon was: "Approx. 200 ft. in diameter and approx. 3 miles from aircraft."

ATC obviously asked why the object could not have simply been an actual balloon, so at 1741 GMT, the pilot responded: "It was not a balloon because it had been paralleling their course for 5 to 6 minutes," The airliner was flying at 31,000 feet on a heading of 260 degrees (almost straight west) at 500 knots (about 575 mph).

That's all we know. The only other thing in the report is that someone on board the aircraft took two photos with "a small camera."

The photos were not included in the file.

July 14, 1974 was a stormy afternoon, with scattered thundershowers across southern Quebec. At 3:36 pm, pilots of two different aircraft encountered something strange flying in their airspace.

According to NRC case N74/052, Capt. Korsvold was flying his Scandinavian 094 airliner over Quebec in a "high level" jet route and was over Charlevoix when he reported seeing a triangular object moving southwest at about 33,000 feet. At about this same time, Mr. C.W. Bacon was piloting a private jet heading for Burlington, Vermont, and was about 35 miles southeast of Quebec City. Bacon agreed the object was triangular and at a bit higher altitude, about 40,000 feet, and to him it seemed to be stationary in the sky. The UFO was in sight for about seven minutes.

Meanwhile, however, during the time the UFO was being observed, air traffic control at CFB Bagotville reported strong interference on a frequency of 121.5 MHz. This was of concern because that is the frequency reserved for aircraft in distress. The signal was also disrupting transmissions at RCAF Station Mont Apica, a NORAD radar base and lasted about ten minutes. It was calculated to have originated from somewhere between 100 and 180 degrees from the receivers, in the southeast. Once the UFO and the interference were gone, all was quiet again.

A more detailed encounter of a UFO by a pilot as recorded in the NRC UFO files is N74/077, which took place in the skies over Bishop's Falls, Newfoundland, on October 10, 1974. John Breen, an air traffic controller at Gander Airport, was flying his private Cessna 172 from Deer Lake home to Gander with his girlfriend Janice Gould in the passenger seat. At 10:10 pm, they were just about over Grand Falls, about 60 miles west of Gander, at about 5,000 feet and going 134 mph., when Breen saw: "a solitary greenish, aluminous light." This light seemed to be moving a few thousand feet below his plane, at perhaps an altitude of about 3,000 feet.

Figuring that his green starboard navigation light was reflecting from something, Breen manually turned off all his navigation lights for a second, only to find the mysterious light below him was still there. Neither he nor Gould could see anything attached to this odd green light as it seemed to speed up and move ahead of the plane, slow down and then move behind them, maintaining a relative position for about 25 minutes.

By this time, they were only about five miles from Gander, so Breen radioed the airport tower to tell them what he was seeing. Robert Lawrence, the controller on duty in the tower at the time, told Breen: "... a target was picked up by ... 6-mile radar, however, the object remained on the screen for only two sweeps of the radar needle." However: "The target did not show up on the screen as an aircraft."

The NRC report notes:

> The target did, however, indicate while on the screen that its course had now changed from a north-west course to a westerly course and that the reason it could no longer be picked up on radar was that it was now believed to be flying at tree-top level. Continued attempts to regain contact with the target on radar met with negative results.

When Breen reached Gander, he circled the airport trying to find the light, but was unable to locate it again. Gander ATC notified NORAD of the UFO encounter, which logged the incident and that may have been the end of the file—until about six hours later.

At 4:15 am on October 11, 1974, the captain and co-pilot of a DC-8 airliner owned by United Airlines (but bearing a Capital Airlines registration) were descending into Gander because of a technical issue. The airliner was flying at about 7,500 feet and cruising at approximately 290 miles per hour, heading west.

As they approached Gander, the air crew saw an object with flashing red and white lights, although the object itself was indistinguishable. It: "… apparently pulled alongside the DC-8 jet liner and continued on a parallel course with the aircraft." And exactly like the case of the Cessna just hours earlier in the same area: "The object in question was further described as being able to keep up to the DC-8, and at times would speed up slightly, just ahead of the DC-8 and then would return back alongside the aircraft."

This aerial cat-and-mouse game continued for five to seven minutes, until: "…the object in question, still travelling alongside the DC-8, entered a somewhat small cloud formation and disappeared." Both pilot and co-pilot insisted the object was not an aircraft.

This view seems to have been supported by the ATC supervisor at Gander, who was now Edward Duhany (perhaps Lawrence had finished his shift). According to the NRC file, he advised: "… no other aircraft were reported to be in the area at the time of the incident. Duhany further stated that their radar monitors at the Gander Air Traffic Control Centre did not pick up any other targets except the descending DC-8."

And, like Breen's observation, this was duly reported to NORAD.

Finally, a military case almost 70 years old offers some insight into what Canadian air force pilots experienced in the skies.

On October 1, 1954, at 9:20 am, a test pilot for the RCAF was flying in a clear blue sky over Montreal in a F86 Mark V Sabre at 30,000 feet.

An experienced pilot, he had flown missions during the Second World War and had since been assigned to the RCAF.

According to a set of documents in the LAC NRC UFO Files, Records 13046-5161-10933 to 13046-5161-10938, dated November 2, 1954, the pilot was on a heading of 180 degrees when he sighted a contrail high over the north end of Lake Champlain, Quebec, heading south-southwest.

At 9:32 am, he climbed to 51,000 feet at an airspeed of 0.7 Mach, or about 540 mph, nearing the speed of sound. The pilot thought the contrail was being made by a single-engine aircraft from what appeared to be a "black dot" that he estimated to be approximately 100 feet in front of the contrail. He thought the object was about the same size as his own aircraft.

The report goes on:

> As the Sabre was at its maximum altitude, he was unable to close on the object which was heading approximately 200 degrees and traveling at about the same speed as his own aircraft at an estimated altitude of 60,000 to 65,000 feet. Being unable to close on the object or climb, he turned onto a heading of 90 degrees and noticed that the contrail made a similar turn. Returning to Montreal, from the Burlington-Vermont area, he noticed that the contrail appeared to climb at a 45-degree angle while on this easterly heading and disappeared. At no time was this object or aircraft painted on any radars.

The pilot had observed the object for about ten minutes, long enough to ascertain it was definitely an aerial vehicle of some kind. But whose?

When he landed and made his report to the command duty controller, the Eastern Air Defense Force was asked if it was theirs, and the reply was negative. Continental Air Defense Command (CONAD), part of the United States Department of Defense, was told of the incident, which checked with Strategic Air Command, with similar results.

Up in the air

The NRC UFO case N79/71 has a few curious elements, but really doesn't seem all that significant at first glance. The file is dated September 21, 1979, but its content comes from a letter received from a witness on August 31, 1979, about an incident that happened on August 17, 1979. The letter was from Elma L'Abbe, who wrote that she was in a small airplane with a companion over St-Jovite, Quebec, when they saw a: "Rolling energy ball with a red radiant side and a white radiant side." The object was 300 feet in diameter and 50 feet wide (presumably meaning a disc) and disappeared into the west after five to eight minutes.

Not much there, but a ball of energy sounds rather interesting. The file did not contain any details on a follow up investigation, but it did also have the letter from Ms. L'Abbe herself, and it painted a very different picture. Although the copy on file is only partially readable, it's enough to show that something very unusual happened over Quebec that night.

L'Abbe wrote:

> On August 17, 1979, I was flying from Saint-Jovite, Québec, to Arnprior, Ontario, [on a heading of] 270 degrees. I was in a single prop fixed wing white with blue markings 1974 Cherokee Warrior aircraft. I was sitting beside the pilot in the cockpit... Please note, neither myself nor the pilot were under the influence of alcohol or drugs. I am 45 years of age. We are both healthy, stable, cool, calculating individuals, not given to hallucinations or hysteria. We have known each other over 25 years. I am, by profession, a medical technologist. The pilot is, by profession, a police officer of approximately 16 years experience... [and] is a pilot of many years' experience.

At about 9:00 pm, L'Abbe said they were flying above St-Jovite, Quebec, above the Gatineau Hills about approximately 40 miles northeast of Ottawa. Visibility was excellent and the flight seemed uneventful. But then:

> I looked out of my window and observed the right wing becoming red in color. I then looked to my left past the pilot's head and observed that the left wing was also red in color... The pilot said to me, 'The aircraft is slowing down, our airspeed is zero and the instruments are behaving strangely.'

> He then said: 'I can't control the aircraft. The controls are jammed or something. We should be falling, yet we aren't.' At that point, we both felt the aircraft being pulled upwards. [Our plane] appeared to be stationary in the sky, but was being drawn upwards.

L'Abbe and her companion were completely baffled, but were even more aghast by what happened next:

> The pilot looked out the right windows and said to me, 'My God, look at the size of it, it must be close to 300 feet in diameter.'

> When I looked, I saw a gigantic red ball of energy close to the right wing and close to the aircraft. It sped away rapidly and as it did it appeared to be white light on the reverse side. The depth of it was approximately 50 feet. It disappeared into a large dark gray cloud to the West of us, only to reappear in the same cloud...

Whatever this was, she seemed to be describing a disc 300 feet in diameter and 50 feet thick. As they watched, it moved as if it was rolling along the cloud, and they were able to see that it was red on one side and white on the other.

Thankfully, the encounter was coming to an end, as the object began moving away from them:

> When it sped away from our aircraft we had a falling sensation. The aircraft was returning to normal. The altimeter read 5,000 feet. We estimated that we must have fallen 1,000 feet before we got this reading. In total, we estimated that we had been drawn upwards 2,000 feet at least. At 4,000 feet we were flying once again, right on course, just as if it had been before this experience... As we descended to land at Arnprior airport, the rolling red and white energy ball disappeared into the orange sky of the sunrise.

The couple were relieved that things seemed to have returned to normal and began trying to figure out what had happened to them. L'Abbe noted that because the experience lasted five to eight minutes by her watch, they ruled out Saint Elmo's fire because of the duration and the UFO's reappearance in the distant cloud. Curiously, the pilot's watch had stopped at 9:00 pm, when the encounter had begun, although her watch was unaffected.

In the days following the encounter, L'Abbe was determined to try and understand what had happened to them. She noted:

> At the advice of my personal physician here in Arnprior, I requested that screening tests be done to determine whether or not the pilot

and myself were exposed to excess radiation and absorbed same. I made this request Monday, August 20, 1979, to Dr. Wate of the Radiation Protection Bureau... and I must say that he was less than helpful or cooperative. He claimed our case to be beyond his realm of experience...

And there the matter rests. We are left with a mystery, ostensibly of a UFO that somehow affected an airplane while in flight. There is no evidence that the plane was ever examined by the NRC or RCMP, and we do not know whether L'Abbe or her companion had any further effects.

4

DOWN BUT NOT OUT

~

Getting down to Earth

As will be described in a later chapter, one of the most-discussed Canadian UFO cases is that of an object said to have crashed into Shag Harbour, Nova Scotia, in October 1967. Canadian airspace seems to be particularly troublesome for UFOs to navigate, as there have been several examples of objects reported to have crashed onto Canuck soil or into our waters.

Sometimes, there are even pieces of recovered debris that attest to the fact something fell from space onto Canada. Such was the case of fragments of a "space vehicle" found near Wollaston Lake in Saskatchewan in 1968. The pieces, some quite large, were transported for inspection to the National Research Council of Canada in Ottawa. One of the pages of RCMP documents about the incident is titled: "U.F.O. Found in Northern Saskatchewan."

The document noted the object was: "... found by an unnamed pilot in the Wollaston Lake area of Saskatchewan, roughly 450 miles northeast of Prince Albert near the Manitoba border. Examination revealed the exhibit had likely formed part of a vehicle that travelled in outer space."

Analysis found that it was 99 per cent pure titanium and was "the largest piece from a satellite that has ever landed on Earth" (at that time).

And here we have a bit of a puzzle. In 1968, a chunk of such a large satellite was considered worthy of detailed analysis by the RCMP and NRC, with many pages of documentation. But only eight years earlier, something that sounded very similar wasn't worth spending much time fretting over.

It's been more than 60 years since the RCMP investigated a report that something unusual fell into Clan Lake, 30 miles north of Yellowknife. Documents in the NRC UFO files show the RCMP and RCAF were both curious about what happened on June 22, 1960.

A look at the two dozen documents regarding the NRC investigation of the case show that it was an ongoing consideration for several years. The RCMP report on the incident contains a lengthy description of what was seen.

ROYAL CANADIAN MOUNTED POLICE

DIVISION FILE No.

DIVISION "G"H,   SUB-DIVISION   DETACHMENT
                 Fort Smith   Yellowknife
PROVINCE N.W.T.   DATE   19-7-60.
RE.

▓▓▓▓▓▓▓ - B: ▓▓▓, Yellowknife, N.W.T.
Report of Strange Object Striking Clan Lake, Clan Lake Dist., N.W.T.
(YELLOWKNIFE DETACHMENT CASE)

18-7-60

1.   With reference to the above, please be advised
that this ▓▓▓▓▓▓▓▓ contacted this office and advised
that on 22-6-60 he had been camping on the shore of Clan
Lake and that after hearing a strange noise he had seen
a strange object strike the water of the lake and after
spinning on the surface for a short length of time the
object had disappeared beneath the surface.

2.   The following self explanatory statement was
given by ▓▓▓▓▓.

STATEMENT OF ▓▓▓▓▓▓▓ - age ▓▓ of Yellowknife, N.W.T.
BEGINS: On June 22nd, 1960 at about 6.00 P.M. I was
dropped off at Clan Lake by Wardair Otter. We piled my
camp gear on the shore and the plane left. About 20
or 25 minutes after the plane left I heard a noise
which sounded to me like a big plane in the distance.
I never paid much attention to this noise until it got
loud. I looked in the sky but couldn't see anything.
The noise appeared to come from very high up. The
noise kept getting louder and louder and I kept watching
periodically but could not see anything. I then heard
something strike the water and when I turned around
I saw a splash and what appeared to be some object with
arms or spokes rotating in the water. The object was
rotating very rapidly and throwing water. Gradually
the object seemed to spin less and finally stopped.
After the object stopped there was a backwash which
came over to where I was. This would be about 1700 feet
from where the object landed. When my partner, ▓▓▓▓▓
▓▓▓▓▓ came we took the canoe and went over to the spot
where the object hit the water. There was grass about
18" high were the object hit and this appeared burnt on
the east, north east side of where the object struck and
the rest of the grass around an area of about 20 feet by
60 feet was cut up in small pieces. We felt around
with the paddles and a pole and found a channel which
corresponded to the cut path of grass. This channel
would be about one foot deeper at one end and about
three feet deeper at the other than the lake proper.
The lake floor appeared to be very much disturbed and
the water very muddy. My partner and I went back
to the spot on two more occasions and looked and felt
around but could not see or feel anything.
       The object I saw in motion in the water appeared
to be about 4 to 6 feet wide. I could not see any color
because of the flying water. I did not see any steam
when the object hit the water.
                                              PTO

FILE NUMBERS, HEADING AND MARGINAL REFERENCE ARE TO BE PROPERLY FILLED IN.

Document 37: "A report of an object that fell into Clan
Lake, Northwest Territories, in 1960." National research
- Radio and Electrical Engineering Division - Unidentified
flying objects, sighting of 6/22/1960 © Government of
Canada. Reproduced with the permission of Library and
Archives Canada (2021). Source: Library and Archives
Canada/Royal Canadian Mounted Police fonds/RG 18 vol. 3779,
file HQ 400-Q-5, parts 1 to 7 [Clan Lake]

That evening, at about 6:00 pm, a prospector named John Person had been dropped off by seaplane at Clan Lake to set up a camp in preparation for his work and getting the camp ready for his partner who was coming later. After about 20 minutes, he heard a noise like another aircraft approaching and looked up to see if he could see it, but there was nothing visible. The noise kept getting louder and he periodically looked up but was unable to locate the source of the sound.

Finally, he heard something hit the water behind him and when he turned around:

> I saw a splash and what appeared to be some object with arms or spokes rotating in the water. The object was rotating very rapidly and throwing water. Gradually the object seemed to spin less and finally stopped. After the object stopped there was a backwash which came over to where I was. This would be about 1,700 feet from where the object landed.

> The object I saw in motion in the water appeared to be about 4 to 6 feet wide. I could not see any color because of the flying water. I did not see any steam when the object hit the water.

When his partner arrived, they both got into their canoe and paddled over to where the object hit the water.

> There was grass about 18 inches high where the object hit, and this appeared burnt on the east-northeast side where the object struck and the rest of the grass around an area of about 20 feet by 60 feet was cut up in small pieces.

They used a paddle and a pole to probe the lake bottom and found there seemed to be a "channel" that was a foot deeper at one end and three feet deeper at the other, compared with the rest of the muddy lake bottom. This channel corresponded with the area where the grass had been cut and otherwise affected. However, they could not detect any kind of object under the water.

The two men spent the next three weeks prospecting and working in the area. When they were picked up and taken back to Yellowknife, Person contacted the RCMP and told them his story on July 18, 1960.

The next day, RCMP Cpl. Matheson flew to the site in a seaplane and stood on its pontoons to examine the lakebed. He reported:

...it would appear that an object did land on the East side of Clan Lake, however, nothing could be found... There is a space approximately twelve feet wide and forty feet long where the reeds are completely gone and the water in this space slightly deeper.

It's important to note that in several documents, the RCMP noted that the witness was a person of good repute and very responsible. He was very familiar with the area and was well versed in bush living so he was considered a very good observer with no reason to make up stories.

On August 15, 1960, Cpl. Matheson returned to Clan Lake to check again for any sign of the submerged object. He probed the underwater mud with a rod but was unable to find anything. He even went over the area with a Geiger counter in case the object was radioactive, but there was nothing detected above normal background levels. He marked the spot with some larger trees in case there was a need for others to search for it later.

Throughout the fall and winter of 1960, discussion ensued between the RCMP and RCAF about what to do regarding the fallen object. Tracking centers in both the USA and Canada were unable to correlate the time and place of the incident to anything on record, and so the Department of Defence did not think the event was of significance to them.

The Director of Air Intelligence for the RCAF agreed that Gordon Brown, a geologist in Yellowknife with Giant Gold Mines, be contracted to fly into Clan Lake with a magnetometer to help search for the object. But because of scheduling problems, this never happened, and it was eventually decided to refer the issue to Dr. Ian Halliday of the Dominion Observatory in Ottawa, who thought the object was likely a meteorite.

The meteorite theory was attractive because if it was hot from entering the atmosphere, it could have sent up a cloud of steam when it hit the lake. It was suggested that this steam would have been misinterpreted as an object with spokes and water being thrown off.

Meteorites are not always that hot when they reach the ground. Furthermore, any meteorite large enough to cause such a big splash and create a channel in the lake bed would certainly have been of interest to the meteoriticists in the National Research Council. Yet any follow-up to the case just fizzled out.

Since National Defence said there had not been any space object tracked in the area, it was not a piece of rocket or satellite. If on the other hand it was a meteorite, given that such chunks of rock and metal are very valuable to scientists, one large enough to have created an underwater gouge on the lake bottom should have been of enough interest to try and retrieve it.

And yet, the interest in any investigation abated after a few years, and was forgotten.

No one seemed to want to know more about the UFO that crashed into Canada's Northwest Territories in 1960.[1]

Besides Shag Harbour (see Chapter 6), the NRC UFO Files has a record of another report of a UFO falling into the ocean, this time off the coast of Newfoundland. According to case N70/057, on Aug. 14, 1970, at 8:45 pm, residents of Little Heart's Ease and St. Jones in Trinity Bay reported a "blood red" fireball with a "trail of lighter colour." It was described as being eight to ten feet long and about four feet wide, with the tail extending several feet beyond the "body" of the object. It was seen for about five minutes as it passed over Little Hearts Ease heading northeast at a height estimated to be about 1,000 feet. The object made a rushing noise and there was a "sound of burning."

The next line in the report, however, adds something that puts a slightly different spin on it: "After it passed over settlement of Little Hearts Ease, it crashed into the water near the mouth of the harbour of Little Hearts Ease. It was described as having a wobbling motion just prior to crash."

Now it's possible that the witnesses on shore were simply watching a very bright fireball or meteor falling to Earth, and it only looked like it went into the water because of their perspective. But a five-minute fireball is rare.

According to the file, when RCMP arrived at the scene, much like in the Shag Harbour incident, they went out in a boat to search the area of the ocean where the UFO had been seen to crash, but they could not find anything. They canvassed residents of the town, and found "a full confirmation of the sighting" based on others' testimony: the observation of a UFO crashing into the ocean off the coast of Canada.

Along the same lines, Case N72/101 is a very short report of an object seen by two RCMP officers on November 17, 1972, near the hamlet of McIvers on Bay of Islands, off the coast of Newfoundland. At about 8:50 pm, they saw an object "12 feet in length, [heading] southwest." This one is tempting to dismiss as a meteor or fireball, except that they reported that the UFO: "Disappeared in water with loud splash."

Case N79/123 records that Chris and Ralph Smith, of Shag Harbour, Nova Scotia (the site of the more famous 1967 UFO crash), also saw a

UFO go into the ocean. On December 3, 1979, at 7:45 pm, they watched a "shiny semi circle," looking "like a parachute" with red and yellow fire beneath it, hovering for five minutes before it "disappeared into the sea."

And then there's the case of the UFO that was seen *after* it had crashed into the water, or so we think.

On July 8, 1971, at about 1:15 pm, miner Claude Girard finished his shift and was near the Hotel Harricana in Joutel, Quebec. He was parked on the road near the bridge over the Harricana River when he saw "an unusual water phenomenon."

On the surface of the water there appeared: "...a circle 15-20 feet in diameter with bubbles coming from around the circumference and from the center of same a jet of water reaching a height of approx. 20 feet.

As Case file N71/047 notes: "When the water jet had settled he noticed in its place an object cylindrical in shape, 6-8 feet in length, rusty black in colour."

As Girard watched, the strange object started to list: "After a short period of time the object leaned to one side and then very slowly took on a horizontal position and then sank."

Within half a minute, the object was gone from view.

The NRC file from the RCMP ends with the cryptic note: "No other relevant info."

There was no indication that any attempt was made to locate the UUO: unidentified underwater object. But since the Harricana River is only about 20 feet deep, would it be worth searching for it now?

A smaller body of water was involved in an incident that occurred just before midnight on May 4, 1975. Paul Dedieu, his brother and a friend were driving near Haywood, Manitoba, when they saw a star that "did not belong in the sky." Case N75/039 notes that as they watched, "red lightning appeared to strike the ship and it took off faster than light itself." Dedieu said it "appeared to be burning molten metal and it crashed in the vicinity of Lake Manitoba" (to the northwest).

On December 20, 1979, at 4:30 am, three people, including one pilot, reported that an object "fell from sky." They were driving near Therian, Alberta, and watched for five to ten minutes as an "elongated" object dropped from 1,000 feet to only 200 feet in altitude, turning red as it did so. The object then made: "Impact with ground a few yards away in the field left of vehicle." The crash was so intense, the "Impact was felt by observers."

NRC case N79/134 is simply stamped: "IDENTIFIED AS METEOR."

The UFO that seemed right on track

In February 1968, the Canadian Forces headquarters in Ottawa received a letter from Mr. R.G. Putnam of Brookfield, Nova Scotia, leading to the opening of the NRC Case file UAR 260A. Putnam was the brakeman on the "Cabot Train" that ran from Truro, Nova Scotia, to Moncton, New Brunswick. He reported an experience he had several months earlier, on October 25, 1967.

In his letter, Putnam wrote:

> On October 25, 1967, 3:15 pm AST... I had the experience of seeing at close range a UFO. It was at the side of the track and at treetop level. When I first looked up at it, I thought of something falling from the sky, as there was green vapour coming billowing from the top of it (which was the exhaust end when in flight).

He went on:

> It followed along beside and at the rear of our train from just ¼ mile past Wentworth or nearly to Westchester and then followed the top of the mountain range toward the west. As it drifted away from our train it tipped to a 45-degree angle, the rear top end to the left, and later rolled on to ¼ turn so the flat sides were up and down.

As Putman watched, a jet descended into view, seemingly to chase the UFO. It dived directly towards the "exhaust end" of the object, which in response "levelled out" and a thin short exhaust appeared behind it. Putnam noted the UFO "took on the shape of a cigar and it just looked like a cloud, with the jet plane pursuing it." In his opinion, the jet caught up with the UFO, but both flew out of sight towards the west by about 3:50 pm after about 35 minutes of observation.

However, there was another aspect of the case that raised it to another level. Putnam wrote that while he was looking at the UFO as it neared him: "It gave off a terrific radiation, as I tried to look at it I covered my face with my hands and peered through my hands with one eye and then the other."

Putnam did not think much of it until:

> One week after, the hair on the back of my hands disappeared and my hands seemed to wither up some—they felt funny. My eyes got

sore and seemed swelled hard. Two weeks later I thought I was taking pneumonia. My chest or ribs in front got sore. My throat got sore and still is. My forehead got greasy and later seemed to dry up. Now my eyes are sore and I had to get my glasses changed but they are still sore.

He added: "I tried to talk to my doctor and have asked him for penicillin but he refused. I guess he thinks I'm nuts."

Concerned for his health and that he accidentally was on the receiving end of some military activity, he wrote: "I reported this to the RCMP and thought the Air Force would contact me and I'd get some help but have heard nothing."

Curiously, there is no record of Putnam's report in the NRC RCMP files related to UFOs—only the Canadian Forces' copy.

In his letter to the Canadian Forces, his desperation is clear: "Can you tell me anything about the thing: what kind of radiation, atomic, electro-magnetic, solar or what? ... I would like to talk to the crew on the plane that chased it sometime. Any help you can give I will greatly appreciate."

Putnam claimed that there were two additional witnesses, a sleeping car conductor and an inspector from Montreal. The file notes: "A letter has been sent to Mr. Putnam acknowledging receipt of his letter and the forwarding of the information." However, there is no indication that this case was ever followed up or the additional witnesses interviewed. One would think that even out of curiosity, someone at the military base or within the RCMP would have contacted him to see how he was doing.

It's doubtful this was just a hoax because Putnam reported it to two different official agencies. If he was mistaken, it's not clear what this might have been. The report on file noted: "No exercises were held by our base in that area at the time specified."

What happened to Mr. Putnam? Hysteria, or was his train really buzzed by a UFO?

5

THE INTRIGUING FALCON
LAKE CASE

~

T he Falcon Lake case of 1967 is one of the most iconic Canadian UFO incidents, concerning the close encounter by weekend prospector Stefan Michalak with what seemed to have been a landed flying saucer in a rugged part of Manitoba. According to Michalak, when he approached too close, the strange craft let out a blast of hot gas which set his clothes on fire and caused burns to his body. The case was investigated by the RCMP and the Royal Canadian Air Force, as well as participation from other agencies including the Manitoba Department of Mines and Natural Resources and Atomic Energy Commission of Canada.

I have discussed the case in several others of my books and it has been portrayed on a number of TV series about UFOs, including *Unsolved Mysteries* and *The Unexplained*. But issues arising during the decades since the event have suggested controversies and promulgated incorrect details in its retelling, so it is worth considering the facts as contained within official and original documents. Rather than recount the case in detail, let's look at the official record in the NRC UFO Files.

Access to Information requests and perusal of records in the National Archives of Canada have uncovered more than one hundred official documents about military and government investigations of the incident. These include a record of interviews and interrogations of people involved and detailed accounts of how RCMP and military personnel conducted their investigations of the case. Civilian records and reports number in the hundreds as well, helping to make the Falcon Lake case one of the best-documented on record, easily surpassing some of the classic and better-known UFO cases such as Roswell and Shag Harbour.

In the final report of the United States Government-sponsored UFO Project, the *Condon Report*, the Falcon Lake case was described as "Unexplained." Its concluding remarks were impressive: "... if (the case) were physically real, it would show the existence of alien flying vehicles in our environment."

And the NRC UFO file on the case, as noted earlier, one document bluntly notes the conclusion of the Canadian government investigations: "Neither the DND nor the RCMP investigation teams were able to provide evidence which could dispute Mr. Michalak's story. Although the investigation has been completed, a satisfactory explanation or conclusion is still lacking."

I will not recount the complete case details here, as they are given in *When They Appeared,* the book I co-authored with Stan Michalak, the witness' son. However, as there are so many documents about the case in the NRC UFO files, it's worth noting in this present volume some of what they contain.[1]

The short version of the incident is that just north of the town of Falcon Lake, Manitoba, on May 20th, 1967, at 12:15 pm, amateur prospector Stefan Michalak looked up and saw two disc-shaped objects, glowing bright red and descending in his direction. One dropped down and appeared to land on a large, flat rock about 150 feet away. It changed colour from red to grey, until it finally was the colour of "hot stainless steel."

Michalak knelt behind a rock outcropping, trying to remain hidden from sight, making a sketch of the object and noting things like waves of warm air radiating from the craft, the smell of sulphur and the whirring of a fast electric motor and a hissing, as if air were being expelled or taken in by the craft. Brilliant purple light flooded out of slitlike openings in the upper part of the craft, and a door opened in the side of the craft through which he could see small flashing lights inside.

Michalak warily approached to within 60 feet of the craft and heard two human-like voices, one with a higher pitch than the other. Convinced the craft was an American secret test vehicle, he called out a greeting as he walked closer to the craft, ending up directly in front of the open doorway.

Suddenly, the craft rotated and an exhaust vent of some kind blasted hot gas that hit him in the chest, setting his shirt and undershirt on fire. Michalak immediately felt nauseous and his forehead throbbed from a headache. Injured and dazed, he stumbled back towards civilization and made it back to the highway where he flagged down a passing RCMP vehicle. The constable assumed Michalak was drunk and left him on the highway. Michalak managed to walk back to his hotel room at Falcon Lake and decided to return to Winnipeg where he was taken by his family to the Misericordia Hospital. He was treated for his burns and released.

The official investigation began with interviews by members of the RCAF and RCMP.

Michalak exhibited some very unusual ailments, including reported weight loss, peculiar burn marks on his chest and stomach, charred hair, an odd rash and recurrent dizziness. He led officials to the site, where the Department of Health and Welfare found such high levels of radiation that for a while they considered cordoning off the area from the public.

If it was a hoax, it is one of the most contrived on record, involving radiation, contaminated soil, medical examinations and a flurry of interrogation by government officials at many levels. Radioactive pieces of metal were even recovered from the site, leading to much speculation on what they are and how they got there.

In fact, in 2019 I located one of the original RCMP officers who investigated the case. More than 50 years after the incident, it still made a significant impression on him, and he stated to me in no uncertain terms that he had no explanation for what had happened to Michalak.

Nevertheless, many armchair investigators have attempted to explain the case without having all the facts available or in some cases selectively ignoring details. One popular explanation is simply that Michalak had hoaxed the entire story. Support for this explanation is that the Condon Report itself noted "discrepancies" in Michalak's story that in its view undermined his veracity.

But what are these discrepancies? One noted by debunkers is the notion that Michalak had said he didn't drink alcohol but the bartender at the Falcon Lake hotel stated he served Michalak many beers the night before the incident. This has been repeated many times in various dismissals of the case, including a featured link in the Library and Archives Canada webpage on the case, which notes:

... Michalak had reported that he went for coffee the night before the alleged sighting; however, the bartender at the Falcon Lake Motel's beverage room claimed to have served Michalak bottles of beer.[2]

In particular, an RCMP document from June 18, 1967, reveals that investigators sought out the person working the bar in the hotel the night Michalak arrived. They asked him about Michalak and he told them that:

...Michalak was in the lounge at the time he took over and that he had served him 3 bottles of beer up until 9:30 PM at which time Michalak left the lounge. It may be noted that this conflicts with Michalak's given statement.

This was because Michalak told the RCMP investigator that he arrived at the motel about 9:30 pm, read his books for at least an hour then went to the bar where he had coffee and talked with the proprietor about prospecting. He said he went to bed shortly after that. But the person at the bar told RCMP:

... Michalak returned at approximately 11:00 o'clock p.m. and had two more bottles of beer in the licensed dining room in the hotel. It was at this time that Michalak had ... asked whether many prospectors work the area north of Falcon Beach.

And, when asked about Michalak's condition at the time, the bartender stated that he thought Michalak was "feeling the effects of alcohol."

In an RCMP document from June 26, 1967, investigators noted: "Falcon Beach detachment have checked beverage room sales slips and Liquor Commission sales slips for that date and there is no indication Michalak bought any liquor to take out."

They were really trying to make a case that Michalak was a drunk and that he was completely unreliable. Adding fuel to the fire was that following Michalak's return from the encounter in the forest, "Everyone that he approached on that day felt as though he was acting as if he was intoxicated although none of the people that spoke to him or were near him could smell any liquor on him."

It's easy to see why they thought he was drunk. Disheveled, disoriented, injured and suffering the consequences of his encounter—he must have been quite a sight. Yet no one could smell any liquor on him. As noted in the RCMP report:

> ... I saw Michalak again on May 27th and asked him about the liquor he was alleged to have consumed on the night of May 19th. He denied having any beer to drink on that night while at Falcon Beach...

Then the RCMP report noted something that is usually not mentioned regarding Michalak's having had or had not anything to drink that night:

> A discrepancy in [the bartender's] version involved the time claim that he had first seen Michalak about 8:00 o'clock p.m. on June 19th, however, Michalak went to Falcon Lake by bus and the bus did not leave Winnipeg until 7:15 p.m. This would be at least a 2-hour bus trip to Falcon Lake which would get Michalak in there somewhere between 9:15 and 9:30 p.m. Michalak's story is that he arrived between 9:00 and 9:30 p.m. and checked into his motel and then went to room 17 and read his prospecting books until about 11:00 o'clock p.m. He then went to the coffee shop in the motel and had a hamburger and a cup of coffee and spoke to the man in the motel about prospecting. He recalls asking the man about any other prospector's working in the area and his knowledge of prospectors in the area. Michalak said he stayed in the coffee shop for about half an hour and then returned to his room in red for an hour longer before retiring for the night.

Michalak's testimony is consistent with what others said, and it's the *bartender's story* which has a discrepancy in time, not Michalak's.

The RCMP report concludes: "This is the main discrepancy in the story. The only other discrepancy in Michalak's story that has been uncovered is his inability to be able to locate the alleged landing spot."

So, the main problem with Michalak's story is that he and the bartender had different versions of what transpired the night before the incident. And the bartender's version has an inaccurate time sequence.

One could ask what the question of Michalak's consumption of beer had to do with the case at all. This was the night before, and everyone agrees that Michalak was out of the hotel bright and early for his prospecting trip, which was the reason he said he was out at Falcon Lake at all. Further, if the questioning was to trip up Michalak on what was assumed to be a hoax story, it's important to note that he told everyone he was there to do prospecting, he had already staked some claims in the area on other occasions, and the rest of the time frame checked out completely. He seemed to be quite transparent in his arrival and time in the area.

It's also worth considering that drinking a few beers would not have any impact on the encounter itself. Rarely in my 40 years of investigation have I interviewed a UFO witness who was inebriated, and the oft-claimed view that UFO witnesses are drunk or on mind-altering drugs is simply not supported by evidence.

If the "main discrepancy" in the case is so minor and perhaps explainable, what about the "only other" one? Namely, why did Michalak have difficulty finding the site in the company of investigators?

I had the good fortune to have been taken to visit the site in the 1970s with some of the original civilian investigators of the case. I was driven out to Falcon Lake in a van along with six other people to the gravel pit north of town. We hiked in from there, wading through swamps and climbing rocky crags for about an hour until I was told we had arrived. We took measurements and photographs of the area, which looked very much like the location of the encounter: a flat rock outcropping and a nearby pond. We hiked back out and headed home.

A week later I was informed we had been led astray; the location we were told was correct was not the site of Michalak's experience at all, even though it looked similar. It took another visit to the area some time later for me to be satisfied I had found the true site some distance away. Since then, I have been there many times, not hiking in anymore but on horseback, and the site is now a tourist attraction as part of a tour by the Falcon Beach Ranch. It's been accurately pinpointed with GPS coordinates, and it matches Michalak's description exactly.

I relate this because some people find it hard to believe that Michalak could have lost his way when taken to the area by RCMP and RCAF investigators. He was unable to locate the site in the company of a well-equipped search party and with a photographer sent to document the expedition from *Life* magazine for a feature spread.

If you were going to be featured in *Life* magazine, wouldn't you want to give them a good story? Instead, *Life* got no story at all, and the photographs of the expedition were never published.

The problem of finding the site was more difficult than most realize. Following his encounter, Michalak was bedridden and weak, having lost weight and unable to hold food down. He was not in any shape to travel, let alone tromp around in the bush. Yet RCMP were anxious to locate the site and visited Michalak's home every day for the next week to see if he was well enough to travel.

RCMP were concerned that the spring growth would make it hard to find the landing site—and it was. They went out several times on their own, guided by a sketch that Michalak made of the area.

Despite ground and air searches, the site was not found. Finally, on June 1, only eleven days after his injuries, Michalak was driven to Falcon Lake then taken up in a helicopter to survey the scene. He later told his family that he had never been in a helicopter before and the view from above only added to his confusion.

The RCMP noted: "This method of searching was unsatisfactory and the terrain looked entirely different from the air and he was not able to recognize any landmarks from the air."

Michalak was disoriented and confused by the new growth that had appeared since he had last been out there. And what's more, his trailblazing was not the best, since he had originally been simply walking through the forest following the many quartz veins in the rocks. One would think that if he was trying to perpetrate a hoax he would have been more organized.

There's also the issue of the map he had drawn. While it didn't seem to match any formation at the time, when the site was found, it was shown to match the area exactly. In fact, when Stan Michalak was taken to the site for the first time, on the 50th anniversary of his dad's encounter, he was astonished at how well the map and his father's description of the area matched the actual site location.

The RCMP and RCAF didn't give up. They went back several additional times on their own until they discontinued their search on June 2, 1967. The site wasn't located until Michalak had regained his strength and went to Falcon Lake on June 23, 1967, in the company of a new acquaintance named Gerry Hart who had access to a free cabin to stay in overnight.

Personally, besides the two official "discrepancies," there are several other issues that I find troubling about the case and its investigation. One is the statement by RCMP Constable Solotki, whom Michalak encountered on the highway when he made it out of the bush after his encounter with the UFO.

It's important to consider Michalak's appearance and state of mind. He had just encountered a strange craft in the forest and was burned by hot gas that came from it. His clothes were charred; his outer shirt was burned and his undershirt was partially burned. His chest and abdomen were burned. He had become violently ill, vomiting several times on his way out. In short, he was in rough shape.

Solotki described Michalak's appearance:

> It appeared to me that Michalak had taken a black substance, possibly wood ashes, and rubbed it on his chest. At no time during my conversations with Michalak would he allow me close enough to him to see whether or not he was injured. I asked him why his hands were not burned if he had touched the spaceship and he would not answer me. I could not smell the odor of liquor on Michalak. His general appearance was not dissimilar to that of a person who has overindulged. His eyes were bloodshot and when questioned in detail could or would not answer coherently.

Obviously, Solotki assumed Michalak was drunk and had somehow burned himself on a campfire. To Solotki, Michalak's blackened chest was interpreted as being an indication of a hoax and not a real injury. Yet when Michalak was at the hospital the next day, as documented by medical reports, he was treated for real burns.

Solotki also questioned why Michalak's cap was in the condition he observed:

> Michalak showed me his cap, the back of which was burnt. I wanted to examine his shirt, however, he would not let me, and kept backing away every time I got close to him. As far as I was able to determine, the back of Michalak's head was not burnt.

Solotki assumed that Michalak's cap was burned when he was facing the "spaceship," and thought he had caught Michalak in a lie because the back of the cap wasn't affected. But during questioning later, it was realized that Michalak had worn his cap *backwards* because he was using his goggles and the peak would have got in the way. Therefore, the burned portion on the back of Michalak's cap was completely consistent with what one might expect.

Also curious was Solotki's description of the cap's colour as grey, although it was reddish-brown. This begs the question of the overall accuracy of Solotki's observation of Michalak, and what else might have been misstated.

Another oft-mentioned concern about the case is the fact that Michalak wrote a book about his experience. On the main Library and Archives Canada page about the case, there is a comment: "The Department of National Defence identifies the Falcon Lake case as unsolved. Stephen Michalak wrote a book about his experience, but claimed to never have financially benefited from his ordeal."

One would think that a plan to make money from a UFO story would be definite proof of the subterfuge, but the facts of the matter suggest otherwise. It was not until after a parade of investigators and curiosity-seekers to the Michalak house that the possibility of a book was considered. And this was because Michalak was getting tired of repeating himself every time someone new wanted to hear about his experience.

Family and friends suggested he write out his story (in his native tongue of Polish) and have it translated into English. The manuscript was then set privately as a thin booklet and a quantity was printed by someone who worked at a newspaper. Michalak then gave away (not sold) the booklets as necessary until the boxful of booklets was empty. It was never reprinted, and Michalak never made a cent from the publication. In fact, he had paid money towards its publication that was never reimbursed.

On the one-year anniversary of his encounter, Michalak traveled with a friend out to the site out of curiosity. They went over the flat rock that was the landing spot looking for any sign that something had occurred there and decided to dig under the lichen and moss that had grown in the cracks and fissures on its surface. About six inches below ground in one of the cracks, Michalak found two W-shaped pieces of metal and hundreds of small metal globules.

Analyses of the metal samples showed they were almost pure silver, but what was more unusual was that they were mildly radioactive. A report from a government mineralogy lab stated they were very pure silver, varying between 93 and 96 per cent in elemental content. The radioactivity was mostly due to U238, or naturally occurring pitchblende ore, which is found occasionally in rock within the Canadian Shield.

The lab report by one mineralogist notes:

> I would interpret the specimens as pieces of thin sheet silver that have been twisted, crumpled, partly melted, and dropped into, or otherwise placed in contact with, nearly pure quartz sand, while still hot. They have subsequently been covered with loosely adhering radioactive material which consists of crushed pitchblende ore...

Memo To: Dr. S.C. Robinson,
Chief, G.M.E.G. Div.,

Page 2
June 13, 1968

From: R.J. Traill

Re: Examination of radioactive metallic specimens submitted
by Dr. Millman.

The pitchblende is cryptocrystalline and thorium-free, and is therefore characteristic of the type found in vein deposits. The unit cell edge was determined as 5.39 ± 0.02 angstroms. This small cell-size is indicative of a
highly oxidized pitchblende such as has been found typically in the uranium
deposits of the Montreal River area and also in some of the deposits of the
Beaverlodge camp in Saskatchewan. Uranophane is a normal alteration product
of the pitchblendes of such deposits, and hematite is usually associated.

Conclusion

I would interpret the specimens as pieces of thin sheet silver that have
been twisted, crumpled, partly melted, and dropped into, or otherwise placed
in contact with, nearly pure quartz sand, while still hot. They have subsequently been covered with loosely-adhering radioactive material which consists
of crushed pitchblende ore, much altered to uranophane and containing associated hematite. These naturally-occurring radioactive minerals are found
typically in the uraniferous deposits of Montreal River area and in parts of
the Beaverlodge camp.

R.J. Traill

RJT:mf

Document 38: "Memorandum from R.J. Traill to Dr. S.
C. Robinson, June 13, 1968. Examination of radioactive
metallic specimens submitted by Dr. Millman." Source:
Ufology Research.

In fact, one of the metal pieces was examined as recently as 2019 using a scanning electron microscope and found to have what appear to be a number of manufactured holes through it, as if it had been a bracket of some kind. But few manufactured brackets are high-grade silver, and how it would end up melted into a crack in a rock that was nowhere near a portable heat source is not easily explainable.

This seems to be an indication of a hoax, but if so, how would someone have melted the metal at the scene without any power supply, and without anyone noticing smoke or evidence of intense heat? Further, the amount of silver was not insignificant and would have been expensive to use in the creation of a hoax.

Little in Michalak's behaviour and profile fits that of a hoaxer. He sought out RCMP himself, traveled to the site with investigators, had been physically injured, and paid out many expenses from his own bank account. He did not benefit from his experience, and in fact his family suffered public ridicule and embarrassment, forcing them essentially into exile as a result of the intense media attention. And, because Michalak's injuries and illness had not abated by 1968, he traveled at his own expense to the noted Mayo Clinic in Rochester, Minnesota, where he was given a thorough physical and psychiatric examination.

Most relevant is the report from the Mayo psychiatrist, who found that Michalak was not someone who would have a tendency to make up stories of alien visitation. The doctor's report noted:

> I found no evidence of delusions, hallucinations... The MMPI was not extraordinary. Despite the fact that his lesions have been diagnosed as obviously factitial, I can find no overt evidence of significant mental or emotional illness.

It's also important to note that in many hoax cases, the perpetrator is not content with a single event. They usually have a history of tall tales, and then after the major claim, have additional claims later in their lives, sometimes expanding on the original story. In Michalak's case, he had never claimed to have seen a UFO before, and did not boast about being selected by the Galactic Council or Federation, had attained alien-induced ESP or other side effects of his encounter. It was a one-shot event, without precedent or sequel.

Taken as a whole, considering all the facts and available evidence, it seems as though Michalak had a real, tangible experience in the rugged forest of Manitoba in 1967. So-called discrepancies in his story can be shown to be either insignificant or due to misunderstandings or misinterpretations of statements by individuals peripheral to the case.

The Falcon Lake case has all the elements that one would want in a UFO case: timely reporting of the incident, eyewitness testimony, physical evidence (including radioactivity, no less), physiological effects in the form of medical injuries, investigations by official and authoritative bodies, documentation of the investigations, a visible and locatable site of the encounter, a cooperative witness who was interviewed at length by various agencies, analysis of the physical evidence, medical records, and a consistent time span that can be followed throughout the incident. How many other UFO cases have all these details?

As with many official investigations, officials opened their examination fully expecting the case to be a hoax, but found Michalak's report to be worth further (or continued) study. Despite what have been described as discrepancies, his story remained consistent from the time he first told it until the time of his death, without embellishment. Offhandedly labeling the case a hoax does not do it justice.

But if it was not a hoax, the question remains: what happened to Stefan Michalak that afternoon?

6

DIFFERENT KINDS OF EVIDENCE

~

Flying saucers over the Rockies

On July 3, 1967, Warren Smith and two companions were hiking together in the Canadian Rockies when they had a UFO encounter that became one of the best cases recorded in the NRC files.

According to case UAR128 in the NRC files (which was not given an N67 file number), the incident took place just southeast of the Highwood Ranger Station on the Alberta side of the mountains. All three saw a shiny, disc-shaped craft in the air that they estimated to be about 25 feet in diameter and about 2,000 feet in altitude, two miles away from them and approaching from the east. Smith took two photos of it as it continued on, lost altitude, passed behind some trees and then rose again. The photos were examined by both Canadian and American authorities and were described as some of the best photos on record at the time.

But that's just the bare bones of the story.

This case began almost a century earlier in 1870, with the Lost Lemon Mine.

It's the stuff of films and TV shows. Frank Lemon and his partner (known only as "Blackjack") were prospectors during a gold rush in the area of Crowsnest Pass between Alberta and British Columbia, decades before 1900. The story most often told about them is that they discovered a rich vein of gold so abundant that estimates of its value range into the billions of dollars.

Alas, Lemon and Blackjack fought over their discovery and Lemon murdered his companion. He ran away to Montana where he lost his mind from paranoia and gold fever, but not before he confessed his crime and the discovery of the gold deposit to a man of the cloth. Lemon died without ever going back to his staked claim but ever since, fortune seekers have trekked into the area in the hope of finding the Lost Lemon Mine despite a legend that says doom will come to those who find it.

Three of those who attempted to locate the treasure were: Warren Smith, a former pilot and a salesman for McGavin's Toastmaster; Craig Dunn, a high school student; and Lorne Grovue, a jack-of-all-trades who had spent the last decade looking for lost treasure. On July 2, 1967, they made camp near the Highwood River because a dowser had told Grovue that the Lost Lemon Mine was near Cataract Creek, only a handful of miles south from there. On the morning of July 3, 1967, they broke camp and headed east through the forest. At one point they encountered a bear and in his escape, Smith fell down a ravine and injured his leg.

At around 6:00 pm, following six hours of hard hiking, they decided it would be best to head back to their camp so they turned back and headed north. After about 15 minutes, Dunn had his attention drawn to something in the sky. He pointed it out to the others, and Smith realized his camera was out of reach in his backpack that was tightly attached to his back. Grovue went into the pack and gave Smith the camera, who quickly took a photo of a disc-shaped object as it moved over the trees. It went out of view and they all expressed amazement at what they had seen. Then it came back, again moving over the trees and much closer to them, so Smith took another photo. Just before it flew out of sight this time, all three men saw something fall from the object to the valley below. They spent some time looking for it but gave up because the forest was so thick.

On the way back to camp they discussed whether they would tell anyone about their experience. They realized that they would be facing mockery and ridicule but at the same time they knew what they saw, and would have photographic proof to support their story. Within a few days, Smith had sent the photos to be developed, and when the prints came back he was disappointed by the lack of clarity—but at least they had a record of what was seen. He showed the photos to a few friends and then eventually decided to give them to the Royal Canadian Air Force along with a report about their sighting.

The NRC teletype from CFB Calgary on September 7, 1967, is covered in handwritten annotations attesting to the interest afforded the case. The description of the case by Squadron Leader (S/L) Bryce Chase is brief; the UFO seen was:

> Circular, shiny, aluminum, approx. 25 feet in diameter. First observed 2000 to 2500 feet above the observer, banked and descended much lower, disappeared behind the trees heading south at high speed.

As for the photos:

> Observer managed to take two photos... Not reported earlier because observer stated that without photographs people would have thought I was out of my mind. Two slides in possession of sender S/L Chase... arranging to have prints made.

There is a handwritten note directly underneath, annotated itself in a different hand:

> Spoke to S/L Chase 11 Sept on 2 points:
> 1 – can the photographs be proven from area in which stated taken? Answer: yes
> 2 – was a check of area for physical evidence been made? Answer: no, but will check further.

FOR. CR V.2000-4.
FILE PRIORITY

NNNNVV AVG002 UU
PP RCCWC
DE RCWDDC 95 07/2335Z
P 072205Z SEP 67
FM CANPERSUNIT CALGARY
TO CANFORCEHED
BT
UNCLAS PSU 767 FOR CFOC UFO REPORT.
A. 3 JUL 67 APPROX 1700 HRS.
B. CLOUDY.
C. WARREN SMITH 3808-17 STREET SW CALGARY, ALTA.
D. APPROX 3 MILES SOUTH SOUTH EAST OF THE HIGHWOOD
RANGER STATION. APPROX 30 MILES WEST OF NANTON, ALTA.
E. WARREN GROUDUE CALGARY ALTA.
F. CIRCULAR, SHINY, ALUMINIUM, APPROX 25 FEET IN
DIAMETER. FIRST OBSERVED 2000 TO 2500 FEET ABOVE
THE ALTITUDE OF THE OBSERVER, BANKED AND DESCENEDED
MUCH LOWER, DISAPPEARED BEHIND THE TREES HEADING SOUTH AT HIGH SPEED.
G. A LITTLE OVER A MINUTE. OBSERVER MANAGED TO TAKE TWO.
PHOTOGRAPHS. NO SOUND NOTED HOWEVER THIS WAS PERHAPS RULED OUT BY
A LIGHT BREEZE BLOWING THROUGH TREES. NOT REPORTED EARLIER BECAUSE
OBSERVER STATED THAT WITHOUT PHOTOGRAPHS PEOPLE WOULD HAVE THOUGHT
I WAS OUT OF MY MIND. TWO SLIDES IN POSSESSION OF SENDER S/L CHASE
C WA WARREN GRODUE

PAGE 2 RCWDDC 95 UNCLAS
CF/PSU CALGARY WHO IS ARRANGING TO HAVE PRINTS MADE. MORE DETAILED
INFORMATION WILL ACCOMPANY PHOTOGRAPHS.
BT

This last point is of some contention. There is no documentation that the Canadian Forces ever conducted an expedition to the site to try and find either evidence on the ground or whatever had fallen from the UFO. However, a document on file refers to a possible reconnaissance of the area by helicopter.

Some media attempted to reach the site but were unsuccessful. In September 1968, some members of a UFO club offered $50 to Grovue if he could lead them to the site of the encounter, but he declined. They went instead with Smith and Dunn, but despite their best efforts, the location where the photographs were taken could not be found.

Another annotation on the telex reads:

> Pls contact S/L Chase and ensure we get these photos, and especially, we attempt to tie these photos in with a landmark. What about other physical evidence, how low was the object, could it have left any visual evidence, such as burns, etc. on treetops, etc. Would like comprehensive report on same.

On October 2, 1967, S/L Chase sent copies of both slides to Ottawa for analysis, noting: "These slides show a very interesting object."

Smith and the others waited for the RCAF to offer some conclusions about the photos, but word had got out about their experience and media wanted to get a look at the images. Also, Grovue noted that when they realized: "...that nothing much was going to be accomplished by the RCAF, the release to the public was made."

So, on October 12, 1967, the three "came out of the UFO closet" at the Calgary Planetarium to a packed house where the photos went on public display. A RCAF spokesman told media that the photos were the best ever seen by the armed forces.

On that same day, in Ottawa, a report on the photo analysis was completed. While the analysts in the Department of Defence could not rule out a hoax, the report noted their study of the photos: "...reasonably substantiate the observer's report." They calculated the UFO could have been an "oblate ellipsoid" with a diameter of 40-50 feet and a thickness of 11 to 14 feet.

The author of the report opined:

> If the story and photographs are a hoax, then it is a well prepared one, that would require on the hoaxer's part knowledge of photography and possibly photogrammetry to support the written and verbal

information supplied. Alternatively, the data supplied has produced a most fortunate and lucky combination of circumstances to make a hoax realistic.

In other words, either the photos were real, or someone went to a great deal of trouble to fake them. However, the University of Colorado, which examined the slides on behalf of the United States Air Force Scientific Study of Unidentified Flying Objects, had a completely different view. It gave its opinion that:

> ...the photographs are also consistent with a hand-thrown model and that there is insufficient information content to rule out this hypothesis. Therefore, the case cannot be said to contribute significant evidence in establishing the existence of unusual aircraft.

In their defence, all three men signed sworn affidavits attesting that they had actually seen what they said they had seen and that Smith had really taken photos of something in the sky. It seems strange that they would have made up an elaborate story about hiking into difficult terrain to fake a UFO sighting, especially one without physical evidence. (Although at least one of them declined to take a lie detector test.)

On October 14, 1967, one of the photos was published in a Calgary newspaper, and soon both images were carried by wire services across the country. This spawned a flurry of interest from literally around the world. Smith and Grovue received correspondence from many UFO groups such as the Aerial Phenomenon Research Organization (APRO), the National Investigations Committee on Aerial Phenomena (NICAP), and from Dr. J. Allen Hynek, whose own group the Center for UFO Studies had yet to be created. Grovue even contacted Maj. Donald Keyhoe, NICAP's director, to see if he would help him in getting a book published about the case. Grovue also wanted to charge Canadian ufologist Bill Allan $40 for the slides, plus royalties from admission charges to public presentations.

Despite all this, the case does give one pause to wonder. If the three men conspired to create a hoax, it seems ill-conceived. They ended up receiving little recompense for their effort, and were subject to intense scrutiny on the world stage. Military technical and analytical resources of two countries were expended in studying the photos, and the mystery surrounding the events of that day remains unresolved.

And the Lost Lemon Mine is still intact.

Unidentified radar returns

As mentioned in the Robertson *Briefing*, one of the six cases classified as unexplained was a set of unidentified radar returns recorded by military and civilian radar in Manitoba in 1967. Details of the incidents are given in the NRC Case file U84, and document what appear to be *bona fide* UFOs over Canadian airspace.

According to documents in the case file, on July 6, 1967, at about 6:00 pm:

> While monitoring A/C FLT 916 Winnipeg to Montreal, Winnipeg radar observed a radar return at 11:00 o'clock to aircraft position at a distance of 70 miles from Winnipeg on a bearing of 093 degrees. Target was observed through seven sweeps and accelerated from an observed 2 miles between sweeps until last observed sweep vicinity of Vivian showed a distance of 10 miles. This represents acceleration from 720 to 3600 knots in one minute 10 seconds. Return was observed by three controllers and two technicians. Technicians felt return was not a running rabbit type of interference. Time of observation approximately 070100Z. No other known traffic in area.

The Air Canada flight from Vancouver to Winnipeg to Montreal, a DC-9 Vanguard, had just taken off from its stop in Winnipeg and was heading east to its final destination. Air traffic controllers in Winnipeg saw an unexpected radar return near the aircraft, also heading east. In the space of 70 seconds, they watched the unidentified radar target accelerate from 800 to more than 4,000 mph before it zipped off the scope near the town of Vivian, Manitoba, about 50 kilometres straight east.

The radar operators were convinced the unidentified target was not a "running rabbit," a term given to radar targets that move generally in a sweeping arc, a kind of interference often caused by radar interference from another radar system. They also noted that there were no other known aircraft in the area at the time. If the unidentified radar return was caused by interference or weather, one could wonder why it did not appear earlier or after the incident. And, if it was interference, its appearance should be of grave concern because radar operators, upon whose judgment many lives depend on every day, were unable to resolve the returns.

If it was only a single incident, the case might easily have been dismissed out of hand. But only a little over two hours later, radar bogies were back in the air.

At 9:24 pm (noted as 070324Z in the file), a radar operator at the airport in Kenora, Ontario, about 200 kilometres east of Winnipeg and only 150 kilometres farther than Vivian, Manitoba, saw an unidentified return on his scope. The target was heading northeast and was 45 miles away when first detected on the Kenora Very High Frequency Omnidirectional Range (VOR) radar, which uses radio transmissions between a beacon on the ground and an instrument on an aircraft to provide information on the heading of the plane. The target moved closer until it was about 40 miles away, then turned and retreated to about 50 miles away.

Eleven minutes later, at 070335Z, Kenora radar picked up an unidentified return that seemed to be following another airliner, Air Canada Flight 405, which was flying west from Toronto to Winnipeg. According to the Kenora radar, the object turned northeast and disappeared from the scope.

Finally, at 070353Z (9:53 pm), yet another unidentified blip followed Air Canada Flight 927, which was also going west on its way from Montreal to Toronto and then Winnipeg. The radar target then turned northeast as well and disappeared.

The report notes: "DOT unable to explain these radar returns. No other known traffic in area and Duluth had no aircraft operating in area at time of radar sightings." Duluth, Minnesota, is about 600 kilometres southeast of Kenora, and did not have any radar returns from aircraft on its scopes.

Pilots of all the aircraft were contacted, but none had reported seeing anything visually, nor did they report anything unusual on their onboard radar systems. However, some of the pilots did report bad weather; the pilot of Air Canada Flight 405 reported: "Weather poor." In fact, one annotation on the file regarding Air Canada Flight 916 reads: "confirmed wx – many a/c picking way through." The abbreviation "wx" means simply "weather," and in this case can be interpreted to mean "stormy weather" (not unexpected in early July), and that planes were having to fly around the storm cells.

The calculations of the unidentified targets were based on the known speeds of the airliners. Air Canada 405 was flying at 325 knots (about 375 mph) and Air Canada 927 was much faster, at about 600 knots (almost 700 mph).

Further investigation involved checking for any aircraft that might have not been regularly scheduled. CFB Gimli, about 90 kilometres north of Winnipeg, was asked about any jets that might have been in the air at the time, and indeed some were doing night flying but were doing so only over the Gimli area. Similarly, the possibility was raised that an American military aircraft could have been in the area, as some planes from the USAF Military Air Transport Service (MATS) did fly through Manitoba and Ontario to a base in Churchill, Manitoba, but no such aircraft were nearby.

In the *Robertson Briefing*, it was noted that the radar operators were: "...certain it was a radar target and not something associated with mechanical, electronic or equipment faults" and that the Kenora target was a "positive radar contact." The inclusion of these radar cases in the *Robertson Briefing* was significant in that they were considered unusual and in need of a formal investigation.

But what about a radar case that was also observed visually? NRC Case U89, which occurred only three weeks later, on July 26, 1967, was such an incident.

That night, PWA Flight 748 was on its way from Calgary to Vancouver, with Captain Shindler at the controls, about a third of the way to its destination. It was 270438Z (8:38 pm PT on July 26, 1967), and the airliner was over the Rockies, somewhere above Westfall River. Shindler reported that he saw a "Little dot with pink light... at about 16,000 ft, zigging and zagging, then straight up and straight down, then horizontal toward horizon."

Shindler watched the odd light for 18 minutes before it zipped away, and then immediately reported his sighting to the RCAF, since the teletype in NRC files has the time as 270457Z and is stamped July 27 at both 6:15 1966 (an error) and 6:30 1967, all in GMT. But then there's the note: "Kamloops radar also observed object. Reported to Seattle sector."

So, does that mean that the ground radar at Kamloops, British Columbia, only a few hundred kilometres ahead, had visually seen the object, or was that on radar? Both situations would be significant.

Strangely, the single page report has no detail on investigation, except for a handwritten note that reads: "We may have followed this report up, however, believe it's too late to initiate investigation action at this date." The annotation is dated "9 Aug 67," only than two weeks later. That would still seem a short enough elapsed time to have made an investigation worthwhile, as other cases in the NRC UFO files were investigated months after they occurred.

Shag Harbour

Also noted in the *Robertson Briefing*, a bright object was seen by several witnesses to fall into Shag Harbour, off the coast of Nova Scotia. Sometimes called "Canada's Roswell," this classic case is a bit better than Roswell because a number of official documents have been located suggesting something unusual really happened, unlike the actual Roswell event. (The latter has been explained by the US government as the remnants of a stray high-altitude balloon, although most UFO fans find that explanation unsatisfying.)

The story of Shag Harbour began in the early evening of October 4, 1967. People all around Quebec and the Maritimes reported UFOs, including pilots of an Air Canada DC-8 who saw a large, brightly lit rectangular object estimated to be flying at around 12,000 feet, moving in a parallel flight path.

Around 9:00 pm ADT, the captain and crew of a fishing vessel near Sambro, Nova Scotia saw several red lights over the water and said their on-ship radar also detected the objects. The RCMP, communicating with the captain via the Canadian Coast Guard, was curious enough about the event to request the captain file a report when he returned to port.

Canadian ufologist Chris Styles, one of the principal investigators of the Shag Harbour incident, himself saw something strange in Halifax Harbour that night. He observed a disc-shaped object, glowing orange and drifting over the harbour. After running closer to the object, Styles could see it was a roughly fifty-foot diameter sized orange ball, moving slowly over the water. No sound could be heard.

Around 11:30 pm, five witnesses observed an object descending at a moderate pace over Shag Harbour. With a swishing sound, the object fell out of the witness's sight, seemingly crashing into the harbour. Moving to the harbour to see what happened, the witnesses could see an object floating on the water, about 200 feet from the shore. As mentioned earlier, it's important to note that, at the time, no one reported seeing the object splash down or enter the water; the crash is only assumed.

Thinking the object might have been a crashed plane, the witnesses phoned the RCMP and the local detachment dispatched a car to the scene. The local police contacted the Halifax station, the headquarters for the surrounding area, and in turn, Halifax contacted RCMP national headquarters in Ottawa. Ottawa then filed a UFO report with the Canadian Forces, who, suspecting a downed plane, contacted the Rescue Coordination Centre back in Halifax.

ICA128PEA133 OEB076 COA038   UU

DE RCEOC 29 05/1320Z
P 051320Z OCT 67
FM RCC HALIFAX   Oct 5 14 19'67

PRIORITY   O.P.I.

TO CANFORCEHED

BT

UNCLAS RCC076

FOR CFOC. UFO REPORT

A 050210Z OCT 67

B NIGHT CLEAR , NO MOON

C CPL WERCICKY RCMP BARRINGTON PASSAGE

D OUTSIDE LOWER WOODS HARBOUR, N S

E 6 OTHER WITNESSES - NAMES KNOW TO RCMP CPL

F DARK OBJECT - IN EXCESS OF 60 FT - 4 WHITE LIGHTS

 HORIZONTALLY 15 FT SPACING - MOVEMENT EASTERLY

LOW ALTITUDE ON DOWN TO WATER SURFACE

G UNKNOWN BUT IN EXCESS OF FIVE MINUTES

H UFO DESCENDED RAPIDLY TO WATER WITH HIGH WHISTLING

 SOUND. BRIGHT FLASH ON HITTING WATER. SINGLE

LIGHT FLOATING ON SURFACE REMAINED FOR LONG TIME

SAND BEFORE RCMP COULD GET BOAT TO IT. AREA

SEARCHED EXTENSIVELY BY CCG LIFEBOAT 101 AND

PAGE 2 RCEOC 29 UNCLAS

MANY SMALL BOATS - NIL RESULTS. POSITION OF

LAST SIGHTING 4330.5N 6545W. ALL OTHER POSSIBLE

LEADS (A/C , FLARES, ETC.) CHECKED - NIL RESULTS.

FOLLOW UP: AT 051215Z COAST GUARD CUTTER 101

PROCEEDING TO AREA WITH RCMP ON BOARD TO RESEARCH

 AREA BASED ON A/REF DATUM POINT.

BT

0 -WA TIME SAN   120

Document 40: "Document filed about the Shag Harbour
UFO crash of October 4, 1967." Herzberg Institute of
Astrophysics - Reports on non-meteoric sightings,
unidentified flying objects, UFO's 10/4/1967 © Government
of Canada. Reproduced with the permission of Library
and Archives Canada (2021). Source: Library and Archives
Canada/National Research Council of Canada fonds/e002749390

MEMORANDUM

V 2000-4 (D Ops)

6 October, 1967

Sec DS

UFO REPORT
LOWER WOOD HARBOUR NS

1.   On 04 October 1967 at 2345 hours local RCMP Corporal
WERCICKY from Barrington Passage NS and six other witnesses
sighted a large flying object. This object, in the time interval
of approximately five minutes, flew down to the water surface,
floated and sank.

2.   The flying object was described as being in excess of
60 feet in diameter and carried four white lights spaced horizontally at a distance of 15 feet. The object, flying in an easterly
direction when first sighted, descended rapidly to the water and
produced a bright flash on impact. One light remained on the
surface for considerable time but sank before a boat could reach
it.

3.   The Rescue Co-ordination Centre conducted preliminary
investigation and discounted the possibilities that the sighting
was produced by an aircraft, flares, floats, or any other known
objects.

4.   Maritime Command were asked, on 05 Oct, to conduct an
investigation into the sighting. At the present time one Officer and
a diving team of three men are on the scene aided by Coast Guard
Cutter 101.

W. W. Turner
Colonel
Director Operations

W. Bain S/L
2-2900

Distribution
Orig
Circ
File

120

Document 41: "Document filed about the Shag Harbour
UFO crash of October 4, 1967." Herzberg Institute of
Astrophysics - Reports on non-meteoric sightings,
unidentified flying objects, UFO's 10/4/1967 © Government
of Canada. Reproduced with the permission of Library
and Archives Canada (2021). Source: Library and Archives
Canada/National Research Council of Canada fonds/e002749391

MESSAGE FORM

FOR COMMCEN/SIGNALS USE

FILE NUMBER

PRECEDENCE - ACTION	PRECEDENCE - INFO	DATE - TIME GROUP	MESSAGE INSTRUCTIONS
PRIORITY	DEFERRED	Ø5212ØZ OCT	

FROM CANFORCEHED

TO CANMARCOM

PREFIX

GR

SECURITY CLASSIFICATION

UNCLAS

INFO RCC HALIFAX

ORIGINATOR'S NUMBER

OPS 533

SUBJECT: UFO. REF RCC HALIFAX RCC Ø76 Ø5132ØZ OCT. (1)
REQUEST SUBJECT UFO REPORT BE INVESTIGATED BY YOUR HQ. (2)
CONSIDERATION SHOULD BE GIVEN FOR AN UNDERWATER SEARCH OF THE
AREA ASAP.

DOPS 4-2

PAGE	OF PAGES	REFERS TO MESSAGE	DRAFTER'S NAME	OFFICE	TEL.
			(W BAIN) S/L DOPS 4-2 2 2986		

R DATE TIME

D DATE TIME SYSTEM OPERATOR

MORRISON S/L

COPY 3

Document 42: "Document filed about the Shag Harbour
UFO crash of October 4, 1967." Herzberg Institute of
Astrophysics - Reports on non-meteoric sightings,
unidentified flying objects, UFO's 10/4/1967 © Government
of Canada. Reproduced with the permission of Library
and Archives Canada (2021). Source: Library and Archives
Canada/National Research Council of Canada fonds/e002749392

Meanwhile, down at Shag Harbour, the local RCMP were thinking of ways to reach the object, whatever it was, believing that a rescue was necessary. Three RCMP officers were now at the scene, including one who had himself observed a bright object moving over the mainland.

For several minutes the officers were able to see a strange yellow light off the shore, and through binoculars were able to see what appeared to be yellow foam around the light. The police roused some local fishermen from sleep and the Mounties secured some boats for a water rescue. Unfortunately, the object by this time seemed to have sunk beneath the surface of the ocean.

Nevertheless, the boats traveled out to where the object was last seen. While the would-be rescuers didn't find the object or any occupants, they did find thick yellow foam floating on top of the water where the object had apparently gone down. The foam was estimated to be around three inches thick, 80 feet wide and a half-mile in length. Bubbles could be seen continually coming to the surface and the smell of sulfur was present in the air. By 12:30 am, the Canadian Coast Guard arrived on the scene and they helped in the search, but by 4:00 am, the search was called off for the night.

The search was restarted again the next morning, this time with the help of a dive team. As many as seven scuba divers searched the depths of the harbour in hope of finding the object that fell from the sky.

Even the military seemed puzzled as to what could have crashed into the water. In a memorandum dated October 6, 1967, it was indicated that:

The Rescue Coordination Centre conducted preliminary investigation and discounted the possibilities that the sighting was produced by an aircraft, flares, floats, or any other known objects.

The search continued through to Monday, when it was finally called off. Nothing was ever found, but rumors circulated that something, or at least pieces of something, were recovered and sent to a naval base in Dartmouth. One witness insisted he saw divers dragging shiny metal material out of the water.[1]

Officially, nothing was recovered from the waters off the coast of Nova Scotia in the search for what crashed back in October of 1967. The USAF-sponsored Condon Committee examined the case (Case #34 in its report) and after a brief review of events concluded its consideration of the case by indicating:

No further investigation by the project was considered justifiable, particularly in view of the immediate and thorough search that had been carried out by the RCMP and the Maritime Command.[2]

No explanation for the witnesses' sightings was attempted by the Committee.

7

SEEING SPACEMEN

~

Good night, nurse!

Doreen Kendall and Frieda Wilson were two nurses working together on the night shift in Cowichan District Hospital at Duncan, British Columbia, on New Year's Day, 1970. At about 5 am, Kendall was tending to one of her patients and opened the curtains in the room to let in some cool fresh air.

When she did, she said: "...there was this brilliantly lit thing looking right at me. The first thing I noticed was this... string of lights around it like a necklace. And then after I got my eyes off those lights, I glanced up and there was a brilliantly lit dome, which must have been made of glass because I could see the interior."

Regarding the strange craft itself:

> There was no noise whatsoever, but of course we were inside the hospital. It didn't shoot any flames and had the lights still on in the dome and around the outside as it rose. I would say that the ship was about 60 feet away from me when I first looked out the window and would be at least 60 feet in diameter. The dome alone would be about as big as the room I was in and the lights were brilliantly white. At

the beginning, I couldn't tell what color the outside of the ship, but as it tilted, I could see that it was metallic, but not as highly polished as the metal on the instrument panel. It was about as high as the third floor eaves are off the ground.

RCMP-GRC 6861   CONTINUATION - SUITE DE C237
                                                                              REV. 1-4-66

CRIT. U.F.O. REPORT - Duncan, B. C., 1 Jan 70   PAGE 3

(CONT'D. FROM PAGE TWO)

                                                    "Duncan, B. C.,
                                                     Jan 12th, 1970.

STATEMENT OF: ■■■■■■■■■■   (■■ ■■■■■■■■)
                               5780 Ludwiga St., Duncan, B. C.

" I was working graveyard shift at the Cowichan District Hospital,
Duncan, B. C. on Jan 1st, 1970. I am a Registered Nurse and was on
2nd North (Surgical Ward). At approximately 5:00 AM I walked down to
the 3rd West Nursing Station. Mrs. ■■■■■ and Mrs. ■■■■■ were sit-
ting there and as I walked up to them, two nurses from the Extended
Care unit, Mrs. WILSON and Mrs. ■■■DALL, came running out of 213
saying "come and see the space ship". We just laughed and joked about
it, but they were so insistant, that we finally ran to the hall windows and looked out. I saw this bright round object heading away from
the hospital above the trees accross the parking lot. It is difficult
to say how big it was, but I remember thinking it isn't a plane, or a
star, or a helicopter (unless it was all lit up inside) and there
was absolutely no noise and it moved very quickly and disappeared from
my vision at the window I was at, so I ran to another vantage point
farther along the hall, but it had disappeared completely.
"   It was very bright yellowish orange and all I could see was light.
This was most unusual and I am unable to explain it.
"   Right after it happened, Mrs. ■■DALL told us it was like a transparent dome or bubble and that she saw two silhouettes in it and that
it had two wings on it, which were lit up. I looked at the clock at
the time. It was 5:00 AM and still dark out and I went back to my
floor and told some of the other nurses about it and got the big "hee
haw". Later, about half an hour, I went back and the two nurses (Mrs.
■■DALL and Mrs. WILSON) were still looking out a window and were still
obviously awe-struck with what they had seen.
                                                 SGD: ■■■■■■■■■■■■■■

WIT: "R.P. Gilchrist" Sgt.,
     R.C.M. Police, Duncan, B. C.

                                                    "Duncan, B. C.,
                                                     Jan 13th, 1970.

STATEMENT OF: Doreen Eve ■■DALL (■■ ■■■■■■■■)
                               3066 ■■■■■■■ Terrace, Duncan, ■.■.

" I am a Licenced Practical Nurse and am employed at the Cowichan
District Hospital. At 5:00 AM on Jan. 1st, 1970 I was on the second
floor doing the rounds of patients in Ward 213 of the Extended Care
unit. Mrs. Friesz ■■■■■ and I were working together. She is the
R.N. I was checking the patient right by the window and, after finished her, I drew the drapes and looked out, and there was this brilliantly lit thing looking right at me. The first thing I noticed was this
brilliantly string of lights all around it like a necklace. When
after I got up, eyes on these lights, I glanced up and there was a
                                                            ■ ■ ■

Document 43: "On New Year's Day, 1970, nurses at a hospital
in Duncan, BC, reported seeing a UFO at close range."
National research - Radio and Electrical Engineering
Division - Unidentified flying objects, sighting of 1/1/1970
© Government of Canada. Reproduced with the permission
of Library and Archives Canada (2021). Source: Library
and Archives Canada/Royal Canadian Mounted Police fonds/
e003000983

U.F.O. REPORT - Duncan, B. C., 1 JAN 70

(CONT'D. FROM PAGE THREE)

brilliantly lit dome, which must have been made of glass because I could see the interior. There were two figures in the dome and they had on dark sort of flying suits and close fitting helmets. They were faced sideways and were tall. And then I saw this instrument panel and it looked to me like it was chrome, as the lights were shining off it. At this time the saucer was tipped towards me allowing a view inside of it. This instrument panel had large circles and small ones and the one figure was working on the panel. I saw both his hands operating the instruments. His hands appeared to be just like ours. They appeared to have fine physiques. The one closest to me turned slightly and appeared to be looking directly at me. I tried to see his face, but couldn't make out the features as there seemed to be a covering over the face. He then touched the other man in the centre of the back. His movements were smooth and he turned and looked at me too. He also had something over his face. Whatever it was, it was neat and tidy and part of his helmet. I wondered at the time if they were having technical difficulties. Their hands were bare and their heads and faces covered.

" After the second one looked at me, he moved this "joy stick" like a gear shift in a sports car. He moved it forward, downward and then upward and the ship started going in small, counter-clockwise circles. As it circled, it was rising slightly and I thought I'd better call someone else to see this, or no one would believe me. Up to this time, I was fascinated and staring out the window. So I turned and called Mrs. WILSON, who was on the other side of the ward. I said "Frieda look". She came right away and said "my gosh Doreen what's that". I replied that it must be a flying saucer. Then some of the other nurses came to the windows and looked too.

" As soon as the saucer sort of steadied itself, it rose steadily and then levelled slightly and still rising, disappeared behind the trees at the side of the parking lot. This took place in the matter of a few seconds. There was no noise whatsoever, but of course we were inside the hospital. It didn't shoot any flames and had the lights still on in the dome and around the outside as it rose.

" I would say that the ship was about sixty feet away from me when I first looked out of the window and would be at least sixty feet in diameter. The dome alone would be about as big as the room I was in and the lights were brilliantly white. At the beginning, I couldn't tell what colour the outside of the ship, but as it tilted, I could see that it was metallic, but not as highly polished as the metal on the instrument panel. It was about as high as the third floor eves are off the ground.

" After it disappeared out of sight, I felt ill for a minute and was very quiet. Mrs. WILSON said to one of the other nurses that she'd have to get another partner, hers was no good now. I was deep in thought and then things returned to normal and I wrote down a memo. of what had happened in a note book.

" I have very good eyesight and was sober and am certain that what I saw was not any mirage, reflection or any plastic bag filled with hot air from burning candles. I was most impressed with the sight of the instrument panel in the ship. It was fascinating. I have never seen anything like this before.

(CONT'D. ON PAGE FIVE)

Document 44: "On New Year's Day, 1970, nurses at a hospital in Duncan, BC, reported seeing a UFO at close range." National research - Radio and Electrical Engineering Division - Unidentified flying objects, sighting of 1/1/1970 © Government of Canada. Reproduced with the permission of Library and Archives Canada (2021). Source: Library and Archives Canada/Royal Canadian Mounted Police fonds/ e003000982

But just seeing the remarkable saucer wasn't the strangest part of her observation. As documented in signed affidavits covering several pages in the NRC files, as given to RCMP, Kendall had a close encounter with the pilots or operators of the UFO. Her testimony according to NRC case N70/003 describes what Kendall saw inside the craft. As it hung in the sky, she noted that: "the saucer was tipped towards me allowing a view inside of it." She was clearly able to see:

> There were two figures in the dome and they had on dark sort of flying suits and close-fitting helmets. They were faced sideways and were tall. And then I saw this instrument panel and it looked to me like it was chrome, as the lights were shining off it... This instrument panel had large circles and small ones and the one figure was working on the panel. I saw both his hands operating the instruments. His hands appeared to be just like ours... The one closest to me turned slightly and appeared to be looking directly at me. I tried to see his face but couldn't make out the features as there seemed to be a covering over the face. He then touched the other man in the center of the back. His movements were smooth and he turned and looked at me too. He also had something over his face. Whatever it was it was neat and tidy and part of his helmet. I wondered at the time if they were having technical difficulties. Their hands were bare and their heads and faces covered.

Kendall said at one point she could peer well into the craft, and that she could see: "to a point just below their knees and noticed they were standing in front of what looked like stools." She also noted: "I noticed how human they looked. Their flesh seemed just like ours... They both had fine physiques."

Kendall interpreted what happened next as that when the first occupant had seen her and poked his companion, the jig was up and they realized they had to skedaddle.

> After the second one looked at me, he moved his joystick like a gear shift in a sports car. He moved it forward, downward and then upward and the ship started going in small, counterclockwise circles.

As the saucer started moving away, it finally occurred to Kendall that she needed to get other witnesses.

> As it circled, it was rising slightly and I thought I'd better call someone else to see this, or no one would believe me. Up to this time I was fascinated and staring out the window. So I turned and called Mrs. Wilson, who was on the other side of the ward. I said, "Frieda, look!" She came right away and said, 'My gosh, Doreen, what's that?' I replied that it must be a flying saucer. Then some of the other nurses came to the windows and looked too.

Wilson's testimony agrees well with Kendall's, in supporting her testimony:

> Mrs. Kendall was looking after a patient next to the windows and I was attending to one on the door side of the ward. I noticed her pulling the drapes on the window and was just standing there looking out not saying anything. Then she suddenly turned around and said, 'Frieda, Frieda, Frieda! Come quick!' So I went over to the window and I saw a large saucer shaped object. It was metallic and had either a glass dome or plastic dome and the bottom part was brilliantly lit, and it was moving off, tilted slightly and moving in a counterclockwise series of small circles as it rose. When I first saw it, it was about 100 feet from the window and slightly above eye level. I said to Doreen, 'What on earth is it?' And she said it must be a spaceship or flying saucer. It was going away, so we decided to go and get some of the other nurses so they could see it too...

The other nurses, however, did not come in time to see very much. Two were interviewed by the RCMP: Mrs. Clackson and Mrs. Appelby. One of them noted:

> We heard Mrs. Kendall call to us from one of the wards in the extended care unit... but we didn't go right away because we didn't think it was anything urgent. Seconds later, she came out into the hallway and Mrs. Wilson was with her. This time, she said, 'Come and see the flying saucer.'

She continued:

I saw big a bright yellow light moving up and away towards the east...
much larger than stars or airplane lights or anything that I've ever
seen before. It disappeared quite quickly in a matter of seconds - a
minute at the most.

The other of the two said:

I saw this big round bright object heading away from the hospital
above the trees across the parking lot. It is difficult to say how big it
was, but I remember thinking it isn't a plane or a star or a helicopter
unless it was all lit up inside and there was absolutely no noise and it
moved very quickly and disappeared... It was a very bright yellowish
orange and all I could see was light. This was most unusual and I am
unable to explain it.

One of the most curious aspects of the case is that Kendall seemed
mesmerized by what she was looking at, to the point of immobilization.
She said she didn't want to move or make any noise to attract attention
from the craft's pilots. She explained she was focused on the instrument
panel in front of the pilots. Because her family was into auto racing, she
was familiar with instrument panels, so she was trying to understand
the mechanics of the craft. The panel was large and took up about
half the interior of the craft, nearly to the top of the dome, and the
instruments were set into the metal panel itself.

Kendall thought that because the pilot in front was staring intently
at the panel, she wondered if they were having mechanical trouble.
She even thought they were going to make an emergency landing on
the hospital roof. But when the pilot in back saw Kendall and poked
his co-pilot, she said he reached down, grabbed a lever beside him and
pushed it back and forth, and the saucer began its spinning. Only five
minutes had elapsed from the time she opened the curtains until the
time that it was lost to sight.

The RCMP interrogated Kendall, Wilson, Clackson and Appelby,
plus another person who saw an odd light that morning as well. RCMP
Constable Gilchrist visited the hospital and surveyed the area to see if
the scenario laid out by the nurses made any sense. And it did:

There are no guy or high tension wires or any other obstructions
which would have been in the way of an object getting into or out
of the location where Mrs. Kendall reports she saw this UFO. The

distance that she claims to have seen it first would be from 50 to 60 feet off the ground and about 50 to 60 feet from each wing of the two wings of the hospital. The distance from the edge of the hospital to the tree line varies from about 90 to 150 feet. The tops of the trees would be approximately 120 to 150 feet above the level of the ground or the parking lot besides the hospital.

In other words, a craft of the dimensions described by Kendall could conceivably have moved over and away from the hospital in the directions she noted. And as for her story itself, Gilchrist stated:

In assessing the reliability of the above witnesses I can only say that they appeared to be all sane, responsible persons and are well thought of by their coworkers and friends generally. Mrs. Kendall's account of what she saw seems to be firmly embedded in her mind, and although there are some very minor differences in the details... they do not alter the fact that what she has said is backed up by the accounts of the other women.

What is also remarkable about this case is that it was never actually reported to the RCMP or NRC. In his report, Gilchrist explains that the story of the nurses' encounter was first carried in the local newspaper the *Cowichan Leader* on January 7, 1070. Subsequently, Gilchrist noted that: "...vague rumors had been voiced around that people had sighted some sort of UFO since the new year."

Because of the local attention, Gilchrist took it upon himself to investigate the claims and he interviewed the witnesses starting on January 8, 1970, filing his official report with Ottawa on January 15.

The case remains one of the most detailed in the NRC files, supported by multiple witnesses. What on Earth (or not) did Kendall see?

A bad date

Some guys just don't have any luck.

It was a Friday night, October 23, 1970, and eighteen-year-old Gerald Adams and his girlfriend Donna Martin were on a date. They were in Adams' truck, parked on a dirt farm road about three or four miles north and half a mile west of MacGregor, Manitoba. It was a very secluded location, far away from farmhouses and well off any well-traveled highway. It was a perfect place for two teenagers to have some privacy.

Until a UFO interrupted them.

Adams recalled that at about 1:00 am (by then October 24): "My attention was first called to the object when we sat up because we noticed a bright light. We thought it was a car coming."

What happened next was one of the strangest Canadian UFO encounters on record, followed by a testy debate between a witness and a debunker.

Adams said: "I estimated that the object was approximately ½ mile away...I estimated this distance because we were half a mile away from the next crossroad and the object seemed to be quite far away in the field."

NRC Case N70/078 starts with a simple typewritten report from the RCMP to the NRC, noting that Adams and Martin were only about 125-150 feet from:

> One oblong UFO 4 to 5ft. high, 8 ft. diameter on ground. Bottom shaped in a tapered bowl fashion – unable to describe top. Nine rods 2 ft. high on top – arranged in clusters of three. Red light on top. Flange around center. Waver motion.

Adams explained: "I was able to make out the form of the object because the object gave off a light which seemed to light up the sky, and also the moon was shining."

The couple didn't know what to think or do at this point. It was obvious their night of intimacy was over, but what was this thing if it wasn't a car or truck?

Adams continued: "As my girlfriend and I sat in the truck watching the object, we talked about what it could be. I told her it might be a UFO. This made her a little nervous."

One can imagine. But undaunted, and wanting to show some bravado, Adams boasted: "I told her I was going to walk over to the object."

However, "She then became scared as she did not want to stay alone nor come with me."

Adams was concerned for Martin, so rather than ignore her display of fear, he drove her home. But when he returned to the scene, the object was gone from its original location to "a couple of miles away and hovering above the ground."

As he drove closer, Adams had an even stranger encounter. He saw:

> One humanoid sighted approx. one-half mile from UFO walking with 'difficulty' heading north. Humanoid 4 ft. high with arms and legs and head in a silver metallic uniform, appeared to be wearing a helmet.

The "humanoid" was crossing the road less than 50 feet away from Adams' truck. When he braked to get a better look, the odd entity had disappeared. Then, he was surprised to see the UFO:

> Take off from second location described as slowly lifting from surface in vertical motion then rapidly departing in a NW direction with great speed and out of sight within 30 seconds.

Adams noted: "This is why I could still see it. I knew it was the UFO because it took off and later disappeared into the night."

Within a few days, Adams reported their encounter to the RCMP Detachment at Carberry and was interviewed at length by Capt. G.M. Winterburn, who, understandably, did not know what to do with the account. However, after consulting with his superiors, Winterburn sent the report to the air force and the NRC. A note in the file reads:

> The RCMP Carberry Manitoba interviewed Mr. Adams but no report of sighting was forwarded to CFOC or NRC. The RCMP have now been notified of the requirement will file a report as per their operational manual CO-AIR.

When the report reached Ottawa, it was Dr. Peter Millman himself, the head of Upper Atmosphere Research for the NRC, who examined the file and listened to a tape recording of the interview of Adams made by Winterburn. On November 12, 1970, Millman mailed a letter to Adams, asking to clarify some details of the sighting and encounter. Millman was deeply skeptical of all UFO reports, and this one seemed to strike a chord with him. Adams quickly replied on November 17, answering Millman's questions and filling in much of the details.

Millman had wanted to know about the exact time of the encounter and the exact direction it was seen. This was because he had a theory that the UFO had a simple explanation. In a response to Adams' letter, Millman gave his explanation:

> On looking for an explanation of what you observed, there is one possibility that occurs to us, and while it may not be the correct

solution to the problem, I will note it here. The direction you gave for the sighting of the object is almost exactly the direction of Neepawa. Neepawa has at least two high towers lit with red obstruction warning lights for aircraft, and there may be other high warning lights in the town. If on the night you were out there occurred a rather rare type of looming mirage, the town of Neepawa would appear quite similar to what you described as seen from your location. As the mirage condition disintegrated the appearance would correspond to what you described after you returned later, and eventually it would disappear.

Neepawa is about 50 kilometres to the northwest, and situated among some hills. While it would not be impossible for a temperature inversion to create a looming mirage of the town, it would be odd that on this particular night Neepawa would be reflected, rather than any other of the towns nearer to the location and flatter terrain.

Further, Adams and Martin had a pretty good look at the object, which he noted was on the field, not above it. He described many details in a letter to Millman, providing a sketch of it and noting, as in the RCMP report:

It was oval in shape and orange yellow in colour. There were 9 red lights on rods on top of the object in clusters of three. There was a dark flange that appeared to go around the object and stuck out a distance of about a foot. Above this appeared a window about a foot high, and a bright yellow light came from this area. The rest of the object was a bright orange colour.

Adams had also commented that there were some bright shooting stars that night, and Millman picked up on this to suggest:

Your comment of the frequency of meteors or shooting stars that night is interesting, since this was close to the maximum of the Orionid meteor shower. Bright meteors from this shower would travel in general from a southeast to a northwest direction, and it is possible that a very bright fireball produced the intense light which first called your attention to the phenomenon, and you may have assumed that the mirage was the landed object.

This seems like a possibility, although the couple were not distracted until the UFO broke the darkness with its light. They were obviously sensitive to any kind of lights in the area, and it is unlikely a bright mirage appeared concurrently with a bright fireball.

As for Adams' encounter with the "humanoid," Millman also had a simple explanation: it had nothing to do with the UFO.

> I have no ready explanation for the small silver man, but I note that your observation of this phenomenon was in a direction at nearly right angles in which you saw the UFO. It is quite possible that what you saw as the little silver man was not associated in any way with the other phenomenon.

Millman also took issue with the comment that "the moon was shining." A simple check of an ephemeris showed that the moon didn't rise until 2:00 pm that night, so therefore Adams' account was suspect. Millman wrote:

> ... it would appear that either your statement of the date, which was Friday, October 23/24, or your statement about the moon, must be in error. Which is the better assumption: that you made the observation on an earlier date, or that your memory of the moon relates to an earlier period than 1:00 a.m. possibly to when you drove back after you had taken your friend home?

Millman's line of questioning assumed the witness' testimony must have been flawed, and was searching for vindication of this belief. But an examination of the RCMP report notes the UFO encounter took place between: "0700Z – 0900Z 24 Oct 70." In other words, the moon would have been visible above the horizon by 0800Z (2:00 am), which would agree with Adams' timeline.

Adams wrote back to Millman on December 3, 1970, and was adamant:

> I received your letter... and do not agree with your conclusion of the light being a mirage of the tower lights from Neepawa. It is too far away to be that and why has no one seen them before? I am absolutely positive that what I saw was no light on a tower, but that of a UFO.

Despite cross examination, the witness stood by his story while the scientist in Ottawa tried to explain it away.

It all depends on whom you believe.

1. The "Non-Meteoric Sightings File" was the top drawer of a single filing cabinet within an office in the Herzberg Institute of Astrophysics, Ottawa. Photo taken in about 1985. Source: Ufology Research.

2. "Sketch of saucer-shaped object seen at Iberville, Quebec, in 1953." From: Intelligence - Sighting of unknown objects, 23 April 1953 © Government of Canada. Reproduced with the permission of Library and Archives Canada (2021). Source: Library and Archives Canada/Department of National Defence/e002751147

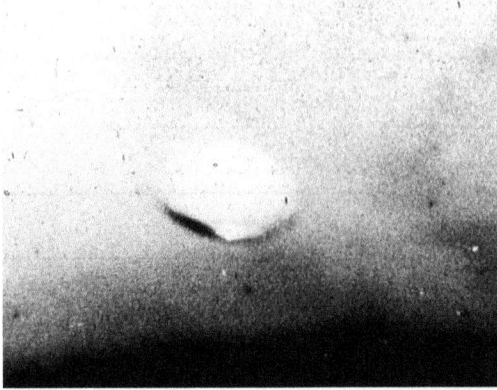

3. "Photo of disc-shaped object seen over Willow Point, BC, in 1972." From: Herzberg Institute of Astrophysics - Reports on non-meteoric sightings, unidentified flying objects, UFO's 4/24/1972 © Government of Canada. Reproduced with the permission of Library and Archives Canada (2021). Source: Library and Archives Canada/National Research Council of Canada fonds/e002745835

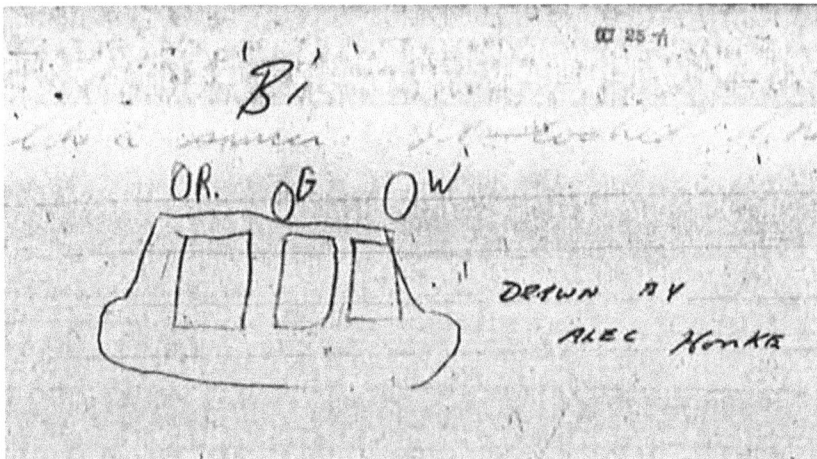

4. "Sketch by witness of object seen near Winnipeg in 1971." From: Herzberg Institute of Astrophysics - Reports on non-meteoric sightings, unidentified flying objects, UFO's 9/19/1971 © Government of Canada. Reproduced with the permission of Library and Archives Canada (2021). Source: Library and Archives Canada/National Research Council of Canada fonds/e002745732

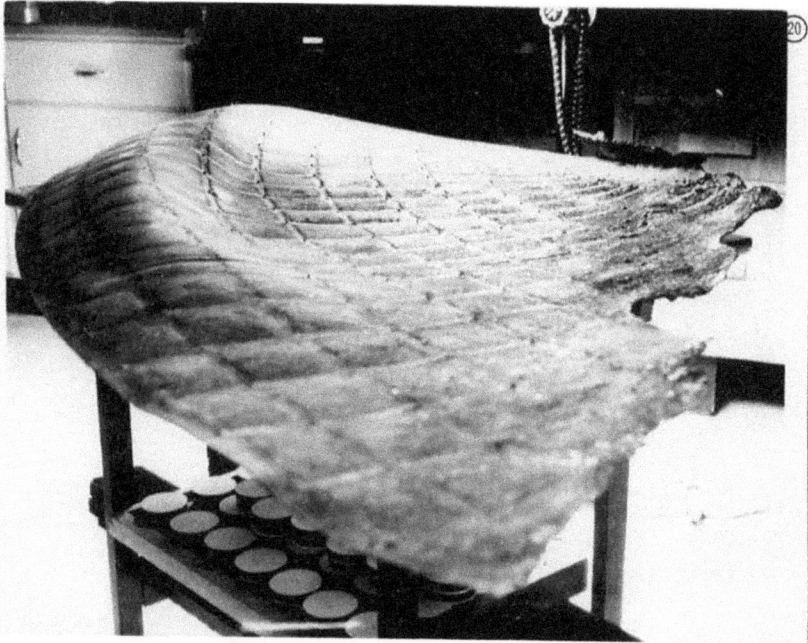

5. "A piece of a spacecraft found near Wollaston Lake, Saskatchewan, in 1968." From: © Government of Canada. Reproduced with the permission of Library and Archives Canada (2021). Source: Library and Archives Canada/Royal Canadian Mounted Police fonds/e003000408

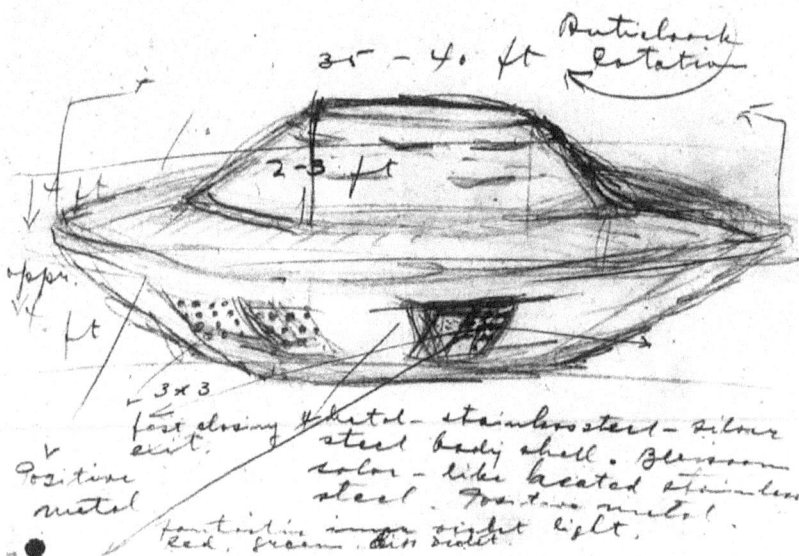

6. "Sketch made by Stefan Michalak of the object that
descended near him."

Source: Ufology Research files.

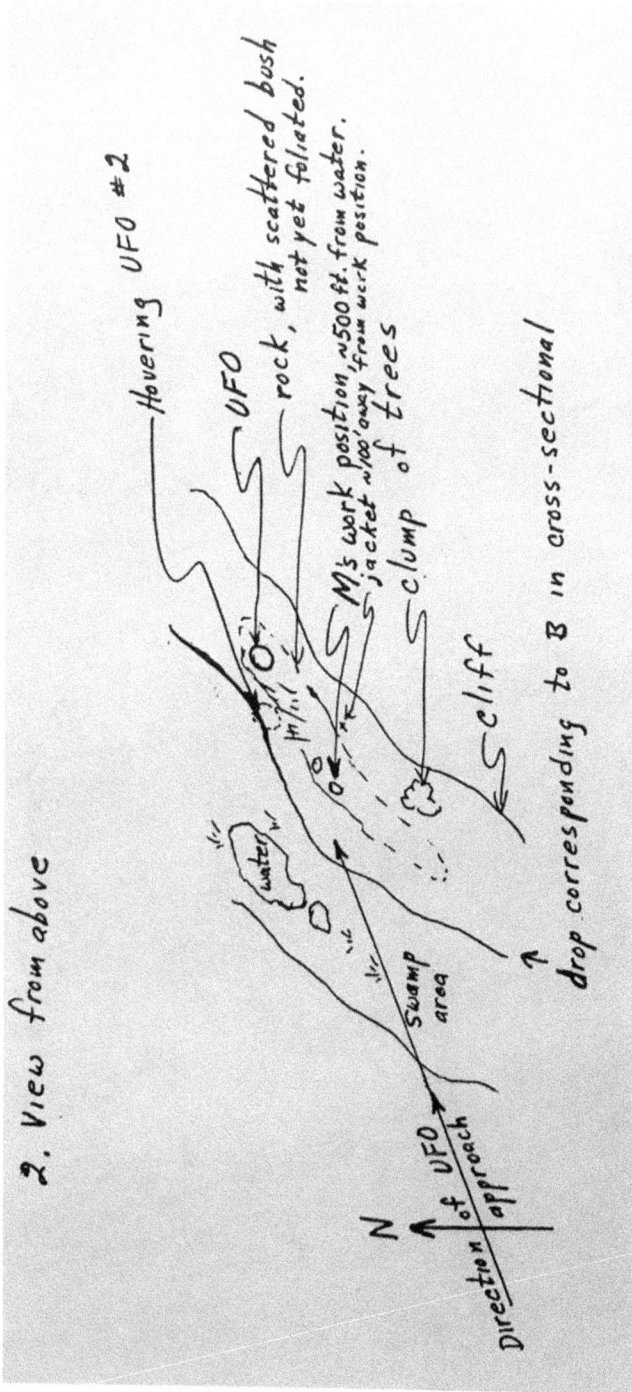

2. View from above

N

Direction of UFO approach

Swamp area

water

Hovering UFO #2

UFO

rock, with scattered bush not yet foliated.

M's work position, ~500 ft. from water.
jacket ~100' away from work position.

clump of trees

cliff

drop corresponding to B in cross-sectional

7: "Sketch of location of UFO landing site as drawn by Stefan Michalak for RCMP investigators."

Source: Ufology Research.

8. "Cap worn by Stefan Michalak, side view."
Source: Ufology Research.

9. "Cap worn by Stefan Michalak,
rear view, showing burned hole."
Source: Ufology Research.

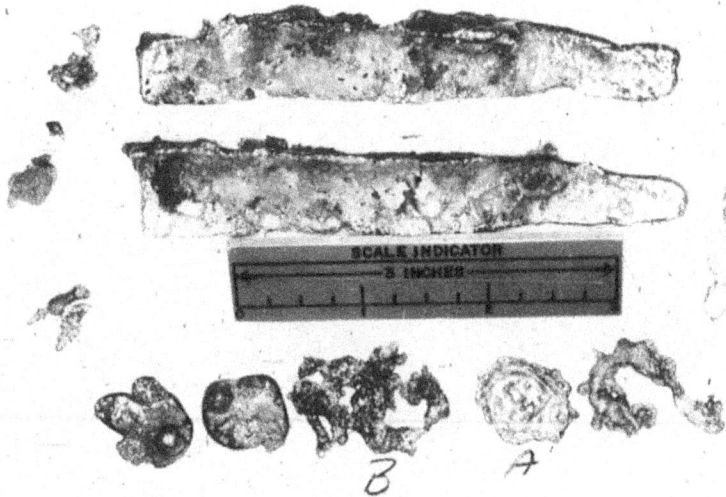

10. "Radioactive silver bars and globules found at Falcon Lake UFO site in 1968."
Source: Ufology Research.

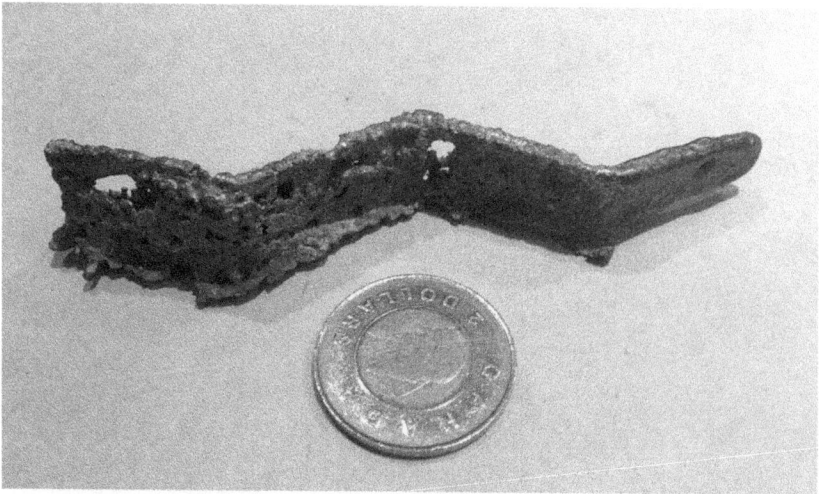

11. "Radioactive silver bar originally found at Falcon Lake UFO site during examination in 2020."
Source: Ufology Research.

12. "Warren Smith photo 1." Published with the permission of the Board of Regents of the University of Colorado.

13. "Warren Smith photo 2." Published with the permission of the Board of Regents of the University of Colorado.

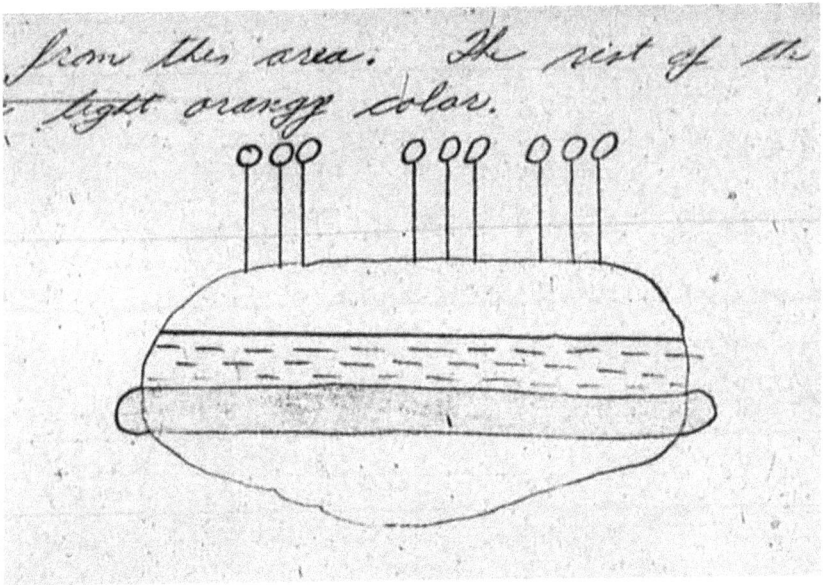

from this area: The rest of the light orange color.

14. "Sketch of object seen on October 24, 1970, near MacGregor, Manitoba." Source: Herzberg Institute of Astrophysics - Reports on non-meteoric sightings, unidentified flying objects, UFO's 10/23-24/1970 © Government of Canada. Reproduced with the permission of Library and Archives Canada (2021). Source: Library and Archives Canada/National Research Council of Canada fonds/e002745547

15. "'Charlie Redstar,' as photographed by Freddie Giesbrecht on July 7, 1975." Source: Herzberg Institute of Astrophysics - Reports on non-meteoric sightings, unidentified flying objects, UFO's 7/7/1975 © Government of Canada. Reproduced with the permission of Library and Archives Canada (2021). Source: Library and Archives Canada/National Research Council of Canada fonds/e002746801

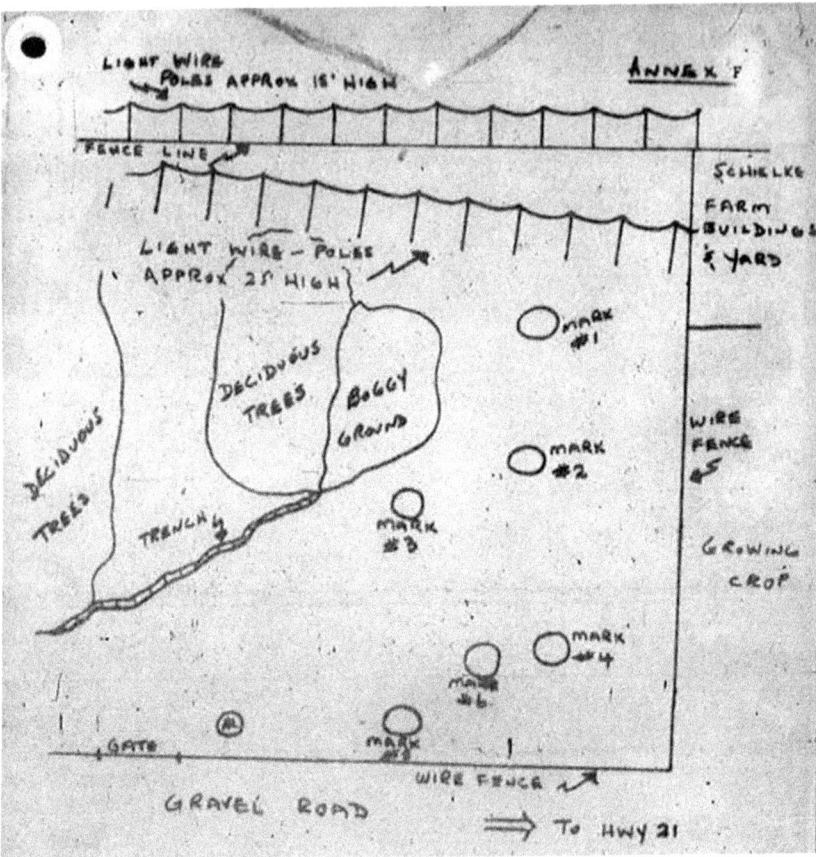

16. "Map of Duhamel 'crop circles.'" Source: Herzberg Institute of Astrophysics - Reports on non-meteoric sightings, unidentified flying objects, UFO's 8/8/1967 © Government of Canada. Reproduced with the permission of Library and Archives Canada (2021). Source: Library and Archives Canada/National Research Council of Canada fonds/ e002749307

17. "Duhamel 'crop circle.'" Source: Herzberg Institute of Astrophysics - Reports on non-meteoric sightings, unidentified flying objects, UFO's 8/8/1967 © Government of Canada. Reproduced with the permission of Library and Archives Canada (2021). Source: Library and Archives Canada/National Research Council of Canada fonds/e002749311

18. "Duhamel 'crop circle.'" Source: Herzberg Institute of Astrophysics - Reports on non-meteoric sightings, unidentified flying objects, UFO's 8/8/1967 © Government of Canada. Reproduced with the permission of Library and Archives Canada (2021). Source: Library and Archives Canada/National Research Council of Canada fonds/e002749311

UNCLASSIFIED

SUFFIELD MEMORANDUM NO. 49/67

ONSITE INSPECTION OF REPUTED UFO LANDING MARKS

AT DUHAMEL, ALBERTA

by

G.H.S. Jones

WARNING
This information is furnished with the express understanding that:
(a)   Proprietary and patent rights will be protected;
(b)   It will not be released to another nation without specific approval of the Canadian Department of National Defence.

19. "Suffield Memorandum 49/67." Source: © Government of Canada. Reproduced with the permission of Library and Archives Canada (2021). Library and Archives Canada/ https://www.bac-lac.gc.ca/eng/discover/unusual/ufo/ Documents/Duhamel-inspection-report.pdf

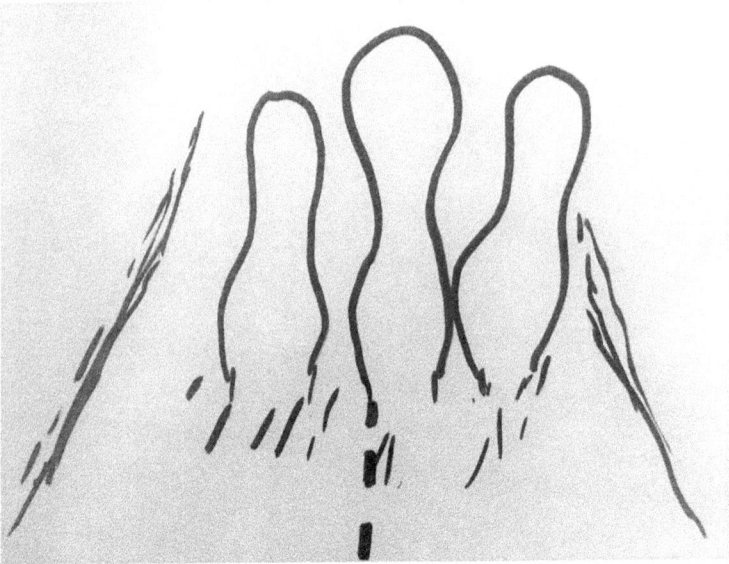

20. "The "bowling pin" creatures seen near Sundown,
Manitoba, in 1977."
Source: Ufology Research.

21. "The 'Mysterious Chunk of Space Hardware' found near
Ottawa in 1960."
Source: Spacelink (ufozine), Volume 2, No. 6, January 1970.

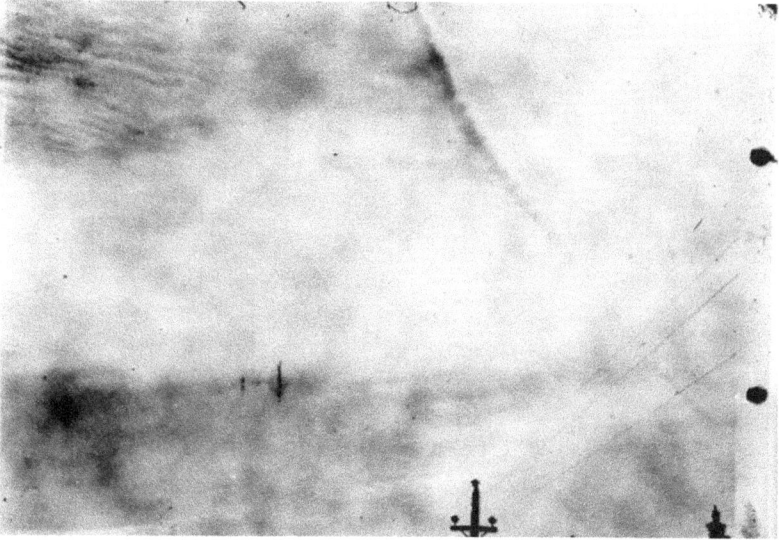

22. "The Harmon, Newfoundland, flying object trail through
the clouds."
Source: Project 1947. http://www.project1947.com/fig/1948air.htm

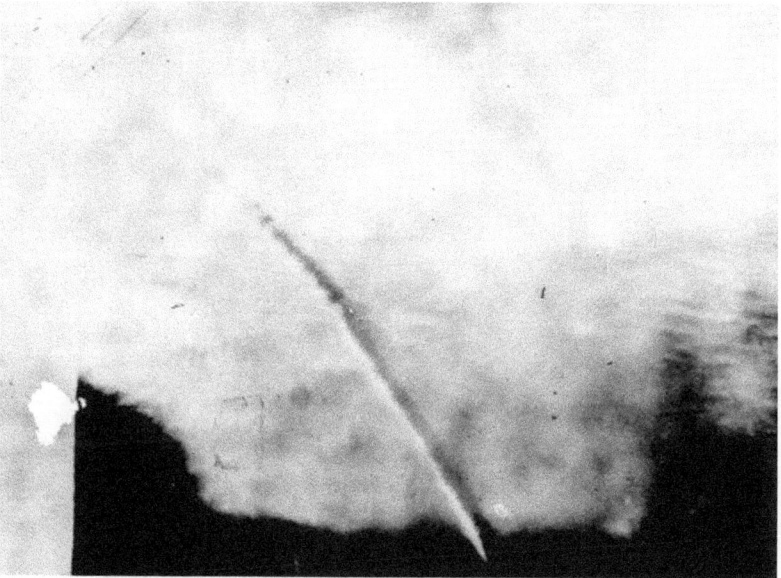

23. "The Harmon, Newfoundland, flying object trail through
the clouds."
Source: Project 1947. http://www.project1947.com/fig/1948air.htm

Monthly Distribution - NRC vs Survey

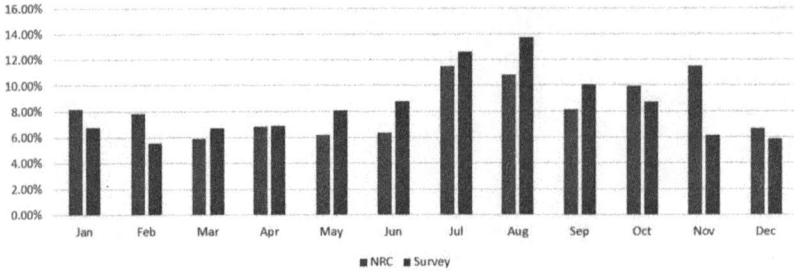

24. "Comparison of UFO reports by Month, NRC vs. Canadian
UFO Survey."
Source: Ufology Research

NRC Vs Survey by Type of Sighting

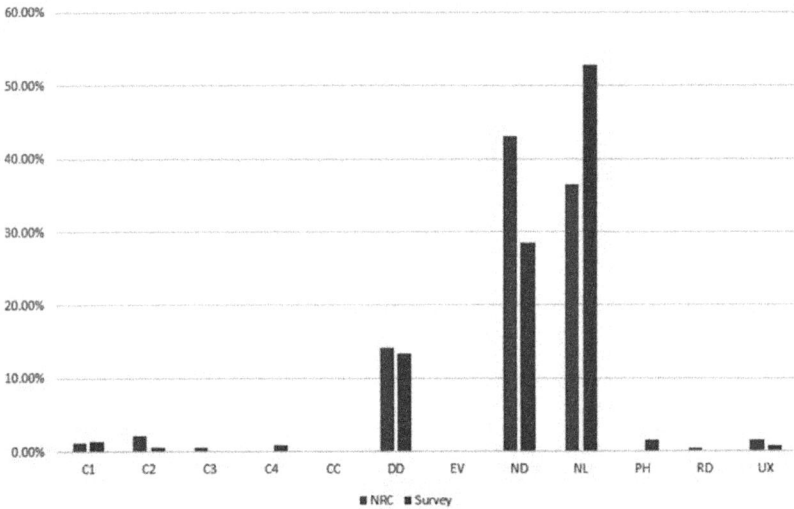

25. "Comparison of UFO reports by Type, NRC vs. Canadian
UFO Survey.
Source: Ufology Research

NRC Vs Survey by Province

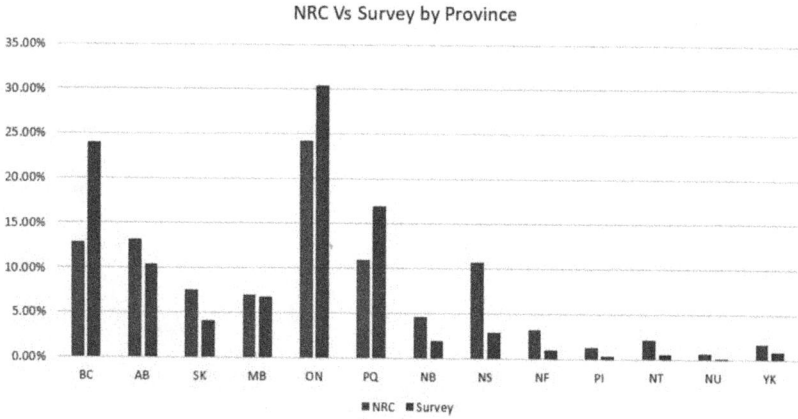

26. "Comparison of UFO reports by Province, NRC vs. Canadian UFO Survey."
Source: Ufology Research

Duration NRC Vs Survey

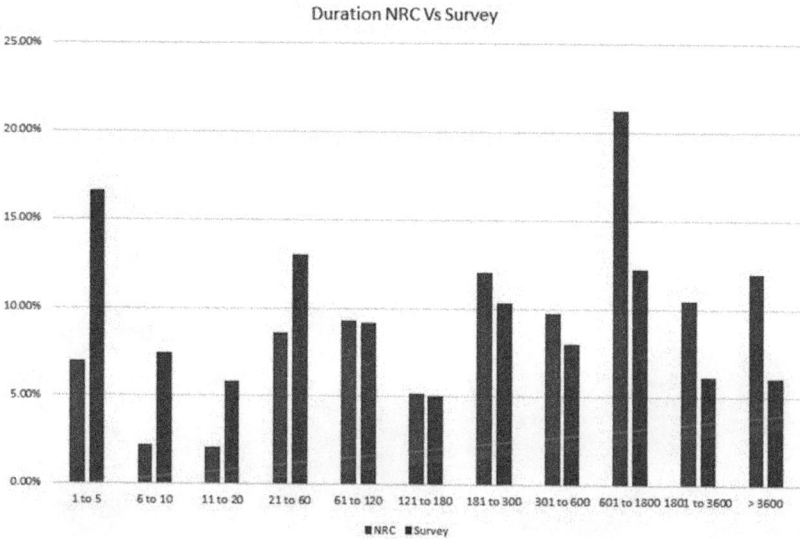

27. "Comparison of UFO reports by Duration, NRC vs. Canadian UFO Survey."
Source: Ufology Research

8

CHARLIE REDSTAR
AND FRIENDS

~

Much has been claimed about the "Charlie Redstar" UFO flap
during the 1970s in Manitoba, sometimes described as one
of the most spectacular UFO flaps in all of Canada. Was it
really as remarkable as has been claimed?

Well, yes and no. The flurry of UFO reports in that part of Manitoba
started in 1975, just as I was starting to investigate UFO reports, and
I took the opportunity to understand the reported Carman UFO
experiences. I went literally into the field, with no preconceived notions
but admittedly at least somewhat caught up with the excitement and
the idea hyped by media that UFOs and aliens were possibly visiting
farms and villages just an hour's drive southwest of where I lived. I
spent many, many hours in the Manitoba countryside and talking with
witnesses of the many mostly nocturnal lights that were seen.

That's mostly what they were—simply lights in the sky. There were a
few notable exceptions, but they were few and far between. And most
cases, it turned out, had simple explanations.

Even some explanations were particularly interesting, however. For
example, I learned from some farmers near the American border, less
than 30 miles away, that sure enough, there were lights moving along
the border and into Canada many evenings. But these were generally

known to be American aircraft flown by the department of Alcohol, Tobacco and Firearms (ATF) from North Dakota looking for drug smugglers. Many farmers I spoke with knew the stories about how marijuana was grown on the Canadian side under railroad trestles and other secluded spots, and then shipped to the USA after harvesting.

During the Carman UFO flap, dozens of witnesses came forward; there are six cases from Carman and five from nearby towns in the NRC UFO files. Anecdotally, however, UFO sightings during the summers of 1975 and 1976 were much more common—so much so that there were actual traffic jams on farm roads (more like dirt tracks) in the countryside, created by city folk wanting to see for themselves what all the fuss was about.

Although the first few years of the 1970s had respectable numbers of UFO reports in Manitoba, they in no way matched the dozens and dozens recorded for the 1967-1969 flap across Canada. But five sightings were reported in February 1975 alone in Manitoba, prophetic in their style and description, and are on file with Ufology Research, though not reported to the NRC.

Early that month, a farmer was walking to his barn north of Lundar when a light that "looked like a ball" swooped low over his head. While gazing up at the object, he felt as if "hot plastic" had been poured on his face. He said it was "suffocating," and that he "couldn't think straight" while it was over him. The light was red and about 14 to 18 inches in diameter.

That may have been the first sighting of what came to be known as "Charlie Redstar," the strange red light frequently seen bobbing over the hillsides in the area near Carman, 70 kilometres southwest of Winnipeg. Because it was seen so frequently according to some witnesses, the light was given its moniker, and when it was seen some people would say, "Oh there goes Charlie again!"

Although the majority of sightings that were part of the Carman flap were observations of distant lights in the night sky, some cases involved the observation of disc shaped objects at close range. Some witnesses said they were near enough to see "portholes" on the sides or underside of the strange craft. There were reports of "Ferris wheels" in the sky, with a myriad of coloured lights moving in slow, ponderous action, very like the vehicles depicted in the movie *Close Encounters of the Third Kind*, although predating the movie's special effects. Most of these cases, however, were never reported to the RCMP and are not part of the NRC UFO files and exist only in private UFO investigators' collections. But the ones that were reported to the RCMP still raise some interesting questions.

The case which is generally taken to be the start of the Carman wave of "Charlie" sightings occurred on March 27, 1975, southeast of Graysville, Manitoba, about 12 kilometres west of Carman. A young girl was awakened by a "shrill, pulsating siren" at about 2:00 am, accompanied by a feeling "like an earthquake." She briefly saw a red ball of light pass her window on its way south, and thought it had set the house on fire because of the intense light flooding in. She thought it came over the house from the north, and last saw it on the southern horizon, "looking like the Sun was coming up."

But the Carman flap really took off from an airport (pun intended). On April 10, 1975, as Bob and Elaine Diemert were walking from their farmhouse to their private airfield called Friendship Field, they were startled to see:

> ... a big red light coming at us, like a big landing light. You couldn't miss it. It was right at eye level, and it was just loafing along. It was close enough already that you could see the dome on the top, but it was all red - pulsing red.

There are several pages of documents in the NRC files regarding this case, N75/039. The saucer shaped object flew towards them from the west, then eventually veered north and travelled "about 300 feet above the treetops," going an estimated 30 miles an hour. The entire sighting lasted no more than five to seven minutes.

Other witnesses were found to corroborate the Diemerts' sighting, but their actual supportive testimony was not as strong as was hoped. Mrs. Corrie Pauls, for example, is considered a witness to a UFO that night, too. However, all Pauls saw was "a red light flashing by," and since she lived literally right next to Diemert's small airport and often saw airplanes with lights in the area, she "didn't pay no attention to it."

The Diemerts observed other UFOs a few more times that month, but the real affront on their airport took place later, beginning on May 7, when sightings began a nightly streak that lasted literally for months. During the summer, people would gather at the Diemert's field, watching for the nightly appearance of Charlie Redstar as he (or it) skimmed low over the trees on the horizon then soared overhead in a grand finale.

Charlie dazzled his admirers practically every night. On May 9, 1975, at about 12:15 am, Constable Ian Lloyd Nicholson of the Carman RCMP

Detachment saw "an object in the west, three or four miles away, and at about 1000 feet [altitude]." Nicholson's account of Charlie Redstar is perhaps the most accurate of all the reports, since he was a decidedly unbiased observer with the least subjective interpretation. On May 13, 1975, he gave a statement describing his experience:

> During town patrol in Carman, at approximately 12:15 am CST, on the 9th May,1975, I was driving out near Friendship Field, an airfield in Carman. At that time I saw a red light in the sky off to the northwest of the airfield. I then proceeded two miles west of Carman, on P.T.H. 245, to get a better view of the object. At that location, I stopped the police car and saw an oval shaped red light with an X-shaped background. The X-shaped light was white in colour, and not attached to the oval shape. In order to get a better view of the object, I then proceeded west on P.T.H. 245, all the while keeping this red object in view. As I proceeded west of Hwy 245, the object seemed to be flying in a northwesterly direction at an undetermined rate of speed. I continued west on P.T.H. 245 for approximately twelve miles, until I lost sight of the object over the trees. The object was in view for approximately twelve minutes… flying in in a northwesterly direction at an approximate altitude of 1000 feet, and there was no noise emanating from the object.

When UFOs are stationary and then seen to move away when being chased, one possible explanation is that they are astronomical in nature. Sure enough, a check of star charts shows that both Venus and Saturn were very low in the northwest at that exact time of Nicholson's observation, the former of which would have been very bright indeed. Did Nicholson mistake Venus for a UFO? It would explain why RCMP at Portage la Prairie about 50 kilometres to the northwest, wouldn't have noticed it, if they were told it was possibly coming from the southeast. Nicholson's description of an X-shaped light is puzzling, however.

And that doesn't explain the many sightings of Charlie Redstar that flew over the Diemerts' airstrip. Today, we might say that they had been watching the antics of a drone, but this was 1975 before such toys and remotely piloted vehicles were available to the public. Of course, the US military had developed and was using drones in the early 1970s, so one could theorize that some could have been employed for reconnaissance from across the border into Canada, but that seems unlikely since such vehicles were being used primarily over battlefields at that time.

There was one curious sighting during the Carman flap that involved multiple witnesses, simultaneous observations from different directions, television news footage, and even possible radiation effects. Because there were so many people involved and the events took place over a large area over a few hours, the reconstruction of the incident is quite difficult, and further complicated by conflicting accounts and statements by the witnesses. Regardless of which version is the most accurate, there is no doubt that something very strange happened on the night of May 13-14, 1975, a few miles northwest of Carman, as recorded in the NRC files as case N75/060.

Because "Charlie Redstar" was being reported so often, Bob Diemert had contacted CKY TV in Winnipeg with the hope that their filming the UFO would prove what was being seen. He told CKY TV that if they sent a news crew to Carman, they would get footage of Charlie for sure.

After convincing the TV station management of the "sure thing," cameraman Bill Kendricks, John Berry and two others from the TV station went to Carman on May 11, 1975, but unfortunately saw nothing of interest. They went out again on May 12 but saw only a "light at the end of the road," a "boring" kind of UFO that is self-explanatory. Berry got in his car and tried to approach the light, but as is typical in this kind of UFO case, it moved away and disappeared ("blinked out") before it could be caught, implying that Charlie possessed some intelligence.

Frustrated, the cameraman who was out with them then went back to Winnipeg and immediately filed for overtime pay, annoyed that he had been on a wild goose chase. The next morning, when the news director received the request for overtime, he was upset at the extravagance that resulted in no worthwhile footage. He then forbade all cameramen from going to film any UFOs unless they went on their own time.

So, under those conditions, on May 13, Bill Kendricks and Allen Kerr (a film lab technician) took a TV camera to Carman and met with others about two miles north of Carman to wait for Charlie to appear. About 11:30 pm they saw a light on the western horizon. The light rose above the trees, drifted slowly south, then briefly flashed a brilliant light and shot "straight up at incredible speed." This swift departure was so fast, only two of the many gathered saw it.

The UFO hunters did not want to give up on UFO watching that night. They decided to split into three groups to try to get a closer look at Charlie, as the RCMP report on file details.

One group, consisting of newspaper editor Howard Bennett, Kerry McIntyre, and 'Red' Storey, headed northwest to end up a few miles

CONTINUATION – SUITE

REF – OBJET:

PAGE

Robert Edward DIEMERT – U.F.O. Sighting

APPENDIX "F"

STATEMENT OF: Ian Lloyd NICHOLSON, Cst.
R.C.M.P. Carman Detachment,
Carman, Manitoba

13 MAY 75.
Carman, Manitoba
TAKEN AT: R.C.M.P. Detachment office, Carman.

Q- In your own words, could you tell me all the facts regarding the U.F.O. sighting near Carman on the 9th MAY 1975?

A- During town patrol in Carman, at approximately 12:15 AM.,CST on the 9th MAY, 1975, I was driving out near Friendship Field, an airfield in Carman. At that time I saw a red light in the sky off to the northwest of the airfield. I then proceeded two miles west of Carman, on P.T.H. 245, to get a better view of the object. At that location, I stopped the police car, and saw an oval-shaped red light with an X-shaped background. The X-shaped light was white in color, and not attached to the oval shape. In order to get a better view of the object, I then proceeded west on P.T.H. 245, all the while keeping this red object in view. As I proceeded west on Hwy. 245, the object seemed to be flying in a north-westerly direction at an undetermined rate of speed. I continued west on PTH 245, for approximately twelve miles, until I lost sight of the object over the trees. The object was in view for approximately twelve minutes. I notified Portage La Prairie Rural Detachment, of the above, and they later advised that they had not seen any objects as described above. The object was flying in a north-westerly direction at an approximate altitude of 1000 feet, and there was no noise eminating from the object.

Q- Is there anything else you can add to this at this time?

A- No, I don't think so.

END OF STATEMENT.

SGN: I.L. NICHOLSON, 30994, Cst.
Carman DetachmentRCMP.

RCMP-GRC C-237 (4/66) 6851 (7530-21-029-4628)

Document 45: "Report by RCMP Constable Ian Nicholson regarding UFO he observed near Carman, Manitoba, on May 9, 1975." Herzberg Institute of Astrophysics - Reports on non-meteoric sightings, unidentified flying objects, UFO's 5/7/1975 © Government of Canada. Reproduced with the permission of Library and Archives Canada (2021). Source: Library and Archives Canada/National Research Council of Canada fonds/e002746725

CANADAS UFOS: DECLASSIFIED

east and just north of the road they believed Charlie was on. They believed they had "scared it into flight" by their tactical manoeuvre, and thought they had come extremely close to the object. Bennett stated in an interview:

> ... I could see this big glow behind some trees less than half a mile away off to the right and ahead of us ... It was smoky red, a hazy glow, and to me the thing was higher than the trees, maybe 50 feet tall. It was about 20 feet thick and was sitting at an angle of about 45 degrees. The edges were fuzzy and not sharply defined. It was much like seeing a drive-in movie screen from the side.

(Several days later, Bennett led investigators to the area where he believed the object had rested. They took readings with a radiation survey meter and at the "landing site," discovered "a series of hot spots about 85 yards apart, each with a radius of approximately 25 feet." However, the readings from these areas were not that much greater than the normal background level, and could have been due to equipment malfunction according to a technician familiar with the survey meter. Radiation anomalies have sometimes been claimed by investigators of UFO landing sites, though this is disputed by skeptics.)

Another group of observers that night consisted of Bob and Elaine Diemert, Mr. and Mrs. Bill Kendricks, and Paul Sanders. They travelled south one mile from Carman and then went west to approach from the opposite side to the first group. To them, the object seemed to be "rising and falling like a blood red Moon through the trees." The group tried to close in on the object, but it suddenly "popped into the air, hovered... and then took off straight for the CBC tower [east]."

The third group included CTV cameraman Allen Kerr who managed to catch the object on film as it "jumped into the sky" as he watched with others at the CBC tower itself. He panned his tripod-mounted camera with the object's movement as it approached and flew overhead. Kerr claims he panned in a vertical angle from about 45 to 90 degrees, held the camera steady for a few seconds then followed it again to about 135 degrees.

The resulting film contained three and a half seconds of footage showing the light initially on the ground, then a few seconds when the camera was held at 90 degrees. The first sequence showed the object on the ground and increasing slightly in size, then jumping to the top of the frame after a flash of light illuminates the horizon.

This "flash frame" was considered by another cameraman to be caused by a defect in this particular type of camera. This explanation was rejected by most of the individuals involved with the sighting, although they themselves admitted they had not seen any such flash of light at the time. A second sequence of film taken that night shows a red, pulsing light following a wavelike motion in its flight across the frames. There also seems to be a series of "echoes" following the object on the film.

None of this detail made it into the NRC files but is from the large file on the Carman sightings that is part of the Ufology Research collection. Although not part of the official record, it's important to note it here because it expands on the RCMP report of the incident. The film itself was never submitted to the RCMP or NRC, but was publicly available.

The film was examined by many people, including myself, as well as the noted astronomer and UFO expert Dr. J. Allen Hynek of the Center for UFO Studies. Hynek was put on the spot by CKY reporters when he visited Winnipeg in 1975 and was asked on camera what he thought of the film sequence. He replied, quite diplomatically, that it was "the best film of a nocturnal light I've ever seen." Even now, there still is little else to say about the film; it is a short sequence showing a small red light moving in the sky.

But what was it? Three groups of witnesses saw the same thing from different locations at the same time; a strange light moved from the horizon then zoomed overhead. An aircraft? But Bob Diemert knew what airplanes look like at night, and it definitely wasn't one of those in his opinion, and in the opinion of the several others present.

In any case, why only a red light? An aircraft should have displayed other colours if it had been seen under similar conditions, which "Charlie" did not. It is premature to suggest that an alien spacecraft flew over the groups that night, but something very odd was seen and photographed.

The sightings of Charlie Redstar continued that summer, and soon UFO watching became a favourite pastime for Carman area residents. Carloads of curious people came each night to see their own UFO zipping through the night sky. The media were having a heyday, both in print and on the airwaves. Ads in local newspapers urged the reader to "Shop where Charlie Redstar shops!" Carman residents even received a visit from a *National Enquirer* reporter who was interested in getting the tabloid's "scoop" on the situation.

A circus like atmosphere evolved; cars lined the dirt roads along favourite hot spots, and traffic jams occurred when Charlie flew by and drivers scrambled to be first to give chase. During these chases, speeds of 80 or 90 miles per hour were not uncommon, and it was perhaps only luck that no serious accidents happened. UFO watching parties took place throughout the region, lasting on occasion through the night and into the dawn. It is no wonder, then, that literally hundreds of sightings of Charlie Redstar and his friends were claimed during that summer, but as noted, few ever were reported to the RCMP.

Apart from Carman, there were a number of remarkable reported UFO sightings that came out of this flap, and a discussion of the Carman flap would be incomplete if it did not include at least some of them to give the reader a better picture of the reports that summer.

For example, at about 7:50 am on June 4, 1975, a man was driving near Holland, Manitoba, and encountered a saucer-shaped UFO hovering in the middle of a farm road. This daylight sighting seems much more significant than most of the Charlie sightings and took place about 50 kilometres west of Carman. The witness was considered truthful and reliable by the RCMP and he was justifiably shocked to have seen the UFO on (or over) the road. It's significant that the witness did not hold a specific or strong view about UFOs, meaning he neither believed nor disbelieved.

Another case that is considered one of the cornerstones of the 1975 Charlie Redstar flap is what was seen by Mrs. Frederika (Freddie) Giesbrecht on July 7 just after 2:00 am. An avid photographer, she was able to capture some photos of a UFO as it sat low in the eastern sky. She described what she saw to an RCMP investigator:

> The colour was yellow, just about white. It was something like Venus. I know that there is no star like that east of Carman, so I got out the camera with the telephoto lens. I also looked through my husband's binoculars. Then I took the first photo at 2:25 a.m. The object disappeared suddenly, then it reappeared bigger, brighter and closer. Then I took the second picture at 2:44 a.m., a minute later at 2:45 a.m. I took the third and final picture.

Even with her zoom lens, Giesbrecht said the object looked like it was "pretty far away." Pressed on this, she said it looked to be "about 15 or 16 miles away." Her photos in the RCMP files show a curious triangular light in a dark night sky, the shape possibly due to movement of the camera.

What did she see? Well, she was quite correct that Venus was not in the eastern sky at the time. However, star charts show that both

Mars and Jupiter were low in the east at that time of the morning on that date, and the latter would have been spectacularly bright, hanging over the horizon.

Treating Charlie as a physical entity was common to many watchers' descriptions. To this day, many local residents insist that Charlie was a real "living" entity that chose to fly over their rooftops. This perception was reflected in many ways; there were songs and poems made up about the aerial antics of the lights, and one religious family published a tract attesting that they had a marvellous vision of the Endtime while watching the skies in the Carman area.

Although Charlie never seemed to leave Carman (the Diemerts and others insist he appeared during the decades since then), after 1975 there were no further reports from the area as recorded in NRC files. In fact, there were only five UFO cases in the NRC files for all of 1976 in Manitoba, and no further cases from Carman at all.

Is Charlie still out there, playing coy?

9

MORE EVIDENCE CROPS UP

~

Well-grounded UFOs

We've looked at cases involving apparent crashes of UFOs, and cases where UFOs have passed uncomfortably close to witnesses in cars and airplanes. There's another category of UFOs called Close Encounters, where objects are seen to land or are found on the ground. Those are in abundance in the NRC UFO Files as well.

On October 14, 1975, the RCMP received numerous calls from residents of Edson, Alberta, about UFOs that they had seen in the sky. Radio station CJYR was flooded with calls that night. We don't know exactly how many and what most had been seeing, but if the report from one resident is any indication, there was some weirdness in the air.

One call was from a man who saw an object described as:

> Size of cattle truck as reported by observer, two red lights lower surface, two clear lights on top. Actual size men on top wearing hard hats. Object airborne then landed on highway. Stopped for short duration. Then proceed north Peers Alberta via highway towards Whitecourt then elevated.

So, a UFO landed and then traveled on an Alberta highway for a while before taking off again. I assume it obeyed all vehicle regulations and speed limits.

On May 22, 1966, somewhere on the highway between Blue River, BC, and Jasper, Alberta, the driver of a vehicle reported that a grey-coloured object the size of a car and "shaped like a bowl" landed on the road, making a whining noise. The brief NRC report N66/024 doesn't mention how long it sat there, and the object didn't make any sound when it took off. However, the person reporting the incident said that the object left behind "three pad impressions about four feet square."

One would think that a case like this, with physical traces left behind, would make it imperative that there be a detailed and thorough investigation. However, there is nothing else in the file to suggest that the case was ever investigated. In fact, a handwritten note on the report reads: "Requested more info from RCC, *i.e.*, name and address of person, *i.e.*, circumstances and any other potential data." (In 1966, RCC was the Rescue Coordination Centre, which was responsible for issues regarding aircraft and possible crashes, so was involved in UFO reporting within the Canadian Forces.)

There's no indication that this case, which was substantially more than just a light seen in the sky, was followed up. Did something land in the Rockies? Was it a hoax? If so, why would someone file a report like this at all, risking serious consequences?

Another case involving a "landed" UFO about a month later, on June 16, 1966, in Glace Bay, Nova Scotia, had a much different response and result. At about 6:30 pm, Mrs. George Evely was startled to see a "red tinted fireball with a faint white tail and trailing grey smoke." It made a buzzing noise as it flew towards the witness from the southwest for about a minute before it fell to the ground only about 100 yards away. On striking the ground it made a noise like a large firecracker and when it fell onto loose gravel it shattered some larger rocks and scattered the gravel in all directions.

The NRC report N66/029 notes: "Object recovered." Mrs. Evely walked over and found a "round hollow object open on one end" 7/8 inches in diameter and ¾ inch long. She dutifully took it to the nearby RCAF Station in Sydney, where she handed it over for examination. Several pages of correspondence detailed how the Commanding Officer at the RCAF Station himself was involved in the investigation.

In the NRC file, an official named L. Guy Eon explains:

The object had been identified as a probable obsolete Canadian Army flare—specifically, [the inner liner of] a cartridge illuminating, 1 inch, J Nk 3T. It might have come from a militia store in Sydney.

In a handwritten memo, one military investigator added: "Too bad it wasn't a UFO!"

At 12:30 am on November 5, 1975, Jim Divall was driving north of Redwater, Alberta. According to NRC case N75/150, he came upon: "A large black object that appeared to be revolving slowly" and "had to drive his [vehicle] into the ditch to avoid hitting it." The UFO was 40 feet in diameter and had no "running lights," so had been unseen until Divall almost ran into it. He got out of his vehicle and watched the object for a few minutes as it made a rushing sound, then it disappeared.

One would think that any report of someone running off the road in order to avoid a crash with another vehicle might have precipitated an investigation by RCMP, but there was nothing more in the file. Even if the assumption was that Divall was somehow mistaken and the black object was actually a Mack truck with no running lights, that still should have warranted some kind of investigation.

Much more information was in the case file that documented what happened at 7:00 am on December 15, 1976, when Arnold Barker was driving a few miles north of Boyle, Alberta. Case N76/115 contains a long handwritten letter he supplied to the NRC describing what he encountered that morning:

While traveling south on Hwy 46, two and three quarter miles south of Boyle, I sighted two bright lights. I thought this was unusual for an airplane because of the type of light. It seemed about ½ mile away, at about a 1:30 o'clock position. The object was flying from [a] west to east direction. I drove until the object was in a 90-degree angle from the truck and road. I then waited until the object was too close to the truck and too close overhead for me to see from my passenger side window.

Up to this point, the object had two lights, one behind the other and both flashing. Each light appeared to be approximately two feet by four feet square, and close together—about three or four feet apart. The light itself was not a blinding light, but a bright white. It was not until the object was directly over the ditch on my right side of the road that I realized it was very low in flight and that it was not a plane.

I jumped out of the truck so that I could get a better look at it as it passed overhead and across the highway. By this time there were no white lights, one in front of the other, but two red lights side-by-side, four feet apart and not flashing. Each red light was in sort of a zigzag pattern about two inches high. The lights seemed to be joined by something that gave off a faint light.

Although my truck was running, I heard absolutely no noise from the object while I was outside. The object appeared to be landing in the field on the east side of the road. Then it stopped about six feet to ten feet from the ground for a moment. It stopped about 100 to 150 feet away from me. I made about six to twelve steps in the direction of the object, thinking that I could reach it. Then it moved in a northerly direction.

I then got into my truck and backed up for about ¾ of a mile to an intersection where I could turn around. I was backing approximately 30 miles an hour and the object by this time was a white light again and stayed behind me at a two o'clock position. I then turned my truck around, still traveling north and the object at more of a one o'clock position, gaining distance from me. I speeded up to 75 mph for 1 ½miles. When I stopped, I sighted the object on the horizon many miles away. The object seemed to travel parallel to the road about 300 yards off to the side some miles and just above the ground.

The NRC report contained additional information, noting that the object Barker saw had been estimated to be approximately 50 feet in altitude when it was traveling across the highway. It seemed to be six feet in length and had two rectangular illuminated modules connected to the very narrow body. The UFO went under a power line near a field fence and came to a stop approximately six feet overtop of the snowdrifts. When the object began moving rapidly away from Barker its lights changed to a reddish color.

In the several documents devoted to this case, investigator RCMP Cpl. Goodall noted that: "Barker is a reliable person (Very) and would not make such a story up [NB: emphasis in original]." Goodall also noted in his own handwriting: "I personally inspected the snow covering the field and found no signs of it having been disturbed."

This case is remarkable for several reasons. First, it involved a close encounter of the first kind, within about 150 feet. Secondly, the RCMP investigator actually took the report seriously enough to visit the site of the encounter to check for evidence, a detail not found in most other NRC cases. And finally, a statement about the witness and his reliability, which suggests he likely did not just make up the story.

One day in mid-July 1969, Bernard O'Brien was on a tractor, cutting grass in a field near Manotick, Ontario, when "a small cloud of dark smoke arose from the ground" as his machinery passed over a particular spot. As noted in NRC Case N69/149, O'Brien thought it best to notify the field's owner, John Fox, who came out to examine the area himself.

Document 46: "Report of ground mark and material found on ground near Manotick, Ontario, in July, 1969." Herzberg Institute of Astrophysics - Reports on non-meteoric sightings, unidentified flying objects, UFO's 9/3/1969 © Government of Canada. Reproduced with the permission of Library and Archives Canada (2021). Source: Library and Archives Canada/National Research Council of Canada fonds/e002745295

Fox found three "near-perfect circles" in the field, two together and the third about 150 feet away. They were each rings of affected grass 15-20 feet in diameter with a width of about a foot. Grass was flattened inside the rings, but the rings themselves were dark in colour and contained "a crystalline substance." This material was puzzling and did not seem to be anything related to normal farming operations. Fox noted the substance was not something used on the farm and "did not know what the substance actually consisted of."

A number of people heard about the discovery, including Salvatore Longo of Ottawa, who had the wherewithal to collect a sample of the crystalline material. The bad news is that he didn't pass along the sample until August 11, almost a month later, and when he took NRC investigators to the site, there was no trace of the strange substance on the ground, probably because of rain during the previous weeks. There was no mention in the NRC report, however, if the rings were still visible.

In this case, the NRC file does have a note about the analysis of the material from the rings. In a letter to the RCMP on October 16, 1969, Dr. Peter Millman, then head of Upper Atmosphere Research at the NRC, explained that the sample of grass and crystalline material was tested and even x-rayed by the Geological Survey of Canada. The results showed "no evidence of a mineral content or any type of radioactivity."

Millman stated: "The results indicate that it was some type of biological mould of which there are many varieties and these may frequently assume a circular pattern," like "the well-known mushroom rings found in Ireland and other parts of the world."

Millman also pointed out that there was no UFO sighting associated with the rings, so the case was closed.

His conclusion, however, is hardly satisfying. One would like to think that farmers used to working their land would know what "mushroom rings" looked like. In this case, Millman was obviously referring to *Marasmius oreades,* also known as the "fairy ring mushroom" that is found throughout North America. It grows in arcs or circles, and often makes the grass in the rings themselves grow a deeper green. The mushrooms themselves are relatively small but following growth they release spores in a circle around them and after several years produce a ring of decent size. In many cases, the rings are indistinct but can be identified by the mushrooms themselves, which are quite edible and much sought after by foodies.

One mushroom expert explained the fairy ring mushroom's most noted characteristic this way:

You can understand the circular growth of the fairy ring by thinking about what happens when a fungus spore lands on your bread or your cheese or your Jello—it germinates then grows in every direction it can. If the substrate is perfectly homogenous, *i.e.*, composed of exactly the same nutrients throughout, this will result in a perfect circle. Slight variations in the substrate can account for different growth rates in different parts of the circle, making it less than perfectly round. Interestingly, if you try to isolate the fungus from the far inside of the circle, you will find that the fungus is no longer growing there, but only on the outside edge. You can also notice the center of the fairy ring is often quite differently colored from the outside of the ring, adding to its mystique.[1]

This doesn't sound very much like what was found in Manotick. But at least the "crystalline substance" was analysed by the NRC.

Something was also analysed from a "landing" near Peesane, Saskatchewan. On May 12, 1975, at 11:30 pm, Mr. and Mrs. Lyle Carson were in their home when they saw a strange green light for about 10 or 15 minutes, somewhere over their farm fields. It seemed to head east and vanish after a while and they didn't think anything of it until a few days later, on May 14, 1975, when Mr. Carson was checking his fences on the east side of their property, about 400 yards from their house. He came across "a perfectly round circle burnt into the grass," apparently more of a ring that was five feet in diameter and six inches in width. NRC case file N75/057 notes that photos and samples from the burned area were taken and sent to the NRC for analysis, although there's nothing in the file to suggest what was discovered.

A similar burned area was found only a few weeks later, on May 30, 1975, near Hazel Dell, Saskatchewan, only about 100 kilometres southeast of Peesane. Russell Worobetz was cultivating some stubble when he found two burned areas in the center of his field on a small knoll. They were both five feet in diameter and situated about four feet apart. Worobetz said he had never seen anyone in that part of his field and that the odd marks must have been created in the spring because they were too fresh to have been made in the fall. Again, photos were taken and presumably passed along to Ottawa. NRC Case N75/072 is classified as a "Suspicious Looking Spot."

Also in Saskatchewan, a somewhat different kind of landing trace was found near the town of MacNutt on December 17, 1974. Early that morning, at about 2:30 am, John Wagner was in his farmhouse and noticed a large, bright glow to the west, like daylight, that lasted for about 25 minutes. The next morning, he found a circular ring in the snow, about 20 feet in diameter. NRC Case N74/117 provides few details other than that local radio and TV stations carried stories about the discovery.

NRC case N78/023 also concerns a UFO leaving a mark in the snow, with considerably more investigation and analysis. At about 9:30 pm on February 2, 1978, Brian Mosychuk was walking in an Edmonton neighbourhood when he saw a car-sized object with blue lights on front and back, approaching from the northwest. It hovered over him and began making a rumbling sound, then a beam of light shot out towards him.

Mosychuk leaned backward to avoid the beam, which shone at his feet in the snow, but could still feel its heat. He ran away in fright, and when he looked back, the object was flying away to the northeast, leaving behind a red trail in the sky. He told his father what had happened, and his dad came out and saw a round circle in the snow.

Police were called and when they came out they found a melted hole about 28 inches in diameter. Samples of snow were gathered, including some with "carbon spots," and taken to a hangar at CFB Edmonton "For contamination check." The report notes: "Sample of snow being kept in Morning Light command post in the freezer."

This last reference is significant in that *Operation Morning Light* was the code name of the international recovery mission to secure pieces of a Soviet satellite which crashed into Canada's north on January 24, 1978, only a week or so earlier. This was an ecological as well as a humanitarian disaster because Cosmos 954 had been powered by a nuclear reactor whose radioactive fragments were scattered through a huge region east of Great Slave Lake, only about 800 kilometres directly north of Edmonton.[2]

More than 4,000 pieces of Cosmos 954 were found, some as small as the head of a pin. Many of these were radioactive, and there was great concern for the health of Canadians living in the area as well for contaminated wildlife habitat.

Clearly, military and RCMP personnel wondered if the melted hole in the snow in Edmonton was somehow related to the crashed satellite. While the real Cosmos 954 pieces were sent to the Whiteshell Nuclear Research Establishment in Manitoba for analysis, we don't know if the carbon from Edmonton was sent there too.

And then there was Langenburg.

On the night of September 1, 1974, Karl Zorn phoned the RCMP detachment in Langenburg, Saskatchewan, asking if they had any reports of UFOs. Constable Ron Morier replied that no calls had come in, so Zorn explained that his brother-in-law, Edwin Fuhr, had been swathing canola that morning and had come upon five "saucer shaped" objects on the ground.[3]

Morier noted in case file N74/067: "Mr. Zorn of course was skeptical as was I of the above story, however he advised that his brother-in-law is a responsible person and not prone to making up stories."

Zorn also told Morier that Fuhr's father had been led by Fuhr out to the field where saw for himself five "definite circular patterns left in the swamp grass."

Morier paid a visit to Fuhr and his family the next day. Edwin Fuhr told Morier that although it was lightly raining the previous morning, he wanted to get his harvesting done. At about 10:45 am, he had been concentrating on swathing the crop when he looked up to see something large ahead of him. His first reaction was that it was probably a duck blind erected by a neighbour or perhaps a poacher so he jumped down from his tractor to get a better look.

When he got within about 25 feet away, he could see that it was a spinning "highly polished" metallic object about four or five feet in height and about 10 or 11 feet in diameter, hovering about a foot off the ground. It had the appearance of an upside-down bowl, with a dull "rim" on its lower edge. He hadn't noticed it before he had driven with 50 feet of it because the canola was almost four feet tall and the object was situated in a "sunken dried slough." Perplexed, he backed away and got back on this tractor. From his higher vantage point, he could see four similar objects nearby, each spinning rapidly. He couldn't hear any sound from them, likely because his swather was still running.

Fuhr said that at one point, he tried to put the swather into gear and drive away, but he couldn't turn the steering wheel or move the throttle at all, which was wide open.

He watched the strange objects for about 15 minutes, transfixed by their appearance. He said he thought one had a "probe" of some kind that poked in and out of the ground intermittently. Then all five of the objects ascended into the air, pausing to hover about 200 feet above the ground for a few minutes with exhaust coming from underneath each one. Suddenly, there was a blast of air and all five gained more altitude and disappeared into the cloud cover.

Morier went to the field and found the circular impressions in the grass. He wrote:

> There were five different distinct circles, caused by something exerting what had to be heavy air or exhaust pressure over the high grass. The grass was flattened in clockwise circles with the flattened portion being approx. 18 in. The total diameter of two of the circles was 12 ft. with the other three being approx. 10 ½ ft. in diameter. The grass in the center portion of the ring was standing and appeared untouched.

```
M•
NRC REED-OTT
PRIORITY LANGENBERG SEP2 UNCLAS                          | N 74/063 |
                                                      RADIO RECORDS M-50
NATION RESEARCH COUNCIL - METEOR CENTER OTTAWA
INFO
F DIV REG                                             SEP 3  8 09 AM '74
YORKTON S/DIV

LAN81 RE SIGHTING G OF UFO 6 MILES NORTH AND HALF A MILE WEST OF
LANGENBURG SASK
   (A) DATE ANDTIME OF SIGHTING 1-9-74 1030AM CST
   (B) CONDITION OF SKY - CLOUDY WITH LIGHT RAIN
   (C) IDENTITY OF OBSERVER - EDWIN FUHR B28-4-38 FARMER
   (D) LOCATION - SWATHING GRAIN. TURNED CORNER IN FIELD AND CAME
                  ON OBJECTS 50' AWAY AND WALKED UP WITHIN 25'
   (E) OTHER TO SEE UFO - NIL
   (F) DESCRIPTION - FIVE SAUCER SHAPED OBJECTS 10/12' IN DIAMETER
                     APPEARED TO BE ROTATING. HIGHLY POLISHED STEEL
                     LIP NEAR THE BOTTOM DARKER IN COLOUR POSSIBLY
                     GREY. HOVERED 2/3' ABOVE THE GROUND AND THEN
                     WENT STRAIGHT UP AND DISAPPEARED IN THE CLOUDS
   (G) DURATION OF SIGHTING - 20 MINUTES
   (H) MARKS - LEFT CIRCULAR MARKS ON GROUND WHICH ARE STILL VISIBLE
       LANGENBURG DET
```

Document 47: "Document regarding the observed UFOs and swirled circles found in a field near Langenburg, Saskatchewan, in 1974." Herzberg Institute of Astrophysics – Reports on non-meteoric sightings, unidentified flying objects, UFO's 1/9/1974 © Government of Canada. Reproduced with the permission of Library and Archives Canada (2021). Source: Library and Archives Canada/National Research Council of Canada fonds/e002746474

Morier took some photos of the swirled patches and when he got back to the Detachment told his commanding officer what he had discovered. But apart from informing Ottawa of the incident, there seems not to have been an impetus to do much else. No soil or plant samples were taken, and the investigation may have ended right there. Only three short pages documented the case in the NRC UFO file. And

Morier did not think any device had been driven or rolled into the field to create the marks.

Word got around, and within a day the field was overrun by curiosity seekers wanting to get a look at the "saucer nests." It wasn't long before the *Regina Leader-Post* broke the story and news reached Ted Phillips of J. Allen Hynek's Centre for UFO Studies (CUFOS) in Chicago, Illinois. Phillips, who specialized in UFO cases with physical effects, visited Langenburg by the third week of September and conducted an extensive investigation with interviews of the Fuhr family and friends in an attempt to find an explanation for the case.

Phillips learned that the night before Edwin Fuhr's encounter, a babysitter at a neighbour's house had heard dogs barking and growling. And on September 3, a sixth saucer nest was discovered beside the original five, followed by a seventh on September 15. In fact, that fall, additional circles were found at Langenberg and nearby towns Young, Peebles, Lake Lenore, and Dinsmore.

The case remains one of the most confounding of Canadian UFO encounters. It occurred during harvest time, and the many visitors and investigators caused great disruption of the Fuhr's livelihood, so it seems unlikely that it was a hoax. Yet most skeptics dismiss it as such.

Before he passed, I had phoned arch skeptic Philip Klass to ask his opinion, since he was well-known for his ability to come up with explanations for classic UFO sightings. The Langenburg case seemed pretty solid, so I wondered what Klass thought about it.

I was not disappointed. Although he had not visited the site or conducted any personal investigation of the case, Klass told me he had telephoned a church in the Langenburg area and spoken with a minister who told him that Edwin Fuhr had been known to play practical jokes on people as a child. To Klass, that was enough to undermine the quality of the Langenburg case.

The RCMP had a different view, however. In his report, Morier noted:

The witness Fuhr has been known by a member of this Detachment for a period of four yrs., and during this time he has not been known to materialize any such stories. He is a responsible person, and his information is considered reliable.

I have personally visited Langenburg on several occasions and met with Edwin Fuhr. During my interviews with him he has always seemed sincere, not seeking notoriety nor embellishing his story in order to entertain. He has taken some ridicule from people in the community as can be expected in such cases, unfortunately, but has withstood them with dignity.

Indicative of the NRC's attitude towards UFOs and their witnesses is the only other document found in the Langenburg case file. It was added long after the incident, in 1977, and consists solely of a page from a popular UFO magazine with an article describing the case. Although published in a newsstand magazine, the article is very factual and contains details of Morier's investigation plus comments from Fuhr that have not been widely recorded elsewhere.

Despite its straightforward presentation of the case, and its title "Mysterious UFO formations found in Canada," the page in the NRC file has an all-caps typewritten annotation that belies a rather derogatory approach to the subject.

PAUL: CAN YOU THINK OF ANYTHING FUNNIER. FOUND THIS IN A UFO MAG. THOUGHT IT MIGHT GENERATE SOME FORM OF DISGUST AND LAUGHTER. – NAP

The derisive nature of the annotation shows that the writer (and probably the recipient) had a predisposition to ridicule the subject of UFOs in general, regardless of the evidence or details. Nothing in the earlier documents within the NRC case files suggested the experience of Fuhr was anything other than factually recorded. Why it would provoke "disgust" is baffling. Was "Paul" so rejecting of the possibility of UFOs as an actual phenomenon that he considered it beneath his dignity? If so, why was he even involved in maintaining the NRC UFO files? As to whom "NAP" might have been, we only know that he enjoyed the joke as well.

Another debunker within the NRC was Dr. Allen MacNamara, a specialist in upper atmosphere research on phenomena such as the Northern Lights. He did not conduct any kind of investigation of the Langenburg incident, yet told a reporter at the *Regina Leader Post* that the markings found by Fuhr were caused by "fairy rings," and were the result of a fungus in the soil.

This is remarkable even for the obvious point that MacNamara was not trained as a mycologist or biologist and therefore could not speak from an academic standpoint on the matter. (Can you imagine a specialist in butterflies having the audacity to give an expert opinion on why your car's fuel injection system was not working?) This was no doubt a parroting of what Dr. Peter Millman had said about marks found in the field near Duhamel, Alberta, in 1967.

It was wrong then, too.

Even if a simple explanation could be determined for the marks in Langenburg, that does not explain the metallic objects that Edwin Fuhr testified he saw.

Until then, the case remains unexplained.

And in fact, the NRC UFO files contain more cases of rings and circular patches in Canadian fields, predating the "crop circle phenomenon" by decades.

Rings in the field

As everybody knows (and most UFO experts tell us), the first crop circles were found in England in about 1980. The strange phenomenon of rings and flattened grain or grass started conservatively with isolated single sites, then became more elaborate as they spread throughout Britain, into Europe and eventually across the Atlantic to North America. Speculation abounded as to whether these "agriglyphs" were a natural phenomenon or an attempt by aliens to communicate with humans or raise our collective consciousness as to the true nature of our universe.

Although historically, that's not how it all started at all.

In fact, rings in fields and swirled patches in grain began to be found in Canada many years earlier. What's more, they were investigated and taken seriously by the Canadian government and military establishment.

As listed earlier in this book, there were numerous instances of precursors to crop circles discovered throughout Canada as recorded in the NRC UFO Files. But there are other cases of odd circular formations found much earlier.

As reported in nothing less than the prestigious journal *Scientific American* in 1880:

> The *Plaindealer*, of East Kent, Ontario, states that a curious and inexplicable phenomenon was witnessed recently by Mr. David Muckle and Mr. W.R. McKay, two citizens of that town. The gentlemen were in a field on a farm of the former, when they heard a sudden loud report, like that of a cannon. They turned up just in time to see a cloud of stones flying upward from a spot in the field. Surprised beyond measure they examined the spot, which was circular and about 16 feet across,

but there was no sign of an eruption nor anything to indicate the fall of a heavy body there. The ground was simply swept clean. They are quite certain that it was not caused by a meteorite, the eruption of the earth, or a whirlwind.[4]

In the 20th Century, there are many instances recorded, too, some associated with UFOs. For example, the *Gleaner* of Huntington, Quebec, reported on August 10, 1954, that:

Close to Hemmingford, Quebec, children named Coupal were in a field, at 9:30 pm, when they said a bright light followed them home to the farm. Father and older son went to the field, and saw orange-hued object rise and speed off into the Western sky. Left grass flattened for forty feet, and with two tracks about fifteen feet long.[5]

It should not be surprising, then, that strange markings in a Canadian field should have attracted the attention of official agencies, especially during 1967, a year when many unusual phenomena were being reported to the NRC.

On Friday, August 4, 1967, a thunderstorm brought a heavy downpouring of rain to south-central Alberta. The next morning, August 5, 1967, Mr. Edgar Schielke was concerned that his cows did not come home by themselves the night before as they usually did. He went out to his pasture to get them, a part of his property he hadn't been to in at least a week.

There, on a bit of a rise in the field was a circular mark about 30 feet in diameter. He was puzzled by the strange mark in the ground and could not figure out how it got there. He went back home after rounding up his cows and some time later was in conversation with a neighbour who offhandedly suggested it had been made by a flying saucer, like those that had been in the news that summer. That neighbour in turn mentioned it to Ray Sanders, a local schoolteacher who happened to have an interest in the subject of UFOs. He immediately contacted the local newspaper and then an Edmonton UFO group which went out to the site and discovered three more similar rings in the pasture.

On August 8, 1967, a reporter from the *Camrose Canadian* newspaper visited the site and took some photos, one of which was published the next day. It was this day, August 9, 1967, that officials were formally notified about the discovery and a telex was sent to CFB Namao instructing them to send someone to investigate on behalf of the RCAF.

Schielke himself was not that interested in the subject of UFOs, and didn't think it was something to get excited about. But others did.

It was August 11, 1967, before a RCAF team arrived at Schielke's farm, and by that time, much of the evidence had been trampled by curiosity seekers. As reported in NRC UFO file U93:

> By the time the inspection team visited the site, it had been, literally, a seven day wonder. Thus, the two pastures concerned had been visited by droves of people, including many who drove cars across the pasture making a variety of car tracks in all directions.

```
PRIORITY

PP ROWTEV
DE RCCWC 373 09/1621Z
P 091620Z AUG 67

FM CANFORCEHED
TO RCCHC/CANLIFTCOM
ROWTEV/CANFORBASE EDMONTON

BT

UNCLAS OFS 421                                    (2) AIO (Maj Bowen)
                          (1)
SUBJECT: UFO                                      For your info and action.

REFERENCE: CANINFO EDMONTON MESSAGE PR 158 082346Z     R McGarva S/L
                                                       B Ops O    3035
1. FOLLOWING IS A REPEAT OF REF MESSAGE:               9 Aug 67
A. 8 AUG
B. N/A                                            (3) B Ad O
C. MR K PATRICE, CAMROSE CANADIAN PHONE 672-4421
D. PASTURE AREA AT DUHAMEL AREA CAMROSE ALTA           Returned as requested.
E. NIL
F. FOUR RINGS IN GROUND AS THOUGH ROUND OBJECT         (W Whitehead)F/O
SETTLED INTO GROUND. DEPRESSIONS HEAVIER TO ONE SIDE.    A/RIO 203
RING DIAMETER OF 34 FT TO 36 FT NO SCORCH. CLEARLY     10 Aug 67
MARKED TEETH OR CLAW LIKE MARKS AROUND EDGE
G. N/A                                            (4) A/Det Comd
H. INFORMANT HAS OBTAINED PHOTOGRAPHS                 1 Tpt Hel Pl Det
                                                      (Attn Capt Walker)
2. MAY SUBJECT REPORT BE INVESTIGATED BY CFB NAMAO AND
REPORT WITH COPIES OF PHOTOGRAPHS BE FORWARDED TO CFHQ  We spoke. Pls investigate
ATTEN DOFS FOR STUDY
                                                          D Lafferty Lt col
BT                                                    10 Aug 67


COPY/GW
```

Document 48: "Document regarding the Duhamel 'crop circles,' from August 1967." Herzberg Institute of Astrophysics - Reports on non-meteoric sightings, unidentified flying objects, UFO's 8/8/1967 © Government of Canada. Reproduced with the permission of Library and Archives Canada (2021). Source: Library and Archives Canada/National Research Council of Canada fonds/e002749308

This report was made by Dr. G.H.S. Jones, who was with the Canadian Forces' Defense Research Establishment Suffield, about 400 kilometres south of Duhamel. He had been tasked with going with the RCAF team to the site for investigation.

Fortunately, despite the intervening days, all was not lost. Jones found that:

> Despite the passage of one week, including heavy rain in the early part of the week, and the droves of visitors, the reputed UFO landing marks remained quite clearly impressed in the ground.

There were not four but six rings found in Schielke's field. Jones described the marks in considerable detail:

> As measured by the *Camrose Canadian*, the marks vary from 5 to 7 inches wide, and the smallest circular mark is 31 feet 9 inches in diameter. Three of the rings are essentially circular—very closely so I would say—while the largest mark is slightly elliptical, varying from 34 feet 5 inches to 36 feet 3 inches.

> A description but not an explanation of these marks is to say that they appear almost identical to the marks one would expect by a very heavily laden wheel with rubber tyre moved in an almost complete and accurate circle. Strangely each circular mark was incomplete on the western side, the circles being only approximately ¾ complete. There was no evidence whatsoever of a single tyre track leaving any of the circles. The marks were predominantly in the form of crushed and discolored pasture grass, but where cow dung lay in the mark this dung (reasonably fresh apparently at the time) was compressed in much the same way as would be done by a wheel passing over it. In the dung there was some evidence—which we were informed was clear the previous weekend both on the dung and grass—of tread(?), lugs(?) or similar protrusions on about a 3-inch repeating pattern.

He then speculated on how the rings could have been made, or not:

> Despite the similarity of the circular marks to the pattern of a tyre track, the four circles were strikingly different from truck tracks. Taken in conjunction with the previously reported "sightings" in the area, the initial discovery of three more marks, and the casual

air of the farmer while his farm became the scene of much visiting, and the speed with which the news media were informed, one must consider the possibility of a deliberate hoax. Such a hoax need not have been perpetrated by any individual who has become obvious in the investigation. Nevertheless, I must admit that I was unable to find anything which would lend strength to this supposition. I believe such a track could be produced by a deliberate hoax, but the hoaxers would require some equipment and a great deal of determination. It would be fair to say that if the mark was produced by rolling contact (a wheel), the load on the wheel even allowing for the rain on the Friday would require to be at least three times the load on a truck wheel. If the track was produced when the ground was very soft after rain, I do not see how hoaxers could have produced these marks in isolation, without leaving some evidence of their approach to the area and departure from it.

Jones seriously considered the mechanism of a hoax but then also allowed himself to speculate on the possibility of an actual UFO or alien spacecraft creating the rings. This in itself is astounding; taking a UFO case seriously enough to think about how an alien craft could have been involved is practically unheard of by scientists outside the UFO community of believers. Jones offered:

...consider the UFO possibility, *i.e.,* something coming vertically down onto a relatively narrow ring support—either metal, or, a faint possibility, a flexible skirt. In order to produce the visible marks, the load per unit area would have to be roughly three times that produced by a truck tyre. If we take the load per wheel as being 500 pounds for rough calculations, with an area of contact of four inches by two inches, this would give a loading of just under 63 psi. Reduce this down to 50 psi, which I consider the absolute minimum needed to produce the visible marks. For simplicity, take a visible mark 30 feet in diameter and of average width five inches. This would give a total area of contact of 5,400 square inches, or a total load for the UFO of 270,000 pounds. This load of 135 tons would be in the right ballpark for a large aircraft, or presumably, small spacecraft.

Jones' report was published as Suffield Memorandum No. 49/67, titled: *Onsite inspection of reputed UFO landing marks at Duhamel, Alberta.* This is curious because there was no UFO sighting to associate with the marks at all, though there had been some UFO sightings that summer in Alberta that could conceivably have been connected.[6]

The entry on the LAC UFO page for the Duhamel rings notes:

> According to the investigator, there was no evidence outside of the circular marks. There were no exhaust blasts, scorch marks or disturbances of the loose surface material. Within the circles, there was evidence that thumbnail-sized pieces of vegetation had been removed by the object that made the marks.

> Although the investigator talked about the possibility of the marks being left by a wheel, it is clear in the report that the marks were more likely left by a 135-ton aircraft or spacecraft.

In fact, Jones was very impressed with the marks. He noted in his report:

> Although I must admit to a first impression of disappointment that I have been brought so far to look at so little, detailed study of the marks and reflection leave me more than a little puzzled.

His final thoughts on the rings were insightful:

> My conclusions from this rather quick investigation are: (1) the possibility of hoax can neither be confirmed or denied. (2) the marks in the ground could have been produced by a wheel and rolling contact, but this wheel would probably require a load of at least half a ton and the wheel would have to be moved in a rather exact circle. (3) the marks could have been produced by a vehicle sitting on a circular base—possibly flexible, provided the vehicle weight at least 100 tons and possibly nearer 200 tons. (4) there is some evidence that "strange phenomena" have been seen recently in the area. This could be a lead-in to a hoax or be genuine. (5) the marks were sufficiently unique in my experience for me to state categorically that if I saw similar marks elsewhere, my tendency to treat the matter as a hoax would be sharply reduced. I have not, however, heard of similar markings in any previously reputed UFO landings. It might be worth inquiring of the competent authorities whether or not similar markings have been observed elsewhere.

The LAC entry concludes:

> The crop circles in Duhamel, Alberta are considered unsolved by the Department of National Defence.

But that's not the end of the story. Following the investigation by Jones and the rest of the team, because it was an unsolved case, the Department of National Defence in Ottawa took a greater interest in the case.

In the LAC NRC UFO Files is a document titled: *Ministerial Inquiry, Mr. W.A. Small – Mysterious prints found on Mr. Ed Schielke's farm.* Dated August 25, 1967, the memorandum was prepared by Commodore F.B. Caldwell, Secretary of Defence Staff. The document detailed the Duhamel case for the Minister of Defence, who at that time was Hon. Paul Hellyer, whose name is mentioned often regarding his interest in UFOs.

The Ministerial Inquiry document noted the department's conclusions about the Duhamel rings, following an examination of Jones' report on the case:

> The report has been studied by members of the Operation Staff and Mr. Greenwood, Director of Scientific Coordination in an attempt to arrive at an acceptable explanation as to what may have caused these mystery marks. From the available evidence it has not been possible to arrive at a conclusion.

MEMORANDUM

V 1540-1 TD 7234 (D Ops)

25 August, 1967

TO: MINISTER'S MILSEC

MINISTERIAL INQUIRY
MR. W.A. SMALL - MYSTERIOUS PRINTS
FOUND ON MR. ED SCHIRKK'S FARM

1.   On the 8 August 1967 CFHQ received a UFO report from Caninfo Edmonton stating that four depressions had been made in the soil of a pasture in the Duhamel area, Camrose, Alberta. The four depressions, in the form of rings, suggested that some unknown large round objects had settled into the ground. The rings covered an estimated diameter of some 34 to 36 feet. The outer edges of the circles contained clearly marked teeth or claw like marks. The foreast further advised that photographs had been taken of the imprints.

Document 49: "Memorandum regarding Ministerial Inquiry into Duhamel 'crop circles.'" Herzberg Institute of Astrophysics - Reports on non-meteoric sightings, unidentified flying objects, UFO's 8/16/1967 © Government of Canada. Reproduced with the permission of Library and Archives Canada (2021). Source: Library and Archives Canada/National Research Council of Canada fonds/e002749320

6.   The report has been studied by members of the Operation Staff and Mr Greenwood, Director of Scientific Co-ordination in an attempt to arrive at an acceptable explanation as to what may have caused these mystery marks. From the available evidence it has not been possible to arrive at a conclusion.

7.   Until the soil sample tests are concluded it will not be possible to say as to whether or not a type of fungus was responsible for the marks in question. However, the impressions which indicate a source of distinct pressure would hardly be related to a fungus action. The marks in question were not caused by a Canadian military vehicle, nor to the best of our knowledge, by a vehicle operated by either a friendly or unfriendly nation.

ORIGINAL SIGNED BY

M. F. WHITING

MAJOR

P.W. Caldwell

Commodore

Secretary Defence Staff

(D.F. Robertson) W/C

2-3427

Document 50: "Memorandum regarding Ministerial Inquiry into Duhamel 'crop circles.'" Herzberg Institute of Astrophysics – Reports on non-meteoric sightings, unidentified flying objects, UFO's 8/16/1967 © Government of Canada. Reproduced with the permission of Library and Archives Canada (2021). Source: Library and Archives Canada/National Research Council of Canada fonds/e002749321

The RCAF was leaving nothing out of its investigation. They even cited another Canadian case as reason to do further tests:

In view of a recent UFO investigation carried out by DND in the Falcon Lake area, 90 miles east of Winnipeg, Manitoba in which soil samples taken from an alleged UFO landing area indicated a higher than normal radium count, it was deemed advisable to instruct CFB Edmonton to obtain soil samples for testing purposes from the pasture area.

Because of the unusual radioactivity associated with the Falcon Lake UFO encounter that took place three months earlier, it seemed reasonable to check Duhamel for radiation too, even though no UFO had been seen to create the marks. It's possible that the Falcon Lake case was ultimately responsible for assuming UFOs could leave behind radioactivity and introducing the idea to ufology.

The other reason for taking soil samples was that within the NRC, as noted earlier, one prevailing theory of UFO-related ground traces was their creation by fairy ring mushrooms. But even the RCAF and NRC had to concede the Duhamel case did not seem to have involved mushrooms.

> Until the soil sample tests are concluded it will not be possible to say as to whether or not a type of fungus was responsible for the marks in question. However, the impressions which indicate a source of distinct pressure would hardly be related to a fungus action. The marks in question were not caused by a Canadian military vehicle, nor to the best of our knowledge, by a vehicle operated by either a friendly or unfriendly nation.

Finally, after much deliberation and consideration, there was a document on file dated January 1968, in which Caldwell noted a letter from Mr. Small. Its last line read:

> DND is unable to arrive at a solution as to what caused the impression on the property of Mr. Ed Schielke of [Duhamel] Alberta.

The best efforts of the Canadian Forces could not explain what had happened on Schielke's farm.

And yet, as noted in many other official documents, according to the RCAF and NRC, UFO reports were of no concern.

10.

THE FALCONBRIDGE RADAR/ VISUAL UFO CASES

~

O ne of the most interesting series of UFO sightings in Canada took place during November 1975. Reports were centered around the major Canadian Forces radar installation at Falconbridge, Ontario, and included many cases from the nearby city of Sudbury. Falconbridge radar was part of the North American Aerospace Defense Command (NORAD) facilities in Ontario, based at CFB North Bay, only about 100 kilometres away.

During the middle of the month, dozens of reports were filed with the NRC, both by citizens as well as military personnel. The fact that this happened near a military base and radar installation makes this UFO flap more significant than other clusters of UFO sightings that were reported elsewhere in Canada that year.

NRC REED OTT

COMM SQN OTT
PUZ 010/11
P R 111630Z NOV 75
FM CFS FALCONBRIDGE
TO RCCWC/NDHQ OTTAWA
INFO RCCPUCX/NATIONAL RESEARCH COUNCIL OTTAWA
BT
UNCLAS GEOPSO 77
FOR CFOC AND NRC RADIO ELECTRICAL ENGINEERING DIVISION
SUBJECT: UFO REPORT
A. 11 NOV 75 1115Z
B. BROKEN CLOUD
C. MAJ OLIVER, CAPT CARSON, CPL LAURITSEN - CFS FALCONBRIDGE
D. OPS BUILDING AT CFS FALCONBRIDGE
E. NIL
F. SPHERICAL SHAPED AND APPEARED TO BE ROTATING. APPEARED TO HAVE
SURFACE AREA SIMILAR TO THE MOON AND WAS ASCENDING AND DESCENDING
G. 2 HRS INTERMITTENTLY DUE TO CLOUD COVER
H. OBSERVED ON HEIGHT FINDER RADAR AND SEARCH. POSITION 210
DEGREES 30 MILES ALT 42,000 FT AT 1115Z. POSITION 200 DEGREES
30 MILES ALT 50,000 FT AT 1120Z. POSITION 190 DEGREES 25 MILES
ALT 72,000 FT AT 1129Z
BT
NRC REED OTT

RADIO RECORDS M-50

Nov 12 8 14 AM '75

N75/154

Document 51: "Document regarding sightings of UFOs near
CFB Falconbridge, Ontario, during November, 1975." Herzberg
Institute of Astrophysics - Reports on non-meteoric
sightings, unidentified flying objects, UFO's 11/11/1975 ©
Government of Canada. Reproduced with the permission of
Library and Archives Canada (2021). Source: Library and
Archives Canada/National Research Council of Canada fonds/
e002746949

```
V+
NFC REED OTT
                                                    N 75 / 155
  COMM SQN OTT            |   RADIO RECORDS M-50
  PUZ 008/11
  P R 111230Z NOV 75
  FM 22ND NORAD REGION HEADQUARTERS NORTH BAY
  TO RCCWC/NATIONAL DEFENSE HEADQUARTERS OTTAWA
  INFO RCCPUCX/NATIONAL RESEARCH COUNCIL OTTAWA
  BT
  UNCLAS 220CC 121
  FOR NDCC AND NRCC RADIO AND ENGINEERING DIVISION
  UFO REPORT
  A. 11/1115Z NOV 75
  B. BROKEN CLOUDS
  C. MAJOR OLIVER
  D. CFS FALCONBRIDGE, ONTARIO
  E. CAPTAIN CARSON, MCPL KREUTZ, CPL LAWRENSON
  F. CIRCULAR OBJECT, BRILLIANTLY LIGHTED WITH TWO BLACK SPOTS IN
  CENTRE MOVING UPWARDS AT HIGH SPEED FROM 42,000 FT TO 72,000 FT.
  (NO HORIZONTAL MOVEMENT)
  G. 14 MINUTES
  H. THIS OBJECT WAS SIGHTED VISUALLY AND BY RADAR BEARING 210 DEGREES
  MAGNETIC AT 30NM FROM CFS FALCONBRIDGE. MAJOR OLIVER TOOK PICTURES
  BUT IS NOT SURE IF THEY WILL TURN OUT. A SIMILAR OBJECT WAS SIGHTED


  PAGE 2 RCCALXX0003 UNCLAS
  BY THE SAME OBSERVERS BEARING 270 DEGREES MAGNETIC BUT AT TOO GREAT
  A DISTANCE TO PROVIDE DETAILS. MANY OTHER REPORTS WERE RECEIVED FROM
  SUDBURY ONTARIO PROVINCIAL POLICE
  BT
  0003
```

Document 52: "Document regarding sightings of UFOs near CFB Falconbridge, Ontario, during November, 1975." Herzberg Institute of Astrophysics - Reports on non-meteoric sightings, unidentified flying objects, UFO's 11/11/1975 © Government of Canada. Reproduced with the permission of Library and Archives Canada (2021). Source: Library and Archives Canada/National Research Council of Canada fonds/ e002746951

RADIO RECORDS M-50

N 75/152

NRC REED OTT   Nov 12 8 13 AM '75

COMM SGN OTT
PUZ015/11
P 111955Z NOV 75
FM CFS FALCONBRIDGE
TO RCCWC/NDHQ OTTAWA
INFO RCCPUCX/NATIONAL RESEARCH COUNCIL OTTAWA
BT
UNCLAS GEOPSO 79
FOR CFOC AND NRC RADIO AND ELECTRICAL ENGINEERING DIVISION
SUBJECT: UFO REPORT
A. 11 NOV 75 APPROX 1000Z
B. BROKEN CLOUD
C. CONSTABLES KEABLES AND WHITESIDE. SUDBURY REGIONAL POLICE
D. 1ST SIGHTING - INDUSTRIAL RD SUDBURY
2ND SIGHTING - SOUTHWEST BY PASS JUST WEST OF HWY 69. IT WAS
OBSERVED SOUTHWEST FROM THIS LOCATION
E. NIL
F. ONE OBJECT AT TIMES IT APPEARED TO BE CYLINDRICAL WITH SHAFTS
OF LIGHT BRIGHT ENOUGH TO LIGHT UP CLOUDS IN IMMEDIATE AREA. IT
APPEARED AT TIMES TO TRAVEL IN CIRCLES. AT ONE POINT IT CAME
QUITE CLOSE. IT WAS STILL VISIBLE TO THE NAKED EYE AFTER THE
SUN CAME UP. THE ABOVE OBSERVATIONS WERE MADE WITH THE USE OF
BINOCULARS
G. FROM 1000Z INTERMITTENTLY UNTIL 1200Z

NRC REED OTT

Document 53: "Document regarding sightings of UFOs near
CFB Falconbridge, Ontario, during November, 1975." Herzberg
Institute of Astrophysics – Reports on non-meteoric
sightings, unidentified flying objects, UFO's 11/11/1975 ©
Government of Canada. Reproduced with the permission of
Library and Archives Canada (2021). Source: Library and
Archives Canada/National Research Council of Canada fonds/
e002746945

TVQ+
NRC REED OTT

RADIO RECORDS H-50

N75/159

COMM SQN OTT
PUZI3/11
P 112010Z NOV 75
FM CFS FALCONBRIDGE
TO RCCWC/NDHQ OTTAWA
INFO RCCPUCX/NATIONAL RESEARCH COUNCIL OTTAWA
BT

Nov 12 8 14 AM '75

UNCLAS GEOPSO 81
FOR CFOC AND NRC RADIO AND ELECTRICAL ENGINEERING DIVISION
SUBJECT: UFO REPORT
A. 11 NOV 75 0600Z
B. CLOUDY (BROKEN)
C. NURSING STAFF AT PIONEER MANOR SUDBURY ONT. (SIX NURSES) THEY
WISH TO REMAIN ANONYMOUS
D. PIONEER MANOR SUDBURY
E. SUDBURY REGIONAL POLICE ON FOLLOW UP REPORT
F. IT SEEMED TO HOVER OVER SUDBURY STADIUM. ONE OBJECT VERY BRIGHT
AND VERY LOW AT FIRST, AND SUDDENLY SHOT INTO THE SKY
G. ONE HR 55 MIN. IT WAS STILL VISIBLE WHEN SUDBURY REGIONAL POLICE
ARRIVED AT 0955Z
.
NRC REED OTT

Document 54: "Document regarding sightings of UFOs near CFB Falconbridge, Ontario, during November, 1975." Herzberg Institute of Astrophysics - Reports on non-meteoric sightings, unidentified flying objects, UFO's 11/11/1975 © Government of Canada. Reproduced with the permission of Library and Archives Canada (2021). Source: Library and Archives Canada/National Research Council of Canada fonds/ e002746961

Document 55: "Document regarding sightings of UFOs near CFB Falconbridge, Ontario, during November, 1975." Herzberg Institute of Astrophysics – Reports on non-meteoric sightings, unidentified flying objects, UFO's 11/11/1975 © Government of Canada. Reproduced with the permission of Library and Archives Canada (2021). Source: Library and Archives Canada/National Research Council of Canada fonds/ e002746953

One Falconbridge report is N75/154 in the NRC files.

In the early morning hours just before sunrise on November 11, 1975, several military personnel, including the high-ranking Major Oliver, watched a rotating spherical object with a bumpy or pockmarked surface, moving up and down between clouds. The base radar painted a return from what they believed was the object at a distance of 30 miles in the southwest at an altitude of 42,000 feet (about eight miles). Over the next 15 minutes, the object on radar gained altitude to 72,000 feet, moving slowly towards the south. In total, the witnesses watched it for about two hours.

Curiously, the following NRC case, N75/155, was almost identical but had actually been filed before the first one. This earlier report seems to be more explicit in terms of noting the observation was 14 minutes in length as opposed to the two-hours in N75/154.

Usually, UFOs that persist for many minutes, especially those lasting into hours, turn out to be stars or planets. And indeed, that night, Saturn was very bright and at 210 degrees in the southwest, while Mars was about 250 degrees in the WSW. But Venus, which was even brighter and low in the southeast, was not mentioned at all.

NRC case N75/152, which occurred a few hours earlier still and reported by RCMP constables on patrol, was also likely a planet. This seems to be the case where the UFO was seen over two hours. This is entirely consistent with a planet or star poking out "intermittently" between clouds, making it appear to observers that it's moving in circles.

A few days later, on November 13, 1975, NORAD issued a press release concerning the incidents:

> At 4:05 pm, Nov. 11, the Canadian Forces radar site at Falconbridge, Ontario, reported a radar track of an unidentified flying object about 25-30 nautical miles south of the site, ranging in altitude from 25,000 to 72,000 feet. Persons at the site also saw the object and said it appeared as a bright star but much closer. Two F-106 aircraft of the US Air Force Air National Guard's 171st Fighter Interceptor Squadron at Selfridge ANGB, Michigan, were scrambled, but the pilots reported no contact with the object.[1]

Of course, there are a few differences between what was reported to the NRC and what NORAD reported. First, the time is different: 4:05 pm (1605Z) instead of 1000Z or 1115Z. Nevertheless, the distance and altitude seem to be the same as the NRC reports. But most significant is the additional information about the US air force involvement, since two American F-106 jets were scrambled to intercept the UFO. From requests for information filed in the USA, it was discovered that a few days earlier, UFOs had also been reported by American military personnel at Wurtsmith AFB in Michigan, only about 300 miles to the southwest, across Lake Huron.

This amazing Falconbridge UFO story involved an object tracked on radar, observed from the ground by military personnel and police, and causing enough concern that NORAD recommended interception by American jet fighters.

The Falconbridge UFO flap has been described as one of the most significant modern-day UFO cases, possibly with implications for national security. In an interview with a reporter, Captain Gordon Hilchie, then public affairs officer for CFB North Bay, the national NORAD headquarters for Canada, said this incident was:

...the first time that NORAD has been on the record as saying, 'Yes, we saw this so-called UFO, an unidentifiable thing, at the same time people outside were saying they saw it too.'

Interpretations of the incidents vary, as might be expected from the pro- and con-UFO communities. But sorting through the facts of the individual reports, we can get a better idea of what really occurred during that time.

Major Oliver was also interviewed by a newspaper reporter, and he explained:

I got a call from my operations officer at about 6 o'clock in the morning... on November 11, and we went up the hill—and we had a number of reports throughout the night from local citizens, and we passed them on to our own National Defence Headquarters, which is normal procedure—and lo and behold, I also saw something.

He went on:

In any event, there were 3 objects sighted. We viewed them through binoculars and weren't able to make any identification at all... We saw the same thing as many of the local citizens saw. There were three objects. One to the east, one to the southeast or perhaps southeast by south, and another one to the southwest. It was impossible to determine range, of course, so therefore it was impossible to determine size. And it was also impossible to determine height. They looked rather large—I suppose the size of a curling rock... it was as though you were looking at a bright yellow object about the shape of a curling rock.

UFO document retrieval researchers Lawrence Fawcett and Barry J. Greenwood, in their book *Clear Intent*, discussed government cover-up of UFO sightings and published documents about the Falconbridge case retrieved through Freedom of Information Act (FOIA) requests.[2] An entry in the NORAD regional Senior Director's log read:

1205Z 11 November 1975 Received unusual sighting report from Falconbridge AFS, Ontario, Canada. Info passed to NORAD Command Director, Intelligence and Weather.

Again, the time of the report differs from that given in the press release. Because 1205Z is Greenwich Mean Time, which is five hours ahead of Eastern Time in Falconbridge and Sudbury, that would make the time of the report 7:05 am, not 6:15 am as in the NRC report. This must therefore be a different and separate sighting.

The next entry in the Falconbridge log read:

1840Z 11 November 1975 Actions pertaining to scramble of JL08 and 09 due to unusual object sighting. With Director of Operations approval. Scrambled JL08/09 at 1745Z, airborne at 1750Z. NORAD Combat Operations Center notified of Falconbridge AFS incident. Aircraft over Falconbridge flying over incident, point no sighting. 1831 aircraft still in area, no radar aircraft or visual contact. Falconbridge AFS still reporting object at 26,000 feet.

According to these entries, it took more than five and a half hours (from 1205Z to 1745Z) for the USAF to scramble jets in response to the initial report from Falconbridge. But the log entry clearly states that the American jets flew over Canadian airspace in response to the UFO, making this a significant international incident.

The pilots reported they did not see anything visually, nor was there anything suspicious on their radar. But because they weren't sent up until after noon, when the Sun would have overwhelmed the light coming from any aerial source such as a planet or star, it is no wonder that they were unable to see anything, even if the Falconbridge ground radar was still painting an object in the area.

The Falconbridge cases took place during a major North American wave of UFO reports. Skeptics have pointed out that on October 20, 1975, NBC had aired *The UFO Incident*, a feature movie that depicted the Betty and Barney Hill UFO abduction story. It was suggested this contributed to the public's heightened interest in UFOs, and it had indeed been followed by several weeks of increased UFO reports across North America.

Arch-skeptic Philip Klass noted that because the Falconbridge AFS had received phone calls from the public regarding sightings of UFOs during the early morning of November 11, the Falconbridge radar operators turned on their height-finder radar and looked specifically towards the south, where the witnesses had said they had seen the objects. Klass said that:

In doing so they observed a target at a distance of about twenty-five miles south-southwest (in the direction of Sudbury), at an altitude of about 36,000 feet, moving slowly from west to east...[3]

Klass explained that Jupiter was an evening star that month and also that Venus was very bright, rising about 2:30 am local time. He concluded that the visual sightings of UFOs were mostly probably one or the other of these astronomical objects.

However, Fawcett and Greenwood were convinced that the objects seen that night were truly anomalous, and offered additional documentation. The Commander-In-Charge of NORAD sent a message to all NORAD units in North America that night, similar to the press release, noting:

This morning, 11 Nov 1975, CFS Falconbridge reported search and height finder radar paints on an object up to 30 nautical miles south of the site ranging in altitude from 26,000 ft. to 72,000 ft. The site commander and other personnel say the object appeared as a bright star but much closer. With binoculars the object appeared as a 100 ft. diameter sphere and appeared to have craters around the outside.

It's worth noting that the UFO was observed through binoculars, which is a clue that points towards it being a star or planet, especially since the "craters" on its surface are normal effects seen on an out-of-focus object. Furthermore, it's impossible to accurately visually estimate the diameter of a light source that is 30 miles away and between five and 15 miles in altitude.

More support to the explanation that the objects seen were astronomical in nature comes from more UFO reports in the NRC files. Case N75/159 is a report from six nurses at Pioneer Manor, a seniors' residence in Sudbury, who that same night collectively reported seeing a bright object hovering in the sky.

They watched it from 3:00 am to almost 5:00 am on November 11, 1975, among some of the first that night to report UFOs. They had reported the UFO to the local police, who in turn filed their own report.

But in the case of the Sudbury police, it becomes more obvious that the UFOs might really have been stars and planets. When they arrived at Pioneer Manor, the two constables saw four different objects in the sky. There was one stationary light in the east. One in the southwest seemed to move in "a jerky motion." The one in the northwest was stationary, as was a dim fourth one in the northeast.

As noted earlier, there were three planets visible throughout that early morning from the general area of Falconbridge and Sudbury. Venus was prominent in the east, and was undoubtedly the first UFO seen by the police. In the southwest was Mars, between the horizon and the zenith, but another candidate, and as bright as Mars, was the star Sirius, just as bright and low in the southwest as well. Either could have been thought to move erratically.

The other two stationary lights were likely astronomical as well. Saturn was slightly east of the zenith, and would have been bright, but not as bright as Venus, Mars or Sirius. Without knowing the exact angles involved, I would have to think the four UFOs were these planets and star, all of which have given rise to UFO reports over the years. And in N75/152, the bright object in the southwest was very likely Sirius.

(It should be noted that Jupiter was indeed prominently in the sky during that week, but it was, as Klass pointed out, an evening star and would have set in the west at about 2:00 am or 3:00 am depending on the landscape. It wouldn't have been seen by the time the police and military personnel were looking into the sky before sunrise.)

Aviation researcher Palmiro Campagna was able to find a copy of the 22nd NORAD Region Air Traffic Control duty log for November 11, 1975, at CFB North Bay, and it gives the authoritative version of what transpired that night. Formerly classified Secret, the duty officer recorded the reports of a strange light in the sky, initially from the Falconbridge radar station.[4]

The first entry showed that at 1118Z, the Falconbridge radar station advised NORAD of the UFO over the base as well as the report from Sudbury police. The description of the object was that it looked like a "large gem with colored lights all around it." The time is in good agreement with that of N75/154 and N75/155.

At 1147Z, Major Oliver of Falconbridge phoned NORAD with his report of the UFO. He said that between 1115Z and 1129Z, he had observed two brilliant lights: one at 200 degrees and the other at 180 degrees, the latter thought to be much further away. Major Oliver took three photos of the UFOs with his Brownie camera, as noted in N75/155, but they had not been developed yet. (It's not known whether anything was found on the film, as there's no record of the photos later. But it would have been unlikely that a simple Brownie camera would have had the ability to take a useful image of a distant starlike light in the sky.)

The log entry notes that observing with Major Oliver were Captain Carson and Corporal Lauritsen (spelled incorrectly as Calson and Lawelenceson). The three of them watched the nearest object (relatively speaking) through binoculars and judged that it was rising vertically "at tremendous speed." On radar, they had a target on the height finder at 44,000 feet and 72,000 feet, just as reported in the NRC file. They thought the UFO was circular, and "well lighted and what appeared as two black spots in the centre."

A news article about the events in the *Winnipeg Tribune* on November 13, 1975, noted:

Ontario police sight 4 UFOs

Sudbury, Ont. (CP) - Police reports say unidentified flying objects were sighted over Sudbury and Halleybury, about 90 miles northeast of here. Reports on the sightings were compiled by regional police, provincial police and staff at Canadian Forces Base Falconbridge. Regional police constables Bob Whiteside and Alex Keable said they saw three objects in the sky Tuesday, and later spotted a fourth. Regional constable John Marsh said he saw lights in the sky to the southwest while on patrol on Highway 17 near Coniston, about miles east of here. He said the object moved in a jerking manner, had pulsating lights and "was different from what you would normally call a star." Four persons at the Canadian Forces Base Falconbridge said they had sighted objects in the sky and on radar.[5]

In total, seven members of the Sudbury OPP observed UFOs that night. Constables Chrapchynski and Deighton reported that four objects were observed clearly in the sky. Constables Keable and Whiteside reported only one object, observed with binoculars. Constable Marsh saw one very bright star-like object moving in a jerky circular manner. Constables Ryan and Lederoute noted only that they saw a single bright object that appeared to be over the north end of the city of Sudbury, moving in a northwesterly direction at a high rate of speed.

The data from the height finder radar at Falconbridge showed the object was initially at 210 degrees and 42,000 feet at 1115Z, 200 degrees and 50,000 feet at 1120Z, then 190 degrees and 72,000 feet at 1129Z. This suggested to UFO researcher Brad Sparks that the UFO had a climb rate of 1,600 ft/min for the first five minutes then about 2,400 ft/min the next nine minutes, and an almost due eastward course at about 70 mph then northeast at about 60 mph. He thinks the evidence points to "a balloon that has been caught in the east-flowing jet stream, having been launched at about 6 am apparently somewhere in the general Sudbury region." Like Klass, he also believes the OPP observations were likely stars and planets.[6, 7, 8]

In summary, the "classic" Falconbridge radar/visual UFO case is much less mysterious than has been claimed. While there is no way to determine if all the objects seen that night were stars or planets, it seems as though many might have been misidentified. Why experienced radar operators would not be able to distinguish between clouds and truly anomalous tracks is somewhat odd, as is the reason why USAF fighters would be sent up to investigate potentially unknown targets after more than five or six hours had passed.

11

CLOSER ENCOUNTERS

~

A UFO hit-and-run accident

In the early morning of March 4, 1977, Mr. Ludwig Siegal was driving eastward towards his farm near Sundown, Manitoba, along Provincial Road 201. About four miles west of the town, at about 6:00 am, Siegal saw a "vibrating" and shimmering oval object directly ahead of him and an estimated 15 feet above the highway. Its colour was whitish cream around its outer edge, darkening to more yellowish towards the middle. It made no noise and Siegal estimated it was "as big as a car," but did not look to be a solid, metallic object.

Siegal reported that he thought: "I'm not really seeing this," and continued driving. When he passed directly underneath the object, he was puzzled that still could not see any solidity to it.

Siegal's account that is recorded in NRC Case N77/040 paints a vivid picture of what can only be described as an alien "hit-and-run" accident.

Approximately two miles further up the highway, Siegal suddenly came upon what he called three "people" standing on the road right in front of his path, in the glare of his car's headlights. They were arranged in a row only 25 feet in front of his vehicle, spaced evenly across his side of the road. Siegal said they looked to be about five feet tall and were

CANADAS UFOS: DECLASSIFIED

shaped like "bowling pins." Later, he told investigators the entities each had a bulbous head, a narrow neck and a flared body "like a skirt" to the ground. No features were visible on the heads.

At first, he quickly began applying his brakes, but he realized his momentum would carry him into the creatures anyway, so he braced for the impact. To his shock, he heard nothing and felt absolutely nothing as he "drove right over" them. They all seemed to simply disappear when they touched the car's front bumper. Siegal compared this to driving over three vertical flashlight beams shining upwards from the road.

Then he received his next shock: when he looked in his rear-view mirror, all three figures reappeared behind his car. As he watched them reappear, that also seemed to be shrinking proportionately, "like they were balloons going down," until they vanished completely.

Shaken up and in an understandably anxious state due to his experience, Siegal drove straight to the house of a friend who lived south of Sundown in Sirko, Manitoba. There, Mr. Siegal told his story to his friend, who listened patiently and saw that Siegal was visibly shaken by his experience. Concerned that Siegal had actually killed some living beings, his friend persuaded him to call the RCMP.

The police arrived in a matter of minutes (responding to the frantic call about someone run down on the highway) and went with Siegal and his friend to the spot where the incident had occurred. By this time, the Sun had risen and the site could be inspected easily. There were skid marks where Siegal had applied his brakes, but no sign of blood, footprints, glass or any other evidence that anyone had been hit by a car. The RCMP officer was also puzzled as to why there were no signs of impact on Siegal's car.

Upon questioning by RCMP, Siegal said he had not been drinking nor using drugs of any kind. Fatigue was suggested as the cause of his hallucination, but Siegal had been up only since 4:00 am after going to bed immediately after supper the previous evening in order to prepare for his trip. He also said he had made the trip on that highway frequently, so he was used to the routine and early hour.

Since the area around Sundown is mostly swamp, the common meme of "swamp gas" (methane) was suggested as the cause of the illusion that made Siegal think he had seen figures on the road. Indeed, because of the bizarre immaterial nature of the UFO and the odd entities seen, this would be attractive as a possible explanation. However, the temperature at the time was well below freezing and there was a good amount of snow cover. Swamp gas generally produces only diffuse glows and not such specifically shaped forms. Furthermore, driving an automobile through a patch of luminous gas would most likely disturb it to the point of instability so even it were the cause, it wouldn't remain intact after Siegal's car passed through it.

In his report to the NRC, RCMP officer B.H. Forster documented the case as best he could, but was obviously just as perplexed as Siegal, about whom he noted: "... from speaking to him, he would appear stable."

Someone in the NRC office drew a question mark on the teletype from Forster that described the incident.

Veterinary injury caused by a UFO

It's not a good thing when a veterinarian has to be called out to a UFO case. But that's exactly what is detailed in more than a dozen pages of documents supporting NRC Case N78/83, which occurred on April 6, 1978.

At about 7:30 pm that evening, Vicki Burns was on her farm near Prince George, BC., and had just bedded down her horses for the night. She was standing outside when she saw a beam of light come from above some trees and shine directly into the barn. The beam was about two inches in diameter in her opinion, and when it was directed into the barn, she heard her horses scream.

According to her statement to RCMP, when Burns ran back inside the barn, she saw:

> The horse nearest the window in the barn in which the beam seemed to have gone through was down with front feet through a plywood wall. It was conscious and struggling to get out. He got out on his own power... The horse in the next stall was laying on its side and was motionless. While I stood there, the horse got up and appeared frightened. After getting to its feet he immediately darted forwards into the screen surrounding the stall.

V*
NRC OTT

RCMPCITY PGEO
33 ROUTINE PGEO DET APR 12 UNCLAS

NRC METEOR CENTRE OTTAWA

N78/083

PG/197/5
RE: REPORTED UFO SIGHTING - NEAR PRINCE GEORGE, BC   Apr 7, 03:3
    06APR78
===
VIKI BURNS OF BERGMAN ROAD APPROXIMATELY FIFTEEN MILES EAST OF PR
GEORGE BC REPORTS UFO SIGHTING AT APPROX 1945HRS ON 06APR78.
BURNS WAS AT RESIDENCE WITH SEVERAL OTHER PERSONS RAYMOND AND ALICE
MILLER, WAYNE AND LENORE LOFTUS, AND JEAN ANDERSON ALL OF PRINCE
GEORGE. SKY WAS CLEAR AT THE TIME. OBJECT WAS QUITE HIGH IN SKY
OVAL IN SHAPE, CHANGED GRADUALLY IN COLOUR FROM RED TO BLUE
THERE WAS NO DEFINITE FLIGHT PATTERN.
                              =8=
VISIBLE FOR APPROX THREE HOURS. BURNS FURTHER STATES THAT A BEAM
OF WHITE LIGHT PRESUMEABLY FROM UFO PASSED INTO THEIR HORSE STABLE
AND SEVERELY DISRUPTED ANIMALS TO POINT OF EXHAUSTION AND REQUIRING
ATTENTION OF VETERINARIAN

FROM FURTHER ENQUIRIES CONDUCTED IT WAS ASCERTAINED THAT ADDITIONAL
PERSONS KENNETH AND CINDY STEPHENS , GEORGE SEVIGNY, GUS STREIBEL,
AND LEO AND MARLENE SELZER ALSO OBSERVED SAME OR SIMILIAN OBJECT
ABOUT SAME TIME FROM ADDRESS 4278 HART HIGHWAY PRINCE GEORGE
THEY STATE OBJECT WAS DISC-SHOD, MOVED FROM EAST TO WEST APPEARED
RED ON SIDES AND ORANGE ON BOTTOM. STEPHENS APPARENTLY REPORTED
INCIDENT TO CFB BALDY HUGHES. BURNS DID NOT CONTACT POLICE UNTIL
THE 10APR78.   FURTHER REPORT TO FOLLOW
   PRINCE GEORGE DETACHMENT RCMP

LINE 14 OF TEXT SHUD READ
SELZER ALSO OBSERVED SAME OR SIMILAIR OBJECGT .....

NRC OTT

RCMPCITY PGEO
O*
NRC OTT

COMM SQN OTT
PUZ 004113
O P 138326* -04 78

Document 56: "On April 6, 1978, a UFO shone a beam of
light into a barn near Prince George, BC, affecting
several horses." Herzberg Institute of Astrophysics –
Reports on non-meteoric sightings, unidentified flying
objects, UFO's 4/6/1978 © Government of Canada. Reproduced
with the permission of Library and Archives Canada (2021).
Source: Library and Archives Canada/National Research
Council of Canada fonds/e002748099

A horse in a third stall seemed unaffected.

Panicked, Burns called her mother, who came over right away. When they met outside, their attention was drawn to a bright white light moving in the sky over the farm. It was "at plane level" and appeared to dart from place to place quickly, moving roughly north to south. Burns phoned an owner of one of the horses, who came over immediately with her husband and two friends.

All six of them watched the UFO moving in the sky, sometimes with the aid of a rifle scope. In testimony to RCMP, the UFO was variously described as a starlike light like a satellite, a disc "like two plates put together," and a simple flashing light high in the sky. They watched it over the course of three hours while talking with one another and attending to the horses.

A somewhat different version of events is also in the NRC files, in a report made to CFB Baldy Hughes by Mrs. Burns. As in the RCMP report, Burns described the beam as "about 2 inches in diameter with no side refraction (like a solid bar of white matter)." It "appeared to come down from trees and bend inwards through barn door" over her shoulder and lasted only about five seconds.

But in the account given to military investigators, Burns had more to say about the horses, noting that she:

> ... was startled by the long screaming of her horses which were inside. She never in all her life had heard any horse let out such type of noise. It was all very frightening... She entered the barn and found the following: one of the younger horses was down on the stall floor in a kneeling position with both hind legs entrapped through the plywood siding of the stall. In the next stall another horse was down and was found to be unconscious. On examination she discovered 2 unexplained bare patches like all the hair had been torn out or burned off. A third horse was attempting to get away from its stall and finally literally tore loose and went charging around the barn as though scared to death. [She] finally subdued it but it would not settle down entirely.

The third horse's demeanour was not mentioned in the original RCMP report.

In the military account, Burns said that veterinarians who examined the horses: "Couldn't believe [the horses'] condition... They appeared stunned, in shock, one listless – not at all spirited (as they normally were). The one that was gone unconscious would not enter its stall again."

However, in Burns' statement to RCMP, she didn't call the veterinarians until the following day:

The following day, I checked the horses and they appeared dopey, uncoordinated and out of character. Upon checking the filly, I noted a circle on either side of its neck, which weren't present the previous day. I photographed the horse. The horses were put outside and in the afternoon, I noticed the filly fall down. I called the vet, and Dr. McKee came and checked the horses. He told me that they seemed to be suffering from severe fright which caused a number of unrelated symptoms. He said that the circles were a form of ringworm.

By April 10, 1978, Burns noted the horses had been improving. It was then that she contacted the RCMP, who came out and interviewed everyone, including the veterinarian. Dr. McKee told them: "...the horses were completely exhausted as a result of shock. The shock has affected their body functions." He could not explain what had caused their condition.

Burns asked RCMP to check for radiation in the horses' stall, probably as a result of attention the incident had been receiving. She had called a radio station the night of the occurrence and as a result, visitors to the farm had offered their opinions on what had transpired. (No abnormal radiation levels were found.)

We are still left with a puzzle as to what affected the horses. Burns' description of a beam that descended from the sky and bent into the barn is very unusual, and even if it did reach a stall, what could it have done to the animals?

And how?

The weird ones

Lights in the sky are one thing, but oddball flying contraptions are another.

Take case N74/099, for example. On November 5, 1974, at 7:30 pm, Jesse and Johanna Chilton of Red Deer, Alberta, were driving south on Hwy. 2 near Olds, Alberta, when they saw: "... a round circular object approx. 9 ft. in diameter proceeding north parallel to them at a height of 25 ft. and about 50 ft. to their right."

As the object approached and then passed them going in the opposite direction to their travel, they saw that it: "... appeared to have several exhaust ports emitting a bright yellow exhaust which feathered out like ostrich plumes."

As it flew past them, they could hear: "intermittent hissing sounds" as it rotated, zipping just above the height of telephone poles beside the road. It was in view for only a minute before it was lost to sight behind them.

The Chiltons' UFO was downright normal compared with what a farmer and his son reported on January 16, 1975, at 5:15 pm, near Rochester, Alberta. NRC Case N75/008 is very brief, and notes simply: "Object shaped like a dinosaur hovering approx. six feet above their heads, was approx. 4 feet high and 12 feet long – noticed only one object, remained there for approx. ¾ of a minute and then disappeared."

Or what about instead of a flying saucer, a flying box, like the one reported in Case N81/60? Just before midnight on July 16, 1981, two teenage boys from Innisfail, Alberta, were coming home from Red Deer, where they had just watched the movie *Raiders of the Lost Ark*. They were passing near CFB Penhold when they were startled by a cube-shaped object 100 feet long with flashing lights attached to "construction on ends." There were also "revolving lights around unseen mid portions."

But then, according to the report:

Sighted originally at est. 300 feet, came towards the car from the front of them, stopped in front of them about 15 feet off ground, hesitated, did a quick circle around them then went out of sight.

It's easy enough to dismiss this as the product of young imaginations, but the NRC report notes: "Boys were emotionally upset. Tears welled up [when they] started to relate information."

And then, because obviously needed: "Neither appear to be under influence of any alcohol or drug."

But what can be said about a report phoned in to Ottawa from two farmers just south of McGrath, Alberta, about an incident that happened on August 2, 1981? As duly recorded by the clerk on the NRC Non-Meteoric Sightings desk, case N81/69 reads in full:

Eight crafts, semi-circular, 400 yards away, 145 ft. long by 40 to 50 ft. wide, fishey gold, 7 landed on shocks, 1 hovered, ramp extended, 10-15 people emerged, 2 aliens left each craft, taking sample soil and water, departed, no sound.

There was, of course, no follow-up investigation.

12

THE BIGGEST PIECE OF A
UFO EVER FOUND

~

Recently, ufology has been abuzz with vitriolic discussions—no, more like arguments—regarding the acquisition and testing of materials thought to be from alien spacecraft. In July 2018, for example, the much celebrated To The Stars Academy (TTSA) announced that it was creating the Acquisition & Data Analysis of Materials (ADAM) Research Project, "an Academic Research Program Focused on Exotic Materials for Technology Innovation." As TTSA explained: "From time to time, various sources have collected material samples reported to have come from advanced aerospace vehicles of unknown origin (popularly known as UAP – Unidentified Aerial Phenomena - or UFOs.)"

The ADAM project had the admirable goal of studying artefacts from UFOs:

Given the potential significance of such findings, To The Stars Academy has made it a Tier-1 priority to use its resources to subject these materials to detailed and rigorous scientific evaluation whenever feasible. As soon as TTS Academy is notified that materials are available, a thorough effort will be made to document their origin and credibility, followed by the establishment of chain-of-custody procedures and ownership protocols. In addition to reviewing the materials for their potential significance as evidence of exotic origin, the analysis will evaluate materials for such characteristics as exceptional strength, lightweight build and any unusual advanced properties that potentially could contribute to the development of exciting new technologies in the future.[1]

The TTSA's ADAM Research Project was designed to focus on the collection and scientific evaluation of material samples obtained through reliable reports of "advanced aerospace vehicles of unknown origin"—or UFOs.

This sounded great! Finally, some tangible evidence from UFOs would be studied by reputable scientists in laboratories, and finally prove that aliens are visiting Earth.

Except, do such artefacts really exist? From time to time, a number of ufologists have presented details of known artefacts from UFOs, suggesting that materials suspected as being made elsewhere than Earth have been known for many years. Included in the list of such artefacts is a set of fragments from Ubatuba, Brazil, found in 1957, that tests have shown to be very pure magnesium with various other trace elements.

One slight problem, which flies completely against the TTSA mandate about chain-of-custody protocols, is that no one really knows the provenance of the Ubatuba fragments. There were no known witnesses to the UFO that dropped them, and the actual date of the UFO event is not known. Nevertheless, the goal of the TTSA is to study and analyse UFO artefacts, so the Ubatuba fragments appear to qualify.

Yet, one Canadian example of a UFO artefact is usually never mentioned in the context of UFO artefacts, even though it was certainly the largest ever recovered, and was easily the most thoroughly examined and tested by scientists. Its story is most remarkable, and it was reviewed by none other than Dr. Peter Millman of the NRC himself, although it was never formally part of the NRC UFO files. In fact, the UFO event that began this story was never reported to the RCAF or RCMP.

It started (we think) in 1960, in Quebec, Canada.

According to the most-cited story regarding the case, on June 12, 1960, between 3:00 and 4:00 am EDT, a sonic boom rocked the area around Quebec City, Canada. At about the same time, a fiery object was said to fall out of the sky and split into two pieces as it fell, one somewhat larger than the other. The object was estimated to have been moving at an altitude of one to two thousand feet. Both pieces were thought to have fallen into the St. Lawrence River near Les Écureuils, about 20 miles upriver from Quebec City.

This account was said to come from a French language newspaper in Quebec, although I have been unable to find any reference to this in any of *Le Devoir*, *La Presse*, or *Le Soleil*, the major French-language newspapers at the time.

Furthermore, a local UFO group investigated the report, but

> ...were unable to find anyone in the Les Ecureuils area who had actually heard or seen the metal fall - strange, in such a small town. So, the manner in which the metal arrived at the scene still remains a mystery.[2]

Nevertheless, the UFO and the objects that fell to Earth were believed associated, and the story of the "Mysterious Chunk of Space Hardware" began in earnest.

The UFO group in question was the Ottawa New Sciences Club, founded by Wilbert B. Smith, the electrical engineer and legendary and controversial figure in Canadian ufology. In its ufozine, *Topside*, the Ottawa group described the discovery of the found objects:

> A local resident, who supplements his income by beachcombing, covered the area pretty thoroughly the first day or two of June. Then came three days of rain during which he did not work the area. When the weather cleared, he found the two pieces of metal on the shale bed... The smaller piece was close to the shore and visible at low tide; the larger one was further out into the river and was often completely submerged.[3]

This "beachcomber" tried to move the larger piece but couldn't, so he:

> ...loaded the small 800-lb. piece and sold it for one cent a pound to a scrap metal dealer in Quebec City where it was erroneously classified as non-ferrous metal. The large magnetic crane used for handling the scrap would not lift the metal due to its low magnetic permeability, so it was pushed into a pile of non-ferrous scrap and eventually shipped to Japan.[4]

That's right; a possible alien artefact ended up in a scrap heap somewhere in Japan, if it ever made it there at all.

But now the good news: the other piece was taken to a government facility where it was analysed. According to *Topside*: "...rumour of the find reached the Canadian Arsenals Research and Development Establishment (CARDE) in the area, who, thinking it might have been part of a space capsule, picked it up for investigation."

(The name of the government division was consistently cited erroneously in all *Topside* issues. CARDE was actually the Canadian Armaments Research and Development Establishment, now part of the Valcartier Research Centre of Defence Research and Development Canada.)

And what did CARDE find? This is what the Ottawa New Sciences Club told its members:

> The metal object proved to be a mass of high strength metal which had fallen, or had been dropped, while in a plastic state, and had splattered like a ball of mud. It was 6ft. in diameter and 2ft. thick at the centre. At the centre of the body there was an outline of a tube about 10 inches in diameter which protruded from the mass about 6 inches. A small electronic potting can was embedded near one of the outer edges. By scratching away the potting plastic, it was possible to identify an electronic component which appeared to be a transistor. There was also the imprint of another electric can which appeared to have been removed by curiosity seekers. It is not considered that the object fell in the location it was found, because there was no crater or splattered material in the vicinity. The tidal flats at this point are solid rock. An analysis by CARDE revealed that the metal is an alloy with high manganese content. CARDE personnel who are familiar with foundry operations consider it to be a normal product of a foundry consisting of slag with semi-molten scrap embedded. Their investigation did not reveal any electronic components.[5]

Well, that seemed to be rather straightforward. Furthermore, it was pointed out that about 100 miles upstream was the Sorel Iron Foundry, which produced material similar to the artefact. End of story.

Not.

Because it was devoted to advancing belief in aliens and UFOs, the Ottawa New Sciences Club rejected the CARDE findings.

> Despite the findings of CARDE, an element of doubt exists as to whether these are completely accurate. Although they considered the object to be of terrestrial origin, laboratory experiments on the metal carried out by the late Wilbert B. Smith and co-workers resulted in a

number of unusual reactions not consistent with the normal behaviour of terrestrial metal. This was most evident when a small piece of the metal was heated with an acetylene torch which caused it to blossom into a miniature white cloud with extremely bright sparks in it - a sort of A-bomb in miniature. WBS concluded that the magnesium went exothermic, reduced the ferrite in the spinel crystal structure, formed the cloud and left the iron free to burn with o2 in the air. He warned that anyone attempting to heat a larger chunk of the metal might very well fry himself! He also considered that the intense heating should have burned the object worse than it did and he therefore reached the conclusion that it could not have been a blast furnace product. Further experiments revealed that some parts of the metal could not stand too much heat thus limiting the possibilities as to why such a manufactured item came to grief. In testing the metal with the acetylene torch, it was noted that the resulting sphere, with its intensely brilliant shower of sparks, burned until nothing remained- no residue or slag, as is common with Earth metals. CARDE suggested that the metal may have been slag from a foundry, brought to the area via an ice floe. The facts of the case, however, do not bear this out. The nearest mills are many miles from Les Ecureuils, and it was the month of June! The material is not a common foundry product, and even if it had been, one wonders why the foundry would waste 3,000 pounds of metal![6]

Wilbert B. Smith was not a metallurgist but an electrical engineer with a Masters degree, working for the Department of Transport, and later the Department of Communications in the Canadian government. He was responsible for broadcast standards and equipment design and testing for radio in Canada, and helped set the frequencies used by radio and TV stations across the nation.

As noted earlier, Smith is most remembered as having been at a broadcasting conference in Washington and made "discreet enquiries" at the Canadian Embassy where he was told: "Flying saucers exist" and "The matter is the most highly classified subject in the United States Government, rating higher even than the H-bomb."

Later, Smith claimed he was in direct contact with aliens, sometimes telepathically, sometimes visually. His information on aliens included such facts as:

There is much evidence that people who build and fly flying saucers are people very much like us. They have been seen on many occasions and there are many claims of personal contact having been established with them. Communications with these people tell us that they are our distant relatives; that we are descendants of their colonists on this planet, and that they still regard us as brothers even though we don't often act like it. There is much evidence that the technology of these people is quite a bit ahead of ours, and that through study of the behavior of the saucers and from the alleged communications we have been able to piece together some of this technology, and it is amazing to say the least. We are informed that these people are really civilized, in that they regard all men as brothers; that they do not have wars, and live under conditions of personal freedom of which we cannot conceive.[7]

He also wrote articles about advanced quasi-scientific concepts such as the interdependence between Reality and Awareness," and how: "The application of the Quadrature Concept to the Third Parameter yields a further parameter which we might describe as Density or gradient, and is really an expression of how Reality is distributed in Space."[8]

Smith also speculated there were 12 dimensions on Earth, and that his research into gravity and higher consciousness was assisted by "extraterrestrial helpers."

That kind of thing.

Anyway, Smith and his contactee UFO group were convinced that the CARDE results were wrong. I went in search of the original CARDE report, and contacted DRDC directly. They replied that no such report on the analysis of a large quantity of metal found in the St. Lawrence River existed in their records. This could be because it simply was not an official research study, but one taken on as a public courtesy.

In an interview with Smith in November 1961, he explained that he had decided that the mysterious chunk of metal was in fact part of an alien spacecraft:

Our Canadian Research Group recovered one mass of very strange metal... it was found within a few days of July 1, 1960. There is about three thousand pounds of it. We have done a tremendous amount of detective work on this metal. We have found out the things that aren't so. We have something that was not brought to this Earth by plane nor by boat nor by any helicopter. We are speculating that what we have is a portion of a very large device which came into this solar system... we don't know when... but it had been in space a long time before it came to earth; we can tell that by the micrometeorites embedded in the surface. But we don't know whether it was a few years ago - or a few hundred years ago.[9]

Wilbert B. Smith died in December 1962, at the age of 52. However, Carol Halford-Watkins, the assistant editor of *Topside* but effectively the president of the Ottawa New Sciences Club, kept the group going in Smith's memory after he passed away. The ufozine continued publishing throughout the 1960s and into the early 1970s, often devoting entire issues to articles such as channelled messages from Nikola Tesla, who had died in 1943.

One discovery about the massive artefact that certainly contributed to the Ottawa group's persistence regarding its non-terrestrial nature was that there were a number of "inclusions" on its surface.

A further mystery, indicating the possibility of exposure of the metal in outer space, is that the outer surface, under powerful magnification, shows minute inclusions which may well be micro-meteorites picked up during a long sojourn in space. The Club has in its possession a series of photographs of the outer surface of the metal, taken with the aid of microphotography, in which these inclusions can be observed quite clearly. The density of these particles is about 30 per square centimeter. Dr. Peter Millman of the Canada National Research Council estimated that micrometeorites of this size would occur through a sq. cm. section at about 10-6 second, so it would take about a year to accumulate such a density.[10]

The calculation was that because there are about 31 million seconds in a year, the accretion rate per centimeter works out to the stated value. However, there is no indication in any of the tests performed on the artefact that any of these alleged micrometeorites were tested and found to be such things.

The May 23, 1967, issue of the *Christian Science Monitor* included an article by noted UFO proponent Dr. J. Allen Hynek, titled, "A White Paper on UFOs." In the article, Hynek described how the Condon Committee was dealing with the problem of not having any physical evidence of UFOs to which they could apply scientific rigour. He noted: "The only UFO 'hardware' so far consists of patent hoaxes. If there were only some 'hardware' to study, how simple matters would be! Hundreds of laboratory tests could be run and the exact physical nature of the UFO could be established." (This comment was printed in *Topside*, Number 24-25, Spring & Summer, 1967, pp. 10-11, and written more than 50 years ago, it's fascinating that in 2022, ufology has finally caught up to Hynek's ruminations.)

Well, that made the Ottawa club members sit up straight. They actually had a chunk of UFO hardware, so they decided that the Condon Committee needed to take a look at it. On June 21, 1967, Halford-Watkins wrote to Dr. Edward Condon at the University of Colorado, describing the chunk of metal and sending along a copy of the 1966 *Topside* article about it.

Halford-Watkins noted:

> If the Colorado group of scientists decide to accept this offer, we shall await in due course and with a great deal of interest, a report on their findings. We sincerely hope that it will be a factual and truthful one, with nothing concealed – but how can we ever be sure of this?[11]

Alas, Condon didn't reply, so on September 11, 1967, Halford-Watkins again wrote him, this time with registered mail. Immediately, Condon's secretary responded, explaining that the Ottawa club's offer had been referred to Roy Craig, a physicist at the University of Colorado and the project's chief field investigator, but a committed debunker. Unbeknownst to the Ottawa group, Craig was at that exact time dealing with the investigation of the Falcon Lake case elsewhere in Manitoba. This was certainly bad timing, because Craig was decidedly unimpressed with the Falcon Lake case and his response reflected his general dismissal of UFO incidents.

Craig answered Halford-Watkins on September 29, 1967, giving them the bad news:

> Your letter to Dr. Condon written on June 21, 1967, recently came to my attention. The piece of metallic material you mentioned, since it cannot be related directly to an unidentified flying object, would not seem of sufficient value to our study to warrant further analysis by us.[12]

Craig recognized the lack of good provenance of the metal chunk, and therefore didn't see much sense in wasting his time with it. Of course, this smacked of conspiracy, according to Halford-Watkins:

This cursory brush-off was not entirely unexpected, as by this time we had gained the distinct impression from colleagues in the U.S. and elsewhere, that the Colorado project was not an all-out effort to solve the UFO mystery and was likely to be over-shadowed by USAF policy.[13]

That wasn't the last word on Condon, however. In June 1968, Halford-Watkins received an "Express air mail" letter from Roy Craig, noting that he was going to be in Ottawa the following day, and "would like to take the opportunity of examining the chunk of hardware on site, and at the same time to take photographs and samples of the metal." She noted:

...we welcomed the opportunity to play our part in assisting the Colorado investigation and duly arranged for [Craig] to be driven out to the site where he took photos of the metal and we chipped off samples for him and supplied him with copies of the last 2 analysis reports.[14]

During his visit, Craig was courteous and polite despite his considerable scepticism, although Halford-Watlins noted:

While not committing himself that the material we supplied on the metal and WBS would be used in his report, he said he would give the matter some serious consideration. We entertained our guest and an interesting discussion on UFOs followed, but as much of this was on a strictly 'not for publication' basis, we can only honour our word to [Craig], who stated it was hoped that the Colorado UFO Report might be ready for publication in September. As for our small contribution and the Colorado Report itself, we can only hope for the best and that it will be factual and objective reporting.[15]

While this sounded promising, Craig's version of his visit was somewhat different:

Mosquitoes by the hundreds were chewing us up as we looked at 'the mysterious chunk of hardware' which then rested in the yard of the home of an officer of the Royal Canadian Air Force. The officer was a member of the Ottawa New Sciences Club. The club secretary and her husband had graciously driven me from my hotel in Ottawa to the Colonel's home to see the mysterious metal and talk with club members.

237

As I looked at the 'mysterious metal,' my hosts offered to get whatever samples I wished to take from it. The chunk did look to me for all the world like ordinary foundry waste. They brought a sledge hammer, with which we knocked off a small protruding piece which I placed in my briefcase for reasons that were not entirely clear, for it seemed the material had already been analyzed adequately.[16]

Judging from Craig's version of the meeting, he was simply just humouring the group and was there out of curiosity since he was in Ottawa anyway. His scepticism was reinforced by the club's spokesman, 'the Colonel,' who was running the group following the death of Wilbert Smith. He explained to Craig:

'We were told, through a medium,' he said, 'that this was part of a spaceship twenty miles long and three miles in diameter which was destroyed (by meteorite collision or other catastrophe) and was derelict in space. The people 'topside' wanted to clear the derelict from space because man was getting interested in flying around there, and they didn't want it to cause mishaps. They sent segments to Earth, Mars, and other planets to get rid of them. These pieces on Earth so originated.'[17]

Craig must have been dying on the inside, for he wrote:

Their faith in revelations received through a spiritual medium during seance obviously was stronger than their faith in man's knowledge of nature as obtained through the methods of his science.

Was it merely because that belief had been held by the late Wilbert Smith, whom they regarded with such high esteem?[18]

Craig then noted what I have termed "ufology and the science paradox":

What puzzled me was the repeated demand for scientific analysis and use of arguments of scientific vein to refute undesired scientific results.[19]

This has amazed me as well. On the one hand, UFO groups and organizations proclaim their approach to the UFO phenomenon is highly scientific and spend time and effort to ensure specific protocols are followed regarding collection and analyses of physical traces associated with UFO cases. On the other hand, some also accept unsubstantiated claims of contact with aliens, subjective testimony by witnesses with low credibility, and encourage speculation about "interdimensional portals," "contact modalities" and "phase-shifting" of alien spacecraft to explain UFO witnesses' observations. The willingness to embrace the possibility of advanced alien technology that seems to violate physical laws in order to account for UFOs that vanish suddenly, enter and leave bodies of water, and are visible only to select individuals, contrasts sharply with the desire to appear and sound scientific.

Craig noted:

> The Colonel expressed to me his feeling that, while his chunk of metal does have all the characteristics of waste from a foundry when viewed in the realm of three-dimensional physical existence, 'when viewed in a wider framework, the interface of this dimension with other dimensions, which parallel the physical, it well may be part of a spaceship.'

> The 'mysterious chunk of metal' was a fetish. Why, then, the insistent demand for repeated physical and chemical examination of something whose ultimate significance was considered to reside in psychic or spiritual realms?[20]

Craig did mention the Ottawa artefact in the *Condon Report*, although it was written before his visit to Ottawa, because he noted: "The Club does not claim that the piece of metal is, if fact, part of a spaceship; however, its members do not reject this possibility." He noted that CARDE "considered the material the normal product of a foundry, consisting of slag with semi-molten scrap embedded in it." He added:

> Since no connection could be seen between the existence of this metal or slag and the UFO question, no further analysis of the material was undertaken by the project. This writer examined the metallic mass at Ottawa and agreed with the CARDE conclusion that it was ordinary foundry waste.[21]

The Ottawa UFO club was undaunted, however. During the three-month period that the Condon Committee was silent to them, the Ottawa group was experiencing some new developments regarding the UFO chunk. What was happening was that Ronald Anstee, who led the

Montreal UFO Society, had been given some pieces from the large UFO artefact and had displayed them at one of his lectures. After his talk, he had been approached by someone who said he knew a professional metallurgist and could get the samples tested independently. This metallurgists's report to the Ottawa group read:

Findings
1. The corrosion on the part was slight and only superficial.
2. The specific gravity was very high.
3. The hardness was Rockwell B 94.
4. Chemical Analysis
Carbon 0.16% Manganese 11.3 SI 0.12
FE Ferrous 88.403 Sulphur 0.017 NI 110

Conclusion:
The chemical analysis does not correspond to any commercial manganese steels as they contain either more carbon and silicon or some nickel and molybdenum. The alloy work hardened very heavily during the process of cutting which is inherent to such an alloy. The slipped lines were more pronounced once nital reagent was used. Since deep electro-polishing was used in this instance, it indicates that the material went through heavy impact that caused the different planes to slip.

The fact that this composition does not correspond to any known commercial manganese steel, is in itself very interesting, but it does not exclude the possibility of unpublished new materials being used by either the U.S.S.R. or U.S.A. in their space probes.[22]

This conclusion led Halford-Watkins to interpret this thusly:

Now, if this metal underwent such heavy impact as to cause extensive slippage, surely it is a reasonably logical conclusion that this hardware must have been part of a spacecraft that came to grief - it is hardly conceivable that a foundry product would be subjected to such extreme impact.

The report states that the metal does not correspond to any known commercial manganese steels and suggests the possibility of an element they know nothing about. This again surely suggests an extraterrestrial metal.[23]

And, therefore, the extraterrestrial hypothesis was reintroduced as viable. To advance the conspiracy theory, Halford-Watkins noted:

> It is possible, of course, as suggested in the report, that it might have been part of a Russian or American space capsule, but if this were the case, why didn't the Canadian Government agency hang on to it? Could it be that, in fact, it was completely unidentifiable and that rather than admit they had proof-positive of a UFO, they preferred to ignore it?[24]

Ronald Anstee was determined to help the Ottawa club, for he then submitted additional samples for testing by "a group of scientists at McGill University in Montreal." Who knows what was found exactly, because Anstee reported that the scientists were "very disturbed at their findings."

The leader of this group of scientists, Professor John Jonas (the only one identified by name at this point), encouraged Anstee to get the Ottawa club in contact with a few government metallurgists to test the samples.

Halford-Watkins wrote:

> The necessary contact was made with these 2 gentlemen and full details, including the latest analysis report, were passed on to them. The 2 scientists expressed interest in the hardware and on Oct. 14/67, arrangements were made for them to examine the mass of metal on site and take samples of it for investigation. Both appeared extremely intrigued by the mysterious circumstances surrounding the finding of the metal and subsequent tests on it.[25]

The Ottawa club was encouraged by this, because:

> Later, word reached us by telephone that they were prepared to carry out extensive tests and analyses of the samples of metal. It was explained that a thorough analysis was normally rather a long and costly procedure and they were of the opinion that such a comprehensive analysis had not yet been carried out on the metal. However, they were, at the time, working on some new experimental equipment by means of which it was hoped to conduct such an analysis with a great saving in time and money. Special parts for this equipment were on order from overseas and it was added that delivery of these parts and subsequent testing of the completed apparatus might take

anywhere up to 6 months to complete. However, when it was ready, the necessary investigation would be carried out and a report of the findings sent to us.[26]

Again, a different take on this is given by Craig:

Eight years after the CARDE analysis, the group was still seeking additional analyses, and the club secretary suggested I might get additional information from Dr. Eric Smith, Chief, Metal Physics Section of Canada Department of Energy, Mines, and Resources. Dr. Smith had samples of the metal and was awaiting completion of installation of new equipment from Japan, with which he would conduct thorough tests and analyses.[27]

This was the government metallurgist Halford-Watkins heard about via telephone. But it doesn't sound like he was impressed with the samples, because Craig wrote:

When I later contacted Dr. Smith, he said he indeed planned to analyze the material, but he wouldn't be at all surprised if it came from the Sorel Iron Foundries, Sorel, Quebec, more than fifty miles upstream from the site where the material was found. He said production of high-manganese steel is one of the specialties of this foundry, and it is standard practice to dig a hole in sand and dump surplus or non-specification molten material into it. A plug often is inserted so the accumulated mass can be grasped for moving by a crane. Such waste is not utilized or recovered because of its uncertain composition. Dr. Smith said, further, that large chunks of such waste are known to have been buried around a foundry of the Sorel type. His description of the material matched the chunk of metal in the Colonel's yard precisely.[28]

Later, Halford-Watkins wrote about how Dr. Eric Smith visited the Club and examined the large artefact.

...in September 1967, Dr. Smith examined the mass on site, took samples and promised a full report on his findings. After two-and-a-half years of continued delaying tactics we are still awaiting his report![29]

The Topside group was persistent. They sought additional testing by anyone who might help them establish the extraterrestrial nature of the 3,000-pound artefact.

In 1969, Dr. Peter Millman, who led UFO investigations at the National Research Council of Canada, "expressed interest in the metal and offered to arrange a scientific investigation into it. Samples of the metal were passed to him by Lieutenant Commander Arthur Bray, a noted Canadian ufologist, to whom Dr. Millman promised a report on his findings."

At a meeting of the Ottawa club, held in the home of Arthur and Dorothy Bray, Millman, an outspoken UFO debunker, had given a talk about the scientific view of UFOs. It was during this meeting that the members had asked him, and he had agreed to try and get the metal analysed.

But Millman's response was even more noncommittal than that of Roy Craig. He effectively played cat-and-mouse with Halford-Watkins for many months.

In late 1969, Brian Cannon, a representative of the Aerial Phenomena Research Organization (APRO) in Winnipeg, Manitoba, had received a letter from Millman about several UFO matters (including the Falcon Lake case, which Millman had dismissed out of hand), in which he stated:

> ...there was 'nothing unusual' about the metal, that it was manganese steel, and apparently ladle residue from the Sorel Foundry in Quebec, which inserts a pipe into the hole where waste molten metal is poured, and after solidification, the pipe is used to lift the mass of metal.[30]

This revelation disturbed Halford-Watkins, who was upset that Millman was telling others about his findings on the metal but had not told the Ottawa group. She sent an angry letter off to Millman, demanding to know what was going on.

Further complicating the matter was the intervention of another UFO fan who wanted to test the metal scientifically. This was Arthur H. Matthews of Lac Beauport, Quebec, who said he could test the metal using a "Tesla Bridge" and determine if the object had ever been in outer space. Matthews was a contactee who channelled messages from Nikola Tesla and had constructed a "Tesla Scope" for communicating with aliens. He claimed that in 1941, aliens from Venus had landed their spacecraft, called the X-12, near his farm and had begun a series of meetings with him during which they imparted esoteric knowledge.[31]

On September 28, 1969, members of the Ottawa club, along with Ronald Anstee, watched as Matthews tested the UFO artefact at their meeting place. But even they were appalled by what transpired.

> The test appeared to consist of stringing wires and a small flat box-like object across the metal, which were linked up to a tape recorder on which Mr. Matthews made two 6-minute recordings. Despite questions, Mr. Matthews declined to explain how the Tesla device worked. All that he admitted was that it had been used to detect flaws in metal railway lines.[32]

Needless to say, Matthews' test:

> ...left some grave doubts in the minds of some of our technical workers who witnessed it, particularly as no scientific proof was forthcoming to support it, and most of them were unable to accept that it was possible to prove that the metal mass had never been in space with a device used primarily for detecting flaws in metal railway lines! It was also noted that the volume indicator on the tape recorder link to the Tesla Bridge showed no signs of life.[33]

But true to his word, Matthews sent Halford-Watkins a report on his test of the metal, in only three days! But, alas, it was not what they wanted to hear:

> It required many hours of careful study to complete the Tesla Bridge, but only 12 minutes to test the block by means of Tesla's instructions. This test was recorded by transfer onto a magnetic tape and my study of this on return to Quebec proves without any doubt that it is a man-made form of iron and is without any doubt composed of Earth found ores. This piece of metal was never in space. Further tests to prove my statement can be done if the complete block is applied to a reverberatory furnace.[34]

Further confounding the matter, Matthews noted in his report that he had been asked to test the metal "by a person whose name he was not permitted to divulge."

Halford-Watkins sent a letter to Matthews, demanding some clarification and wanting to know who "Mr. X" was. He replied: "I have referred your request re my findings on the metal to the federal authority who requested the test, as these findings are confidential."

So, as Halford-Watkins noted to the Topside readership:

> Here was news indeed. So, the mysterious Mr. X was a federal authority! As Dr. Millman has the responsibility for government UFO research, and by Mr. Matthews' own admittance, he made two telephone calls to the National Research Council on arrival in Ottawa prior to the test, we could only assume that Dr. Millman must be the federal authority concerned.[35]

And voila! Millman was definitely part of the conspiracy to suppress the truth about the artefact. Halford-Watkins even sent a letter to Millman on December 9, 1969, explicitly accusing him of being Matthews' "Mr. X."

By early 1970, with no reply from Millman, Halford-Watkins declared victory.

> To date, two months later, no reply has been received to this letter, which was not entirely unexpected. Did Dr. Millman find our questions too sticky to answer, or was he adopting the safer course of the old adage that says "silence is golden?" We are not blaming him personally for this somewhat cavalier attitude towards a public request for information - in fact, we have some sympathy for the embarrassing position he now finds himself in. Even as a senior civil servant, he still has to take his orders from a higher authority and as long as governmental silence policy exists on such matters, this situation will continue, although we believe the day will finally dawn when governments will recognize their moral responsibilities and give the public the true facts.[36]

About the same time, however, Arthur Bray received a letter from Millman, noting that the samples tested by Dr. Ian Smith, Head of the Metal Physics Section, Federal Department of Energy, Mines and Resources in Ottawa, showed "no evidence of extraterrestrial origin." On learning of this, Halford-Watkins wrote:

> Dr. Millman stated that competent scientists experienced no difficulty in recognizing the non-terrestrial nature of certain space material.

He also deplored the mystery which had been built up around the chunk. These two latter statements we regard as the biggest enigma of all. If it is such an easy matter for scientists to determine the Extra-Terrestrial nature or otherwise of material tested, why has it taken the government over 9 years to produce a simple statement of the facts of the case, thereby itself creating much of the mystery that has surrounded the metal?[37]

She added later:

...we admit to being somewhat puzzled at the delay if, as alleged, the results of the study show no evidence of extraterrestrial origin - or could it be that proof of this would not stand up to close scientific scrutiny? And thus, as all along the line, it has been governmental silence which has created much of the mystery that still surrounds the 3,000-pound chunk of unidentified hardware.[38]

Here, she may have had a point. Millman was dodging the issue and adding to the confusion through his reluctance to reply directly to her. She published excerpts from correspondence between Bray and Millman that show his dance of vagueness.

In his letter dated January 1970, Dr. Millman stated: "I should remind you that in the case of material from space such as moon rocks, meteorites, re-entry debris from spacecraft, there has been no difficulty experienced by competent scientists in recognizing its non-terrestrial nature and identifying it as different to terrestrial material."

And yet, in a letter dated September 9th, 1969, Dr. Millman had this to say:

I think I should mention here, however, that even with a complete examination and analysis of such a specimen, it is not a foregone conclusion that we can give an absolutely definite yes or no concerning its terrestrial or extraterrestrial origin.[39]

Halford-Watkins was justifiably confused by the apparent contradiction:

In view of these two apparently conflicting statements, we can only ask two questions: 1) how come they are suddenly so certain that the metal is not of extraterrestrial origin? And 2) will the real Dr. Millman please stand up?[40]

Even that wasn't the end of the matter. Yet another set of tests were done by an American UFO group, the Unidentified Flying Objects Researchers Alliance (UFORA) of Alliance, Ohio. Its director, Paul J.L. Rozich, provided a lengthy report on his testing, the first time they had received something of such depth.

Rozich detailed his various investigations, including non-destructive testing with an x-ray vacuum quantometer. He reported:

Major Constituents	Minor Constituents
Iron (Fe)	Cobalt (Co)
Nickel (Ni)	Silicon (Si)
Manganese (Mn)	Magnesium (Mg)
Chromium (Cr)	Sulfur (S)
	Potassium (K)

No traces were found of Aluminum (Al), Sodium (Na), Phosphorus (P) or Chlorine (Cl).[41]

Halford-Watkins was encouraged by this result. She noted:

But perhaps the most significant finding of the report is, in fact, a non-finding, i.e., according to the major test conducted on the metal by the X-ray vacuum quantometer, no traces were found of aluminum, calcium, and copper which normally one would expect to find in a terrestrial alloy of magnesium![42]

How she knew this, I am not sure. But she was astute in her realization that the analysis of an alleged UFO artefact requires detailed and advanced studies.

Taking an open-minded view of the general metal analysis situation, we are the first to realize that numerous difficulties lie in the way of establishing definitely whether or not a metal sample is of extraterrestrial origin. The obvious reason for this and as pointed out in an earlier issue, is that there is every possibility that other planets have the same elements as those of planet Earth.[43]

She cited the work of Dr. Allen R. Utke, whose article in the December 1970 issue of the ufozine *Skylook* included his observation that:

Most scientists are convinced that the same 92 natural elements found here on Earth are found everywhere in the universe with no new natural elements yet-to-be-discovered. We would only begin to suspect extraterrestrial origin if the sample, upon extensive analysis, was found to be one of the following: 1. An uncommon element, absolutely pure or of unusually high purity. 2. A mixture of elements or an alloy with a highly unusual or previously unknown composition and or set of properties. 3. A compound or mixture of compounds with a highly unusual or previously unknown composition or set of properties. 4. A material with a highly unusual or previously unknown atomic or molecular structure.[44]

She added:

Dr. Utke concedes that the only evidence which would probably convince scientists of an extraterrestrial origin is a sample whose isotopic distribution differed significantly from that of the same elements on Earth.[45]

And even if such evidence was found, Halford-Watkins doubted that it would prove alien visitation.

The crucial question is, however, even if 100% foolproof evidence were established, would the scientific establishment be prepared to admit it, or would they produce their usual flow of phony alibis to wriggle out of acknowledging the existence of extraterrestrial material?

However, despite the odds against us, we in private UFO research should press on regardless and with sincere prayer that in the final analysis, the truth will prevail![46]

This was the last publication of anything related to the Ottawa club's UFO artefact. The group ceased publication of *Topside* in 1971, and they appear to have disbanded shortly after.

What happened to the 3,000-pound chunk of metal is not known. Canadian ufologist John Magor noted in one of his books that it might be languishing in the backyard of one of the club's homes in Ottawa, forgotten and overgrown with grass and weeds.

The story of the testing, retesting and debate over the origin of the chunk is testament to how some in ufology cling to their beliefs against scientific reason, but also how scientists fail to make their case to those attracted to the subject and undermine their own position.

In the last published issue of *Topside*, Halford-Watkins concluded her review of the UFO artefact with a statement that could be as accepted by UFO believers today, as in 1971:

> From knowledge of the personal experiences of the late Wilbert B. Smith, of one thing we are sure - those government scientists engaged on UFO research, who work so mysteriously behind the silence curtain, have been well aware of the existence of extraterrestrial material for a long time now![47]

The determination of the Topside group to reject scientific analyses of the "mysterious hardware" has a modern-day counterpart in those who reject science in favour of belief in various aberrant ideas. Halford-Watkins' statement that "truth will prevail" against all odds and in counter to facts seems rather familiar. Her Topside group knew they were in the right and that it was science which was wrong.

Perhaps new analyses will settle the matter. Arthur Bray was a pilot in the Royal Canadian Air Force during World War II and later a pilot in the Royal Canadian Navy. He took an avid interest in UFOs, investigating many cases, and amassed a large collection of research material. In 1994 and also in 2004, he donated his collection to the University of Ottawa. Among his papers and files were details of his investigation into the Les Écureuils chunk of iron, which he believed might have been extraterrestrial. Included in his donation were actual pieces from the metal, which obviously await modern day testing.

But apart from Bray's pieces tucked away in a box within an archive, somewhere in Ottawa, Canada, may still be a 3,000-pound mass of metal that is one of the first UFO artefacts to have been scientifically tested. The story of claims and counter claims regarding its composition remains unresolved according to some ufologists. But this story is so similar to that of present-day debates about UFO artefacts, it should be held up as a lesson for those involved in the field today.

It was either foundry slag or a piece of a UFO, depending on whom you believe.

13

OFFICIAL INVESTIGATIONS

~

The RCAF UFO investigation team

Buried within the NRC UFO files is a case that demonstrates how UFO reports were investigated by military officials, and which has deep-rooted connections to other cases in Canada during the national UFO wave of 1967. It occurred near Rivers, Manitoba, and involved multiple witnesses, many of whom were military personnel, plus alleged physical effects and traces. Although rarely mentioned by researchers, it's a case that has many elements of a classic of ufology.

The report in Library and Archives Canada notes that the incident occurred at 0645Z (12:45 am) on August 28, 1967. There were six witnesses, three of whom were military personnel: LAC J. Hebert, LAC K. Taylor and CPL A Fedun, all stationed at CFB Rivers, plus civilians Judy Ross, Leslie Dowdell and Jacqueline Dowdell, all of Rivers. Hebert and Ross were driving one mile east of Rivers, Taylor was eight miles east, Fedun was in the town, and the Dowdell siblings were at their home in the town. In other words, there were six witnesses scattered across four different locations. In addition, two more military personnel, CPL K. McArthur and Commissionaire G. Stefanson, each at different locations on the Rivers base, reported hearing an "explosion" that rattled windows and created "vibrations."

PRIORITY

NNNNVVVVV   PCBØ75VVVV   PWA144SHAØ26   AUG 28 18 48'58

PP RCCWC

DE RCWPSH 21 28/1719Z

P R 281545Z AUG 67

FM CANFORBASE RIVERS

TO RCCWC/CANFORCEHED

INFO RCWPC/CANTRAINCOM

BT

UNCLAS A1497

FOR CFOC. UFO REPORT.

A. 28 AUG Ø645Z APPROX.

B. CLEAR. VISIBILITY 15 MILES PLUS.

C1. 92Ø78 LAC J HEBERT, CFB RIVERS

C2. MISS JUDY ROSS, RIVERS MAN.

C3. 86349 LAC K TAYLOR, DUTY DRIVER CFB RIVERS.

C4. 44168 CPL A FDUN, CFB RIVERS.

C5. MSTR LESLIE DOWDELL AND MISS JACQUELINE DOWDELL, DEPS RIVERS CAMP

D1. ONE MILE EAST OF RIVERS, MAN.

D2. SAME WITH HEBERT.

D3. HWY 25 APPROX 8 MILES EAST OF RIVERS. REPORTS APPROX TIME AS Ø71ØZ.

D4. 15 NAMAO RD, RIVERS CAMP. REPORTS APPROX TIME AS Ø63ØZ.

D5. 5Ø CHURCHILL DRIVE, RIVERS CAMP. REPORTS APPROX TIME AS

APPROX Ø53ØZ.

O.P.I. CFOC

CFHQ OPERATIONS CENTRE
AUG 27 28 1 55 '67
0 5 0 0

96

Document 57: "Document regarding UFOs seen by military
personnel and civilians on August 29, 1967, near
CFB Rivers, Manitoba." Title: Herzberg Institute of
Astrophysics - Reports on non-meteoric sightings,
unidentified flying objects, UFO's 8/28/1967 © Government
of Canada. Reproduced with the permission of Library
and Archives Canada (2021). Source: Library and Archives
Canada/National Research Council of Canada fonds/e002749328

PAGE 2 RCWPSH 21 UNCLAS

E. 57562 CPL KA MCARTHUR, ME DISPATCHER CFB RIVERS REPORTS HEARING QUOTE EXPLOSION UNQUOTE APPROX Ø7ØØZ ACCOMPANIED BY VIBRATIONS AND WINDOWS BEING RATTLED. MR G STEFANSON, COMMISSIONAIRE CFB RIVERS, REPORTS SIMILAR SENSATION AT APPROX Ø645Z.

HEBERT OBSERVED AN ULTRA VIOLET COLOURED LIGHT COMING FROM DIRECTLY ABOVE HIS CAR WHICH REMAINED STATIONARY FOR 3Ø-5Ø SECONDS AND MOVED AWAY BEFORE LIGHT DISAPPEARED. IT WAS ACCOMPANIED BY AN INCREASE IN HEAT IN CAR

F2. MISS ROSS DESCRIBES A WHITE FLASHING LIGHT, ROUND IN FORM. SHE FEELS IT WAS STATIONARY FOR A PERIOD BUT NOTICED NO TEMPERATURE CHANGE.

F3. LAC TAYLOR REPORTS A RED BALL OF FLAME TRAILED BY A BLUE LIGHT OR TAIL AT 3 - 4ØØØ FT ALTITUDE.

F4. CPL FEDUN DESCRIBES A ROUND BALL OF ORANGE WHITE FLAME WITH A REDDISH ORANGE TAIL WHICH WAS EITHER VERY LARGE OR VERY LOW AND WHICH FLARED UP AT MID POINT OF ITS ARC. FLAMING WAS CLEARLY VISIBLE AND VERY NOTICEABLY BRIGHTENED SKY. DIRECTION OF TRAVEL WAS SSW TO NNE AND PASSED NW OF POINT OF OBSERVATION.

F5. DOWDELLS FIRST SAW OBJECT THROUGH UPSTAIRS WINDOW RISING FROM WEST. THEY WENT OUTSIDE AND OBSERVED OBJECT PROCEED IN ARC TOWARDS NE BECOMING DIMMED AS IT TRAVELLED. OBJECT DESCRIBED AS

Document 58: "Document regarding UFOs seen by military personnel and civilians on August 29, 1967, near CFB Rivers, Manitoba." Title: Herzberg Institute of Astrophysics – Reports on non-meteoric sightings, unidentified flying objects, UFO's 8/28/1967 © Government of Canada. Reproduced with the permission of Library and Archives Canada (2021). Source: Library and Archives Canada/National Research Council of Canada fonds/e002749329

PAGE 3 RCWPSH 21 UNCLAS

VERY BRIGHT WHITE STAR WITH ORANGE COLOURING IN IT. OBJECT WAS
ROUND POINT OF LIGHT WITHOUT TAIL. ARC DESCRIBED AS WAVERING WITH
ALTERNATE DIMMING AND BRIGHTENING AND APPEARANCE OF STOPPING
OCCASIONALLY.

G. AS ABOVE.

H. LAC HEBERTS CAR DETAINED AT ME SECTION. BODY REPAIRMAN STATES
LIGHT DUST ON TOP OF CAR IS UNLIKE ANY OTHER IN HIS EXPERIENCE.
THERE IS SOME BUBBLING OF PAINT ON TOP. THIS INCIDENT REPORTED TO
TCHQ BY BASE DUTY OFFICER. TCHQ INVESTIGATING TEAM SCHEDULED
TO ARRIVE RIVERS 1200 HOURS THIS DATE

BT 61

C WB RIVERS ARRIVE

Document 59: "Document regarding UFOs seen by military
personnel and civilians on August 29, 1967, near
CFB Rivers, Manitoba." Title: Herzberg Institute of
Astrophysics – Reports on non-meteoric sightings,
unidentified flying objects, UFO's 8/28/1967 © Government
of Canada. Reproduced with the permission of Library
and Archives Canada (2021). Source: Library and Archives
Canada/National Research Council of Canada fonds/e002749330

As far as we can piece together from NRC UFO case file U96, the
sequence of events went like this...

At 0530Z, the Dowdells:

> ...first saw [the] object through upstairs window, rising from [the]
> west. They went outside and observed [the] object proceed in an
> arc towards NE, becoming dimmer as it traveled. Object [was]
> described as very bright white with orange colouring in it. Object
> was round point of light without tail. Arc described as wavering

with alternate dimming and brightening and appearance of stopping occasionally.

Ms Dowdell explained later: "I saw three or four dancing lights... They reminded me of fireflies... These lights moved in either a zig-zag, unpredictable, sudden linear way or in swoops and waves... dancing or flitting across the west to northwest sky."

As she watched: "They would disappear then reappear and then they seemed to all coalesce into a single disc/flattened orb of lights in an ovoid shape like a mandarin orange. This light approached us from the north and slowed until it hovered in place over top of the garages situated slightly to the Northwest of us. This glowing light melded into a shimmering light of indeterminable color. As soon as my brain recognized it as orange, it had already changed to blue, to white, to yellow, to red. The light approached us but there seemed to be no defining shape or structure to it. The color melded or flowed into itself as it halted and hovered there in the sky."

The light then moved off: "After about a minute or two... this light (which at that point had been stationary for about two or three minutes) moved away and gathered speed so that it quickly zoomed off into the north sky. It travelled faster than any aircraft I had ever seen, even US fighter jets. It moved eastward and then seemed to just hover and move around over the town of Rivers."

Ah hour later, at 0630Z, Cpl Fedun saw:

> ...a round ball of orange, white flame with a reddish orange tail which was either very large or very low and which flared up at mid point of its arc. Flaming was clearly visible and very noticeably brightened sky. Direction of travel was SSW to NNE and passed NW of point of observation.

At 0645Z, Commissionaire G. Stefanson reported hearing a loud noise similar to what McArthur would report later. Also, at 0645Z, LAC Hebert "observed an ultraviolet coloured light coming from directly above [his] car which remained stationary for 30-50 seconds and moved away before [the] light disappeared. It was accompanied by an increase in heat in [the] car." However, his companion Judy Ross only saw "a white flashing light, round in form. She feels it was stationary for a period but noticed no temperature change."

At 0700Z, CPL K. McArthur reported hearing an "explosion" that rattled windows and created "vibrations."

Finally, at 0710Z, LAC Taylor saw "a red ball of flame trailed by a blue light or tail, at 3-4000 ft. altitude."

The first problem to deal with is the discrepancy with regard to the differing times of observation. Even if we assume the Dowdells' time of observation is an hour out, there's still the matter of reconciling 0630Z to 0710Z, at least half an hour. It's reasonable to assume that the military observers would be accurate in their times, so it seems possible there was more than one object seen and the Dowdells saw something different from what was observed by the other witnesses. It's strange, though, that the Dowdells, who were diligently watching the sky that night and were at a point overlooking the base that they did not report hearing the rumbling noise an hour later.

The NRC report provides some insight into the actual investigation of the case by military personnel. The U96 file notes:

> LAC Heberts car detained at ME section. Body repairman states light dust on top of car is unlike any other in his experience. There is some bubbling of paint on top. This incident reported to TCHQ by base duty officer. TCHQ investigating team scheduled to arrive Rivers 1200 hours this date.

There are a number of remarkable things to note here. First, Hebert's report was taken seriously enough that his car was impounded as evidence. Second, the military vehicle repairman noted there was odd dust on the car and bubbling of paint on the roof. Third, this was considered such a significant case that RCAF Training Command Headquarters (TCHQ) in Winnipeg sent an "investigating team" to Rivers, which was about 250 kilometres away, or at that time about a four to five hour drive.

What's most significant is that the documents provide the names of the investigating team. In addition to the text of the telexed report to DND, there are handwritten notes on the documents. The handwritten script is quite readable and notes:

S/n Bissky
S/n Bouthier
F/n Smith
From CantrainCom
Visited Rivers 28 Aug

In other words, three personnel were immediately dispatched to the scene from Winnipeg. Since Rivers is at least a four-hour drive from the TCHQ, if they were to arrive by 1200 hours (6:00 am), they would have to have left Winnipeg no later than about 0800 hours, or within the hour that the sightings were reported to CFB Rivers, which according to the file was about 0645 hours. They had to have been roused in the wee hours of the morning, packed into a military transport vehicle and driven out, all within approximately an hour.

This also says something about the team. To have been essentially at the ready, they might have had to be pre-selected, identified as a team and prepared for "action." Even arranging a transport at short notice is impressive in itself.

It's very interesting that the makeup of the team includes a familiar name. The Rivers case in August 1967 occurred only three months after the Falcon Lake incident in Manitoba, only about 400 kilometres to the east of Rivers. It made sense, then, that Squadron Leader Paul Bissky of CFB Winnipeg was part of the investigation team. Bissky, a devout skeptic, was one of the RCAF leads in the Falcon Lake investigation and was already familiar with handling UFO cases. In fact, it's tempting to suggest that he was part of an *ad hoc* UFO investigation team. Thus, getting a call to ship out to investigate a UFO at practically a moment's notice would have made sense for a select group of RCAF personnel.

An additional handwritten note on the page reads:

Telecon w/Robertson & Rivers Stn ADS
Telecon w/Robertson & S/n Bissky 1615Z 29
Aug. Their message 5247 on its way to CFHQ

The documents indicate that there were two telephone conversations: one between the CFB Rivers commander and Wing Commander D. F. Robertson at Canadian Forces Headquarters in Ottawa, the other between Robertson and Bissky, obviously to give him his "marching orders" on the Rivers incident. Robertson himself was also involved in the Falcon Lake case and reviewed all materials relating to that case investigation as well. Perhaps Robertson was in effect the head of the RCAF UFO investigations.

At any rate, when Bissky and his two companions arrived in Rivers, they conducted only a brief investigation before they returned to TCHQ. Their report, dated August 29, 1967, with a time of 1555Z, noted:

TCHQ team conducted short investigation at Rivers and found:

A. No evidence of radiation on suspect car

B. No magnetic field surrounding car which were unlike patterns of similar autos

C. No blistered paint anywhere on car to indicate excessive heat application

D. Dust on car appeared to be ordinary western Canadian dust and which more than likely was picked up while in the gravel pit and travelling to and from Rivers.

E. LAC Hebert is not suffering any ill effects resulting from his encounter. He was to have a white blood cell count conducted and if any abnormality, to be reported. He complained of a severe headache to approximately 12 hours after allegedly sighting the brilliant ultraviolet light

F. Suspect sightings were of a falling meteorite which may have fallen in the Rivers vicinity. Have advised Prof. Leith office, U of Man, in accordance with CFAO71-1. Prof Leith away on vacation and will not be back for one week.

No further action contemplated on this case at this time.

So the team drove out all the way to Rivers but did only a "short investigation." In fact, a handwritten document by Robertson in the file, dated the next day, August 30, 1967, explains: "Cantraincon elected, on their own initiative, to conduct a fast investigation into subject UFO reports."

The report states they did only a visual inspection of the dust on the car, without taking any samples for laboratory analyses. Their opinion that the dust was just from gravel outweighed that of the carpool jockey, who had certainly seen gravel dust before, as indeed CFB Rivers was only a few miles from a gravel pit. But what had happened to the blistered paint?

At least they also tested for abnormal radiation and magnetism. This certainly was because Bissky was aware of the unusual radioactivity found at the Falcon Lake UFO site that he had investigated personally. The test for change in the car's magnetic field was a bit strange, as while there had been several Canadian cases in 1967 where witnesses claimed odd magnetic effects on their vehicles, there was no consistent explanation as to why this would occur in a UFO case. Further, tests of magnetic fields did not show any abnormalities. It's possible this was just a hunch on the part of Bissky and his team, but this raises the question: how does one quickly test for abnormal magnetic fields? With an ordinary compass? Or did they actually have at their disposal a magnetometer or a gauss meter, such as those used by ghost hunters today?

Curiously, Ms Dowdell later stated that the car may actually have been examined after all. She claimed: "There was active speculation around town that the government would cover this up. I remember seeing the car on the train bed car some time in the next days in town with the tarp over it and so did most of the townsfolk of Rivers."

Finally, the TCHQ team noted that LAC Hebert was going to have a blood test to check his white blood cell count. Again, this was definitely because Stefan Michalak had his white blood cell count checked, from speculation that he had been subjected to radiation. However, there is no record of Hebert being examined by the base physician. And why wasn't Hebert's companion, Judy Ross, similarly tested?

Regardless, Bissky and his team decided that the case was nothing more than a "falling "meteorite" (or rather, a meteor). Dr. Ed Leith was a geologist at the University of Manitoba whose expertise included meteoritics, and he was the National Research Council of Canada representative in Winnipeg. Leith was known to be a vocal skeptic and debunker of UFOs as well.

The meteor explanation is viable for the observations of the fireballs with tails passing from the southwest to the northeast. The 30-second duration of the light above the car isn't compatible with meteors or bolides, although UFO witnesses' perception of duration has been suggested to be often in error. But Ross said the light seemed to have been stationary, too. It would have been useful to get more testimony from her as well since her observation differed slightly from that of Hebert.

There was no evidence to suggest that the TCHQ UFO investigation team conducted anything more than a cursory investigation of the case. They didn't interview witnesses in detail, didn't arrange testing of any samples from the car and didn't try to establish a definitive timeline of events.

Despite this, a handwritten summary of their conclusions was sent to Ottawa by E.W. Greenwood, DSC/DCOps. The document, dated September 4, 1967, read:

DOPS 4C
W/C Robertson
1. Reference UFO Report Rivers, Man.
2. The actual sighting reports conform with the appearance of a fireball, and the two observations of "explosion" noises not only fit the fireball pattern but suggest a good probability that some of the incoming material would reach the ground!
3. The only important confusion is the reported time — 5:30 to 7:10 AM. If the times are reliable, we have another coincident meteor or UFOs. Quite possibly the times are guesses — this might be checked.
4. Prof Leith can take up the fireball investigation.

According to this, the final document in the case file, the incident was solved as a fireball/bolide event, even though the observations did not completely fit the explanation. Robertson even acknowledged that the time differences might suggest that two separate objects were involved. At the very least, Dowell's testimony is definitely at odds with the meteor explanation.

If the objects seen were meteors, were there two of them, an hour apart? One fireball and something else? And was Hebert's estimate of duration of the event radically in error? What exactly did he and Ross see? A brilliant, slow-moving object, or simply a bright flash that they assumed lingered because of a sudden shift in night vision adaptation?

If the meteor explanation was valid, what of the "explosion" that rattled windows? It is rare for witnesses to hear the sonic booms of fireballs, as most are high in the atmosphere, even those that explode or fragment. Whether or not Leith investigated or tried to locate pieces of the meteorite through a ground search is not known.

The Rivers case gives some insight into how UFO reports were investigated by the Canadian military. It is especially noteworthy because it involves multiple witnesses, military witnesses, and alleged physical and physiological effects. It remains a curious case, although evidence suggests that at least some witnesses' observations were those of a bright, fragmenting fireball. It is too bad it wasn't more thoroughly investigated.

Squadron Leader Bissky and his team might have been the Canadian equivalent of the USAF Project Blue Book, or perhaps the forerunners of Mulder and Scully themselves.

Project Blue Book in Canada

Between 1947 and 1969, more than 12,000 UFO reports from around the world were gathered by the United States government as part of its various projects looking into what people were claiming to have seen in the skies. The most notable of these was Project Blue Book which has been fictionalized in two very different TV series over the years, one emphasizing how the USAF explained most cases and in the other, definitely not.

Most reports in Project Blue Book were American cases, but a large number of reports were regarding UFO sightings elsewhere around the world, including Canada. In fact, there are 255 Canadian cases in the Blue Book files, of which 12 (or about five per cent) were labeled as "Unidentified."

One of these was case 969, which occurred on September 13, 1951. According to Brad Sparks' *Comprehensive Catalog of 1700 Project Blue Book Unknowns*, it took place in Goose Bay, Labrador, at the 1932nd AACS (Army Airways Communications System) Station at Goose AFB.[1]

At about 9 pm AST, T/Sgt Warner B. Maupin and Cpl. John W. Green, operators of GCA (Ground Controlled Approach) radar, tracked two objects on a collision course, then one evaded to the right upon the request by radio of one of the radar operators. No aircraft were known to be in the area except a C-54 *en route* to landing at Goose AFB which arrived during the second radar tracking (there was a third object tracked at 10:15 pm). The first target painted a strong and steady radar return at 4,000 feet and 140 mph, covering seven miles in three minutes. About three minutes later, a second target was observed with a weak intermittent return above 5,000 feet level of GCA radar. The third target, with similar altitude and speed appeared after the first two had disappeared. There were no visual observations despite efforts by the radar crew, tower crew and C-54 crew.

While this case occurred on Canadian soil and there are cases in the NRC UFO files from this time period, this incident and other similar Blue Book cases involving radar and military personnel are not part of the latter documents.

Like the above case, ten of the 12 Canadian cases labeled as Unidentified in Project Blue Book were from Newfoundland and Labrador. This is undoubtedly because of the strategic importance of the American military presence in that region and its concern for monitoring for "alien" incursions into North American airspace.

In May 1953, a trio of these unidentified cases from Goose Bay were recorded in Blue Book:

On May 1, 1953, about ten miles south of Goose Bay AFB, at about 11:35 pm AST, USAF 59th FIS pilot Capt. R. L. Emberry and radar operator 1st Lt. J. R. Morin were in a F-94 jet interceptor flying at 24,000 feet. Both men and a control tower operator saw a white light that they thought was an unidentified aircraft with a bright visible afterburner, but unlike any known aircraft. The object was about 10,000 feet below the jet and somehow managed to evade interception by the F-94. Both the object and the F-94 climbed to 40,000 feet but the object seemed to outpace the jet and continued to climb until out of sight after approximately 30 minutes of observation.

On May 4, 1953, near Goose Bay AFB, at 1:50 am AST, a Canadian civilian woman saw a football-shaped, metal colored object when it was caught in the glare of a rotating beacon. The object was traveling south at high speed but at a relatively low altitude and disappeared into stratus cloud that was hanging over the base. The witness reported hearing a sound "like tins striking together."

And on May 12, 1953, about 39 miles northwest of Goose Bay AFB, at 3:20 am AST, an unidentified object was tracked on radar by USAF F-94 pilot Lt. D. C. Rogers and radar operator Lt. J. A. Lane. The pilot attempted to intercept the object but was unable to make visual contact.

Three years later, Blue Book case 3969 recorded that on February 12, 1956, about 40 miles southeast of Goose Bay at 10:55 pm AST, two fighter planes were flying at an altitude of 20,000 feet when USAF F-89D pilot Bowen and radar observer Crawford suddenly saw a green and red object. They were astonished to watch as it rapidly circled their jet, and at the same time the crew of the other jet tracked it on radar but could not see it visually. About 15 minutes later, radar operators at Goose Bay painted a stationary target about 40 miles southwest of the base. The two F-89 crews vectored towards the object and had radar contact as well, but when they got within eight miles of the radar target, it vanished.

Blue Book listed cases of unidentified objects over Newfoundland as well. Even just one example gives you a taste of what was being reported by American airmen stationed in Canada, yet not reported to the RCAF for inclusion in the Canadian UFO files.

On July 5, 1955, at 3:00 am AST, two American aircraft were flying over Newfoundland on a refueling mission out of Harmon AFB, near what is now Stephenville on the west coast of the island. USAF 97th Air Refueling Sq pilot Lt. Homer H. Speer and co-pilot Lt Paul Daily of KC-97, with the callsign Archie 29, and pilot Lt. Robert W. Schneck and co-pilot Lt. David Cueldner of KC-97, with the callsign Archie 91, were both at an altitude of 20,000 feet.

Both crews observed two stationary lights to the northwest, over the Gulf of St. Lawrence. They reported their sighting to Harmon AFB at 3:05 am, describing what they were seeing to 2nd Lt. Charles H. Denney, Senior Director, USAF ADC site N-23, Air Defense Direction Center, 640th AC&W Sq, Harmon AFB, operating search and height-finder radar and a backup height-finder. Denney's radar painted an object at 3:07 am, with intermittent contact until 3:56 am, but also detected four or five additional objects in the area.

Archie 29 was in the best position to close on the object and was ordered to do so by Harmon AFB, vectoring to its position 290° from the radar site at a distance of about 80 miles. It was then that the objects started moving to the northeast, accelerating to 275 knots (300 mph), a speed faster than Archie 29 could attain. The object reversed its course and headed south, and Archie 29 got within 18 miles of it, maintaining visual contact.

Lt. Speer gave a play-by-play of the object's changes in direction to the radar site by radio, and Denney noted the changes matched those painted on the radar scope. The height-finder radar had a brief contact with the object at 35,000 ft. The object began climbing at 3:38 am and jet fighters were scrambled but were unable to make radar or visual contact. Lt. Speer lost sight of the object when it had reached about 40,000-50,000 feet, but radar then tracked the object as it accelerated to 1,600 knots (1,800 mph), moving off to the northeast.

At the same time, radar also painted five smaller objects at 5,000-10,000 feet, briefly detected on the height-finder, and thus below the KC-97s, only 60 miles from the base. These objects seemed to be moving very fast, changing direction and azimuth, jumping on and off scopes, forming a circular pattern then changing to a line. They would travel 10-20 miles then change direction while at a speed greater than 1,500+ knots (1,700+ mph). Radar tracked about four objects at point of initial sighting on 40° true heading, speed 300 knots (350 mph).

Other objects were detected at 3:40 am moving at 50°10' N, 57°50' W, along the Long Range or Northern Peninsula. One C-119 aircraft *en route* from Goose Bay to Harmon passed within five miles of the objects, but it was not known if the crew saw them. Radar targets were confirmed by 1st Lt. Anthony G. Scarpace, Ground Electronics Officer of 670th ACW Squadron, who found the radar was operating properly and there were no inversion effects present. The case was investigated by Northeast Air Command (NEAC) AFSSO (AF Special Security Office), reported to USAFSS (US Air Force Security Service), NSA and CIA.

While citizens of Newfoundland were sleeping, American jet fighters had been scrambled to pursue unidentified flying objects that had been seen visually by flight crews and also detected on radar as they traveled overhead in the night sky. Furthermore, when the radar was examined and tested, it was found to be working normally and that atmospheric inversion of the radar returns was not responsible for the incident.

In 1961, Major Edwin A. Jerome, USAF (Ret.), told a UFO organization that in the summer of 1948, a high ranking inspection team was visiting Goose Bay's radar facilities as part of a tour looking at refueling and servicing capabilities for all military and civilian aircraft on North Atlantic air routes. During the inspection of the USAF radar, the operator painted a target on his scope going from the northeast to the southwest, with an impossible speed of 9,000 mph. This caused considerable concern since the base personnel wanted to look good in front of the inspection team, and the airman technician was berated for his error. However, the target appeared a second time and visiting officials observed the target on the screen themselves but dismissed it as poorly calibrated equipment.[2]

But when they went to the Canadian side of the base to inspect the parallel RCAF facility, they learned that the equipment there had also just tracked the same or similar object and both scopes had painted the target as moving at speeds faster than anything known to be possible. The next day, to everyone's chagrin, both radars again reported an anomalous object, this time moving slowly over the base at about 10 mph at 45,000 feet. While the first object was suggested to be a meteor, this one was explained as high flying seagulls. No official report on this incident is in Blue Book or NRC UFO files.

In a review of American military cases of UFOs over Canada, mention should also be made of the first photographs of a flying saucer in North America, taken in Newfoundland as well. This was very early in modern UFO history, on July 10, 1947, only a few weeks after Kenneth Arnold saw flying discs over Mt. Rainier in Washington State, and only a few days after the infamous Roswell crash had made headlines.

Briefly, on that date at about 5:30 pm ADT, two Pan American Airways mechanics and a Trans World Airlines mechanic were driving up a mountain road six miles south of Harmon Field, an American Air Force Base near Stephenville, Newfoundland. Messrs. J. E. Woodruff, J.N. Mehrman and A.R. Leidy reported seeing a silver, disc-shaped object flying high overhead in a horizontal arc over the base and towards the north northeast and its size was comparable to a C-54 transport aircraft. As it flew past, it left behind a trail about 15 miles long. Mr. Leidy, one of the witnesses, had a camera with him and managed to take two Kodachrome pictures of the trail before it dissipated.

From their report:

> On the evening of 10 July 1947, we were coming up over the mountain between here and Stephenville Crossing. The car was going uphill, and we could see the sky through the windshield. [Deleted] said: "Look at the cut in the sky." I looked and saw a blueish-black vapor trail. The clouds were very scattered and were about 8,000 to 10,000 feet. The object passed through and cut the cloud leaving a gap where you could see the blue sky, like a knife had cut it. The edges were feathered similar to a weld, as if you cut a weld in half. The estimated course of the object was approximately north-northeast. The trail was blueish-black and colors were very easily distinguished from the blue sky. The trail was more or less a band across the sky in a straight path. There was no noise.

The case was of considerable interest to American officials, who had concerns that the "new phenomenon" of unidentified flying objects was evidence of Russian incursions into North America. The photos of the Harmon object's trail were viewed as very valuable in assessing the situation, and the Blue Book files contain dozens of pages of correspondence discussing the witnesses' testimony and what the object may have been.

In fact, the Harmon case figured prominently in an intelligence summary prepared for the US Air Training Command (ATC), dated July 16, 1947. The document not only described the investigation into the Harmon photos but put them into context of other reports elsewhere in the world and also noted a Newfoundland case from the day before the Harmon photos, also not in the NRC UFO files.

Flying objects reports summary: The following is a digest of the only current reports that have been received through the intelligence system of this command concerning unidentified flying objects. On 10 June 1947, rumors were drifting into Budapest from rural areas in Hungary to the effect that "silver balls were flashing across the sky in daytime." No accurate description or confirmation of this report was obtained. A Newfoundland constable named [deleted] has reported to personnel of the 1380th AF base unit, ATC, Newfoundland base command, Fort Pepperrell, that on 9 July at 2330 hours local time (0200Z), he observed for a few seconds four "egg-shaped phosphorus-colored discs" followed 10 minutes later by a fifth similar object moving through the air in the vicinity of Grand Falls, Newfoundland. According to the constable, all objects were flying east, moving very fast, and parallel to the ground, at an altitude of 30,000 feet. The first four were in trail formation. The constable described the shape of these objects as being like a "barrelhead or egg" with "black spots on the tail end" but "leaving no smoke trail." The Newfoundland base command reports also mentioned a second unidentified observer of these objects, who described them as being "three-leafed" in shape. A check of weather records reveals that CAVU weather prevailed in the Grand Falls region at the time those objects were reported as being seen. [Deleted] for Trans World Airlines and [deleted] for Pan American Airways, both stationed at Harmon field, Newfoundland, report that on 10 July at 1730 hours local time 2000Z, they observed over that installation a circular wagon-wheel shaped disc of silver color which, at its estimated altitude of 10,000 feet, appeared to be of equal size to the wingspan of a C-54. Weather records indicate that the weather at Harmon during the time this incident occurred was clear with scattered cumulus clouds at an altitude of from 8 to 10,000 feet. These two men report that the disc was first sighted when it appeared about 6 miles south-southwest of Harmon; the two observers report that the disc seemed to "cut the clouds as it passed" over on a north-northeast course leaving a "blueish black trail approximately 15 miles long" which is described as similar in appearance to the beam seen for an instant after a high-powered landing light or searchlight has been switched off. Personnel of the 1388th AAF base unit ATC, Harmon Field, Stephenville, who relayed Mehrman's and Woodruff's report to this office state that Kodachrome pictures were taken of the disc which are now being developed, probably by Eastman at Rochester, New York, and that [deleted] will forward the prints as soon as received.[3]

There are a few discrepancies in the details, but there's no doubt that something had flown over Stephenville that afternoon. The American investigators checked that there were Canadian or British aircraft flying in the area at the time because it was viewed as likely that an aircraft of some kind was responsible. In fact, one Blue Book document noted:

The bluish-black trail seems to indicate ordinary combustion from a turbo-jet engine, athodyd motor, or some combination of these types of power plants. The absence of noise and apparent dissolving of the clouds to form a clear path indicates a relatively large mass flow of a rectangular cross section containing a considerable amount of heat.[4]

Despite this, the official Blue Book explanation of the Harmon case was that the object that caused the smoke trail was simply a meteor or fireball:

Incident #26 - Harmon field, Newfoundland - 10 July 1947

The evidence presented here, and incident #27, #27a, which refers to the same object, favors the hypothesis that the trail of a fireball was seen. The photographs submitted show a typical fireball trail. The quote feathered edges quote left on a cloud which the object broke through could easily have been caused by a fireball.

According to one researcher, the conflicting explanations seem to be because of some politics within the American military administration itself:

The T-2 [Air Force Technology Transfer Program] team excluded a meteor or fireball scenario in their own minds despite the fact that an astronomical event became the official conclusion on the case file. Behind the scenes, T-2 and Washington were still focused on a Soviet connection. Wright Field investigators spoke with the commander of Harmon Field and others to make sure that no British or Canadian aircraft had been in the area at the time. And since they knew no American aircraft were to blame, they privately concluded something of "foreign origin" made that curious split in the clouds over Newfoundland.[5]

So, was it a fireball or an airplane?

One of the most curious Canadian cases in the Blue Book files was not considered unidentified but was categorized as having an explanation. A man from Caledon East, Ontario, wrote a letter to the USAF in which he described his encounter with "a real flying saucer" at 3:50 pm ET on October 31, 1958. The case file about his report read:

> Elliptical object estimated at 10 ft by 20 ft... Aluminum, speed fast & then slow. Observed at alt. of one mile and then descending to 13 ft. Direction of travel NE. Color silver. Rose by secret method of jerks & flops. No sound until object exploded. 10 min observation during daylight. Made seven attempts to land in a field 500 ft from witness and then halted one ft above the ground where it remained motionless for exactly 5 mins. At this time a red glow started at 1 end & when the entire obj was glowing it then exploded. Witness ran away. Has told everyone in the neighborhood but can't convince anyone it wasn't an hallucination. Apparently, the witness believes he saw an obj of some sort. No attempt at a hoax is indicated. If the event depicted actually happened, there would have been some remains [from] the fire or explosion, if nothing more than charred ground. Case listed as Other, psychological causes, rather than hoax, since the witness is convinced the object was actually there.[6]

There is no indication this case was investigated in any way; it was simply assumed that the man had imagined his entire experience.

Finally, a case in Nova Scotia that appears in Blue Book files was originally reported to the FBI in Chicago by an American citizen who had been vacationing in the Maritimes. On July 17, 1952, at about 6:30 pm AT, a woman was leaving Yarmouth Harbour aboard the SS Yarmouth and was standing near its bow looking toward a point of land extending out into the sea. In the clear, blue, cloudless sky, she saw seven "flying saucers":

> The half circles were arranged in a perpendicular formation with their flat sides down. She could not recall whether they were touching or not. The full circles were near the half circles and slightly to their right and were arranged in an inverted triangular formation with two of the circles above and one below at the point of the triangle. The circles were separated by approximately one diameter. She stated that she first sighted these objects over the point of land described above

but that she could not estimate the distance from her. She added that these objects hovered momentarily in the air, then flickering slightly but retaining their relative position to each other as if they were part of a "picture," they slowly descended. She added that she did not know whether they suddenly disappeared above the land or whether they sank beyond the point into the sea but that when they were close to the horizon, they disappeared.[7]

The woman said the discs:

… seemed highly polished and silvery in color and seemed to reflect the rays of the sun, which was a short ways above the horizon directly out to sea. She added that these objects had a distinct shape and that she could see them clearly. She estimated the period during which she observed them to be of about two minutes' duration and stated that all of these objects disappeared at the same time.

The FBI sent the report to the USAF District Commander, who then passed it to the Commanding General of Air Material Command at Wright-Patterson Air Force base in Ohio.

Some well-known and well-investigated Canadian cases were not part of the Blue Book files. Both the Falcon Lake and Shag Harbour incidents were not investigated by USAF personnel, but at least Falcon Lake is noted briefly, and it was included in the USAF-sponsored Condon Report when it was published in 1969.

Nevertheless, the Canadian cases included in Project Blue Book that are not in the NRC UFO files show that while there was a degree of cooperation between American and Canadian military intelligence operations, it was not complete. Canadian UFO cases seem to have been communicated to the USAF, but cases reported to American installations on Canadian soil were another matter.

14

UFOLOGY RESEARCH ANALYSES OF THE NRC UFO FILES

⌐⌐

The thousands of UFO reports in the NRC files just by themselves show that a wealth of data is available to researchers looking to better understand what Canadians have been seeing in the skies over the decades. But what can we learn from the data, exactly? Do the reports give us insight into what UFOs really are? And what do these numbers mean?

I faced a similar question when I first began studying Canadian UFO reports in the 1970s as I started investigating cases and poring over documents. I and my ufology colleagues were receiving reports and gathering information, but we really didn't know the broader perspective or the extent to which Canadians were seeing UFOs and what common characteristics the reports may have had. There were stories about UFO sightings in newspapers, magazines and on TV newscasts, but without access to actual data, it was hard to know what was really going on.

At a gathering of Canadian UFO researchers in the late 1980s, known as the Manitoba Conference on Ufology, we discussed the possibility of conducting a national survey of UFO sightings, and how we could use data from this study to come to some understanding of the nature of UFOs. From this simple beginning, the Canadian UFO Survey was born. Participating UFO groups and investigators put their differences aside and shared basic UFO report information that became part of the Ufology Research of Manitoba (UFOROM) database. Things like witnesses' names and contact information were not needed in such a database, so not only was witness anonymity protected, but local groups and researchers could retain authority over their information.

The Canadian UFO Survey has been produced every year since 1989 and has as of 2021 amassed more than 22,000 UFO case reports. This far more than even the USAF's Project Blue Book acquired during its tenure before it closed in 1969. Data for the Survey were taken from all known published or publicly available sources of UFO reports, using a simple coding scheme based on Dr. J. Allen Hynek's UFOCAT for the Center for UFO Studies in the USA. Sources have included civilian UFO groups' records, but also documents from official government agencies such as the National Research Council, Canadian Forces and Transport Canada.[1]

Only basic data were entered into the UFOROM database such as date, time, location, number of witnesses, colour of object, etc. But from this set of simple data, a number of interesting details have emerged over time. For example, we know that numbers of UFO reports in Canada vary with time and the months of the year, and are correlated with population. (The Survey has been described in detail in other books and is available to view online. The reader is invited to examine the data and annual studies to see what has been found.)

When Ufology Research dived deep into the NRC UFO files, some parallels with the Canadian UFO Survey data became evident, but there were also some differences. The monthly breakdown for the NRC UFO Files was noticeably different than that of the annual Canadian UFO Survey. Like the Canadian UFO Survey, NRC cases showed an expected typical peak in UFO report numbers in the summer months of July and August, which could be interpreted that more potential witnesses are out in summer rather than cold winter months. It's common for witnesses to be gazing at the midsummer night sky while relaxing at the cottages or while camping, but less likely during the deep freeze of January and February in Canada.

Cumulative data for the Canadian UFO Survey show a peak in reports in summer with 12.6 per cent of cases in July and 13.7 per cent of cases in August. The NRC cases had 11.5 per cent and 10.8 per cent, respectively. However, the NRC cases also showed an identical peculiar peak of 11.5 per cent in reported UFO sightings in November. In the Canadian UFO Survey, November data is only 6.1 per cent, and why NRC cases would show an increase is unknown.

The types of UFOs reported can be classified into a handful of basic categories, primarily Nocturnal Lights, Nocturnal Discs and Daylight Discs. In the Canadian UFO Survey data, Nocturnal Discs represent 28.4 per cent of all cases, and Nocturnal Lights are 52.8 percent, more than twice as many. This makes sense because most reported UFOs are only lights seen in the night sky.

The distinction between the two categories is that a Nocturnal Light is simply a distant light seen at night that the witness can't identify. A Nocturnal Disc, on the other hand, is a UFO seen at night that has a definite shape and is not simply a light. When we look at the types of UFOs in the NRC files, there is a higher number of Nocturnal Discs (43 per cent) compared with Nocturnal Lights (36.5 per cent).

A review of Nocturnal Disc reports in the NRC files explains why the numbers are so high compared with Nocturnal Lights: many witnesses observing UFOs at night seemed to estimate them to be at great heights (often citing altitudes of 10-20 thousand feet and higher), but nevertheless described the observed objects as "round." We know, however, that determining the shape of a distant light is of course quite impossible to judge accurately, and the witnesses were likely interpreting the lights as larger objects. When such cases were entered as data, because there was a shape assigned to them, the default would have been Nocturnal Disc rather than Nocturnal Light.

An analysis of NRC UFO reports by province also has some significant differences from the annual Canadian UFO Survey data. The annual Survey shows that the number of UFO cases is related to the population of a given area, and the provinces with the largest populations have the largest number of cases. Similarly, within a province, the largest population centres have the largest number of UFO reports. It's easy to see why this would be so; the more people around to potentially see a UFO in the sky, the more likely there will be reports. This has been true throughout the 30+ years of the Canadian UFO Survey, although there have been some localized UFO flaps with increased numbers from time to time.

Whereas the annual Canadian study clearly shows the population effect that is normally found in UFO data, the NRC analysis has a different distribution altogether. In the NRC files, Alberta cases outnumbered those of more populous BC, and Quebec just barely had more cases than the much lower in population Nova Scotia. Ontario had almost twice as many reports as any other province, including BC and Quebec. Finally, regions with low population densities such as Newfoundland and Labrador had a relatively large number of cases, as did the Northwest Territories.

Some reasons for these anomalies are fairly evident when the data are examined in detail. Alberta is the site of Cold Lake, the large Department of Defence military base where classified aircraft are said to be tested. It is not impossible that many UFOs reported in Alberta could have been tests or training flights.

The joint USA/Canada military base at Goose Bay in Labrador was a staging and refueling point for overseas flights, so many UFOs near there could have been military or commercial aircraft. And the high number of UFOs in Ontario is likely from two factors: the NRC was based in Ottawa and numerous UFO reports were telephoned directly to Herzberg as local calls; and CFB Falconbridge near Sudbury is a major military installation, associated with North American Aerospace Defense Command (NORAD).

Other geographical anomalies are less easily explained, however, especially the overrepresentation of the Maritime provinces in the NRC files in general. Again, this might be partly because of the significant military presence on the Eastern seaboard.

The tabulation of Strangeness as a variable shows that most NRC reports were low in this quality, consistent with the fact that the NRC was looking for meteors and fireballs, and so received many reports of starlike objects and shooting stars. Strangeness is an indication of how unusual a case seems to be. For example, a single distant light in the night sky that is stationary for three or four hours and seen by one witness is not especially odd, and might get a Strangeness rating of about one or two. On the other end of the spectrum, a case where a witness reports close contact or interaction with telepathic humanoid aliens inside a spacecraft could probably be given an eight or nine. (Don't even ask about a case that is considered a ten!)

In the Canadian UFO Survey, the number of UFO reports according to Strangeness rating show an inverse relationship: the higher the Strangeness rating, the fewer reports. The one exception is in very low Strangeness cases which are relatively few in number compared with those of "moderate Strangeness." This is probably because for a witness to see and report a UFO it must already have to be at least a bit out of the ordinary, otherwise it would not be considered strange at all!

During the 30+ years of the Canadian UFO Surveys, the average Strangeness rating has decreased slightly, from about 4.25 to about 3.5. This is possibly due to the decrease over the years in the number of Close Encounter cases and an increase in the number of sightings which are simply lights in the sky with often simple explanations.

Another finding that came out of looking at the NRC data was that the Reliability rating of NRC cases was quite high. The Reliability rating is a measure of how much information exists about a specific case. For example, a case with a low Reliability rating of one or two usually is something like an anonymous phone call to a UFO investigator or organization, stating only that a UFO was seen, without any details or without providing any contact information. A high Reliability case is one in which details of a sighting are known, the witness has been interviewed thoroughly and there is a wealth of documentation about the incident.

NRC cases were generally high Reliability because the actual UFO case data were present, with witnesses' comments and affidavits, observation details, and analyses by RCMP — and in many instances the witnesses themselves were pilots, police, or other highly qualified observers. Not many cases in the Canadian UFO Survey rise to that level of Reliability, given that reports come in through a variety of ways, and only a small fraction are from official sources. Reliability of Survey cases declined over the decades from a high near six to between four and five, reflecting a reduction in the number of UFO cases that are adequately investigated or originate within official agencies.

Analysis by colour showed that most objects reported in both the NRC files and the Canadian UFO Survey were either multicoloured or white. A multicoloured object was usually one that witnesses said had either several lights of various colours or that the object changed colours while under observation. In many cases where this was so, the object viewed was a star or planet low on the horizon, changing colours because of atmospheric distortion.

Since most reported UFOs are nocturnal starlike objects, the abundance of white objects is not surprising. Orange is often associated with the appearance of candle-heated paper lanterns, sent aloft during celebrations such as weddings and memorials. It should not be surprising that daylight discs are most commonly described as black or silver, since many turn out to be aircraft, and most airborne objects will appear dark when viewed in a bright daytime sky. Other colours such as red, blue, and especially green often are associated with bolides (fireballs) — pieces of comets that burn up when encountering Earth's atmosphere at high speed.

The typical number of witnesses in individual NRC cases is somewhat different from results found in other analyses of UFO data including the Canadian UFO Survey. For the NRC cases, the average number of UFO witnesses was 2.47, meaning that the norm was for at least two witnesses of a UFO, and usually more. This means that there was at least one supporting witness who could verify that the object was under observation, as in the case of two people out for a walk when one sees a UFO then nudges his or her companion to look as well. In many NRC cases, the multiplicity of witnesses for UFO reports was because RCMP constables or officers were called out in response to a citizen's "complaint" of a UFO, and the RCMP personnel arrived in time to observe the UFO as well.

This result differs from the Canadian UFO Survey, which has been recording an average number of witnesses as less than two for several years. One important consideration is that the Survey started long after these NRC records. It is possible that the NRC cases had more witnesses because making an official report was supported by the additional witnesses, whereas a typical UFO report today may only have a single witness who reports his or her experience directly to a UFO organization, through email to a website, or directly to a Facebook group. Statistically at least, UFO experiences seem to have become more personal and more of an individual phenomenon in more recent years.

Duration is another category of UFO data collected; this is because UFO researchers have found that the length of time a UFO is observed can be a clue to its possible explanation. As mentioned earlier, a long-duration UFO sighting of the order of a few hours more than likely has an astronomical explanation such as a star or planet. Very short duration sightings of only a few seconds are often meteors, bolides or fireballs.

For the Duration of the NRC cases, two things stand out: the general long period of time that UFOs were seen, plus a paradoxical peak in cases that were less than five seconds in duration. The peak for sightings lasting between one hour and 1.5 hours (and longer) is probably attributable to observations of stars and planets. The very short duration cases were, as noted earlier, probably bolides and fireballs. It is the cases in between that are interesting, in that they were long enough to rule out fireballs and chunks of comets entering the atmosphere, but shorter than observations of stationary astronomical objects.

The time-of-day distribution of NRC cases shows a normal bell-shaped curve, centred around 11 pm, except for an odd hiccup at 6 pm. Otherwise, UFO cases are, as expected, mostly nocturnal lights seen late at night and into the early morning. The Canadian UFO Survey also found a standard bell-shaped curve, so that fewer sightings are reported in late morning or around noon but more are seen and reported once it's dark. It's possible the unexpected peak of NRC UFO reports at 6 pm is due to twilight and darkness occurring close to when many Canadians are traveling home for dinner, therefore looking into the night sky. But why is there no parallel Survey peak? (And no, the number of UFO reports does not increase right when bars and pubs tend to close.)

Witnesses' descriptions of the shapes of UFOs vary greatly. UFO researchers know that the shape of a perceived object depends on many factors such as the witness' own visual acuity, the angle of viewing, the distance of viewing, and the witness' own biases and ability to put into words what he or she has seen. Nevertheless, in combination with other case information such as duration, shape can be a good clue towards a UFO's possible explanation.

In the Canadian UFO Survey, about 40 per cent were of "point sources"— that is, "starlike" objects or distant lights, and this is also about the same percentage in the NRC data.

The classic "flying saucer" or disc-shaped object comprised less than five per cent of all Canadian UFO Survey cases and even the "triangle" shape, which some ufologists have suggested has today supplanted the classic "saucer," was only four percent of all cases in 2021.

The breakdown of NRC data by reported shape of UFO shows a similar distribution. The most reported "shape" is simply a point source, reflecting the reality that most UFOs are starlike objects in the night sky. The next most common shape was "round," but this is problematic, as many witnesses thought that a distant starlike object was "round," something impossible to determine when the observed UFO was also "miles away" or even, as some witnesses reported, "in orbit."

The distribution of UFOs across provinces has already been discussed, but NRC data also included specific population centres as sighting locations. As in the Canadian UFO Survey, cities with the largest metropolitan populations have the most UFO reports, with two significant anomalies: in the NRC files, Winnipeg was third behind Montreal and Vancouver, but ahead of Toronto. It is possible the Toronto catch basin was not defined broad enough to include all bedroom communities.

The breakdown by Evaluation (or Conclusion) for UFO reports is often hotly disputed among UFO fans and researchers. The Canadian UFO Survey has four operative categories:

Explained, Insufficient Information, Possible or Probable Explanation, and Unknown (or Unexplained). It is important to note that a classification of Unknown does not imply that an alien spacecraft or mysterious natural phenomenon was observed; no such interpretation can be made with certainty, based solely on the given data (though the probability of this scenario is technically never zero).

In most cases, an evaluation was made subjectively by both contributing investigators and the survey data handlers and analysts. The category of Unknown was adopted if a report contained enough information such that a conventional explanation could not be satisfactorily proposed. This does not mean that a case will never be explained, but only that a viable explanation was not immediately obvious.

The level and quality of UFO report investigation varies because there are no explicit and rigorous standards for UFO investigation. Investigators who are "believers" might be inclined to consider most UFO sightings as mysterious, whereas those with more of a skeptical predisposition might tend to subconsciously (or consciously) reduce the Unknowns in their files.

In the Survey, the percentage of Unknowns each year has varied from as high as 23 per cent to only a few percent. Curiously, however, the percentage of Unknowns relative to the number of cases each year has decreased with time, so that the more cases which are reported in a year, the fewer are unexplained. This may mean that an increase in UFO reports could be caused by the public becoming more aware of ways to file UFO sightings with UFO organizations, perhaps because of increased media coverage of the phenomenon. Another way of looking at this would be that the increase in explained cases or IFOs is because better investigation is being done by serious ufologists.

Because the NRC files are historical records with gaps in available data for each case, it was impossible to evaluate most of them post-hoc. However, even with this limitation, some cases had enough documented investigation and detail that an evaluation was possible. About five per cent of the total number of cases in the NRC files were considered Unexplained, such as those where there were many documents detailing the RCMP or RCAF investigations.

The fact that there are unexplained cases in both the Canadian UFO Survey and the NRC UFO files is not proof of alien visitation but simply an indication that some reports cannot be resolved. We can put this into perspective by using an analogy of homicides under criminal investigation by police departments. Some cases remain "on the books" without resolution, not because aliens were the murderers, but because the evidence does not point to a specific culprit or cause with enough authority or evidence to make a conviction.

POSTSCRIPT

~

I
t could all have been settled back in 1947.

One of the documents within the NRC UFO files might suggest that the debate about the nature of UFOs could have been settled right at the beginning of the "modern" era of ufology, but it was never followed up.

On September 5, 1947, a letter was received by the Royal Canadian Air Force that was very succinct and to the point. It had been written by a resident of St-Thomas-D'Aquin, a neighbourhood in the north part of Saint-Hyacinthe, Quebec. The author of the letter to the RCAF was very brief; her (or his) letter was translated from French and the translation is in LAC.

The letter read, in full:

Sir:

I beg to inform you that I found a Flying Saucer on my property.

If you are interested, please, get in touch with me, and I shall send it to you.

Faithfully yours,
[Redacted]

That's it.

There was nothing in the file to suggest the letter was acted upon, although a handwritten note on the translated letter read: "This is perhaps a meteorite and Dr. Millman of the Dominion Observatory may be interested."

A few things to note: First, a meteorite is simply a rock. Why would anyone call one a flying saucer? Second, if this was a joke, writing a letter to the air force seems like carrying things a bit far. Third, the letter was taken seriously enough by the RCAF that it was translated — all 31 words of it. It was even considered worthwhile to suggest that Dr. Millman, an expert in meteorites, might be interested in the rock, if that's what it was. Fourth, and most importantly, it doesn't sound like anyone actually took the letter writer up on the offer.

It's too bad. Maybe the mystery of UFOs might have been solved in Canada in 1947.

Or not.

NOTES

~

Introduction

1. Helene Cooper, Ralph Blumenthal and Leslie Kean. Glowing Auras and 'Black Money': The Pentagon's Mysterious U.F.O. Program. *New York Times*, Dec. 16, 2017. https://www.nytimes.com/2017/12/16/us/politics/pentagon-program-ufo-harry-reid.html

2. "From the Office of House Minority Leader Gerald R. Ford, R-Mich." March 25, 1966. In: Gerald Ford UFO Documents. *The Black Vault.* https://documents.theblackvault.com/documents/ufos/FordUFO.pdf

Chapter 1

1. Hayes, Matthew (2019). *A History of Canada's UFO Investigation, 1950-1995.* PhD Dissertation, Trent University, Peterborough, Ontario.

2. Letter to the Office of Information at the Department of National Defence, 4 March 1965. © Government of Canada. Reproduced with the permission of Library and Archives Canada (2021). Source: Library and Archives Canada/ Department of National Defence/vol. 17988 file HQC 940-105, part 2 [CBC]

3. Title: Unidentified Flying Objects: Suggested Statement by the Minister of National Defence, April 20, 1965 © Government of Canada. Reproduced with the permission of Library and Archives Canada (2021). Source: Library and Archives Canada/Department of National Defence/e002799662 to e002799665 [Arnell statement for MoD]

4. Dittman, Geoff. (2006). Government UFO Investigations. In: Rutkowski, Chris and Dittman, Geoff. *The Canadian UFO Report.* Dundurn Press, Toronto. pp. 220-239.

5. Friedman, Stanton T. (2008). *Flying Saucers and Science*. New Page Books, NJ. p.40.

6. *Huffington Post*. June 5, 2013. 2013. "Paul Hellyer, Ex-Defence Minister, Believes In Aliens." https://www.huffingtonpost.ca/2013/06/05/paul-hellyer-aliens-ufos-video_n_3390295.html

7. "Former Canadian Cabinet Minister Paul Hellyer Lunch 'n' Learn." August 18, 2016. https://www.rostie.com/former-canadian-cabinet-minister-paul-hellyer-lunch-n-learn/ and: "Transcription of Paul Hellyer testimony: People's Disclosure Saturday, 11 May 2013 http://removingtheshackles.blogspot.com/2013/05/transcription-of-paul-hellyer-testimony.html

8. Herzberg Institute of Astrophysics - Reports on non-meteoric sightings, unidentified flying objects, UFO's 7/7/1967 © Government of Canada. Reproduced with the permission of Library and Archives Canada (2021). Source: Library and Archives Canada/National Research Council of Canada fonds/e002749793 to e002749819 [Robertson Briefing]

9. *Scientific Study of Unidentified Flying Objects*, Conducted by the University of Colorado Under contract No. 44620-67-C-0035 with the United States Air Force. Dr. Edward U. Condon, Scientific Director, 1968.

10. Druffel, Ann. (2003). *Firestorm: Dr. James E. McDonald's Fight for UFO Science*. Wild Flower Press, Columbus, NC.

11. Tennyson, Rod. August 15, 2018. "1960s: Dr. Gordon Patterson establishes The UTIAS UFO Project." University of Toronto Institute for Aerospace Studies. https://www.utias.utoronto.ca/2018/08/15/1960s-dr-gordon-patterson-establishes-the-utias-ufo-project/

12. "Red Pill Junkie." February 1, 2021. "Dr. Avi Loeb and the Scientific Study of UFOs." https://www.dailygrail.com/2021/02/dr-avi-loeb-and-the-scientific-study-of-ufos/

13. For example: Schreyer, Edward. Notice Paper, No. 487, October 18, 1967. House of Commons Votes and Proceedings, 27th Parliament, 2nd Session: 1-64. https://parl.canadiana.ca/view/oop.proc_HOC_2702_1/1045?r=0&s=1

15. For example: Mather, Barry. Unidentified Flying Objects, February 6, 1969. House of Commons Debates, 28th Parliament, 1st Session: Vol. 5. p. 5234. https://parl.canadiana.ca/view/oop.debates_HOC2801_05/692?r=0&s=1

Chapter 2

1. McMillan, Tim. The witnesses. *Popular Mechanics*. Nov. 12, 2019. https://www.popularmechanics.com/military/research/a29771548/navy-ufo-witnesses-tell-truth/

2. Roos, Dave. When UFOs Buzzed the White House and the Air Force Blamed the Weather. Jan. 15, 2020. https://www.history.com/news/ufos-washington-white-house-air-force-coverup

Chapter 4

1. Clan Lake, Northwest Territories, June 22, 1960. Library and Archives Canada. Canada's UFOs: The search for the unknown. http://www.collectionscanada.gc.ca/ufo/002029-1000.01-e.html

Chapter 5

1. Michalak, Stan and Rutkowski, Chris. (2019). *When They Appeared: Falcon Lake 1967: The Inside Story of a Close Encounter.* August Night Books, London.

2. Falcon Lake, Manitoba, May 20, 1967. Library and Archives Canada. Canada's UFOs: The search for the unknown. https://www.bac-lac.gc.ca/eng/discover/unusual/ufo/Pages/GeoMaps.aspx#mb

Chapter 6

1. Ledger, Don. (2007). *Maritime UFO Files.* Nimbus Publishing, Halifax.

2. *Scientific Study of Unidentified Flying Objects,* Conducted by the University of Colorado Under contract No. 44620-67-C-0035 with the United States Air Force. Dr. Edward U. Condon, Scientific Director, 1968. Chapter 2: Case Studies During the Term of the Project, Case 34, North Atlantic, Fall 1967, pp. 538-540.

Chapter 9

1. Volk, Tom. Tom Volk's Fungi. *Marasmius oreades,* the fairy ring mushroom. March 2003. http://botit.botany.wisc.edu/toms_fungi/mar2003.html

2. Gummer, W.K. et al. (1980). *Cosmos 954: The occurrence and nature of recovered debris.* NASA STI/Recon Technical Report.

3. Rutkowski, Chris. (1997). "The Langenburg CE2 Case: When UFOs left their mark." In: Evans, Hilary and Stacy, Dennis. *UFOs 1947-1997.* John Brown Publishing, London. 1997. pp. 120-130.

4. _____. (1880). *Scientific American,* Volume 43, no. 2, July 10, 1880, p.24.

5. Wilkins, Harold T. (1967). *Flying Saucers Uncensored.* Pyramid Books, NY. pp. 237-238.

6. Suffield Memorandum No. 49/67 © Government of Canada. Reproduced with the permission of Library and Archives Canada (2021). Source: Library and Archives Canada/https://www.bac-lac.gc.ca/eng/discover/unusual/ufo/ Documents/Duhamel-inspection-report.pdf

Chapter 10

1. Fawcett, Larry and Greenwood, Barry. (1984). *Clear Intent.* Prentice-Hall, NJ. pp. 46-48.
2. Ibid.
3. Klass, Philip. (1983). *UFOs: The public deceived.* Prometheus Book, NY. pp. 107-109.
4. Campagna, Palmiro. (2010). *The UFO Files: The Canadian Connection Exposed.* Stoddart Publishing Company, Toronto. pp. 127-136.
5. _____. (1975). "Ontario police sight 4 UFOs." *Winnipeg Tribune,* November 13, 1975.
6. Sparks, Brad. Dec. 11, 2000. [On the Falconbridge UFO case] http://www. ufoupdateslist.com/2000/dec/m12-002.shtml
7. Wilson, Daniel. March 1, 2010. Fw: Nov. 11, 1975; CFS Falconbridge, Ontario, Canada http://www.nicap.org/reports/751111falconbridge_rep.htm
8. Dean, Paul. Feb. 6, 2017. "OPREP-3" - A Classified US Military Reporting Channel For UFO Incidents? Part 9. http://ufos-documenting-the-evidence. blogspot.com/2017/02/

Chapter 12

1. To The Stars Academy. 2018. *An Introduction to The ADAM Research Project.* July 26, 2018. https://dpo.tothestarsacademy.com/blog/ an-introduction-to-the-adam-research-project
2. _____. (1966). "The mysterious chunk of hardware at Ottawa." *Topside,* no. 20, Spring 1966, pp. 4-6.
3. Ibid.
4. Ibid.
5. Ibid.
6. Ibid.
7. Cameron, Grant. (undated). "Canadian Program Director Discusses Communication with Aliens." http://www.presidentialufo.com/old_site/ smith_interview.htm

8. Smith, Wilbert B. (1964). *The new science*. Fenn-Graphic Publishing Co., Ltd., Ottawa. http://www.rexresearch.com/smith/newsci~1.htm

9. _____. (1961). "Wilbert B. Smith." http://roswellproof.homestead.com/debris8_misc.html#anchor_3697

10. _____. (1966). "The mysterious chunk of hardware at Ottawa." *Topside*, no. 20, Spring 1966, pp. 4-6.

11. _____. (1967). "The mystery of UFO hardware." *Topside*, no. 24-25, Spring/Summer 1967, pp. 10-11.

12. _____. (1968). "Unidentified hardware mystery deepens." *Topside*, no. 27, Winter 1968, p.4

13. Ibid.

14. _____. (1968). "Latest report on the mystery metal." *Topside*, no. 29, Summer 1968, pp. 11-12.

15. Ibid.

16. Craig, Roy. (1995). *UFOs: An Insider's View of the Official Quest for Evidence*. University of North Texas Press. pp. 121-132.

17. Ibid.

18. Ibid.

19. Ibid.

20. Ibid.

21. Craig, Roy. In: *Scientific Study of Unidentified Flying Objects*, Conducted by the University of Colorado Under contract No. 44620-67-C-0035 with the United States Air Force. Dr. Edward U. Condon, Scientific Director, 1968. Chapter 3: Direct Physical Evidence. Parts of UFOs, or UFO Equipment, pp. 133-135.

22. _____. (1968). "Unidentified hardware mystery deepens." *Topside*, no. 27, Winter 1968, pp. 4-9.

23. Ibid.

24. Ibid.

25. Ibid.

26. Ibid.

27. Craig, Roy. (1995). *UFOs: An Insider's View of the Official Quest for Evidence*. University of North Texas Press. pp. 121-132.

28. Ibid.

29. _____. (1970). "More mystery added to Ottawa's mysterious chunk of hardware." *Topside*, No. 33, Winter/Spring 1970, pp. 13-17.

30. Ibid.

31. Matthews, Arthur H. (1973). *The wall of light: Nikola Tesla and the Venusian space ship, the X-12.* IOP Technologies Inc. https://xn--stverstuuv-fcb.de/media/files/Tesla-buch-englisch-matthewswallight.pdf

32. _____. (1970). "More mystery added to Ottawa's mysterious chunk of hardware." *Topside,* No. 33, Winter/Spring 1970, pp. 13-17.

33. _____. (1971). "New developments on Ottawa's mystery metal." *Topside,* no. 35, Winter 1971, pp. 29-33.

34. _____. (1970). "More mystery added to Ottawa's mysterious chunk of hardware." *Topside,* No. 33, Winter/Spring 1970, pp. 13-17.

35. Ibid.

36. Ibid.

37. Ibid.

38. _____. (1970). "Latest report on Ottawa's mystery metal." *Topside,* no. 34, Summer/Fall 1970, pp. 22-23.

39. Ibid.

40. Ibid.

41. _____. (1971). "New developments on Ottawa's mystery metal." *Topside,* no. 35, Winter 1971, pp. 29-33.

42. Ibid.

43. Ibid.

44. Ibid.

45. Ibid.

46. Ibid.

47. Ibid.

Chapter 13

1. Sparks, Brad. (2016). *Comprehensive Catalog of 1,700 Project Blue Book UFO Unknowns: Database Catalog* (Not a Best Evidence List) Work in Progress (Version 1.27, Dec. 20, 2016). http://www.cisu.org/wp-content/uploads/2017/01/Sparks-CATALOG-BB-Unknowns-1.27-Dec-20-2016.pdf

2. Hall, Richard, editor, UFO Evidence, National Investigations Committee on Aerial Phenomena, Washington, D. C., 1964, page 82-83 http://www.project1947.com/folio/1948_labrador.htm

3. Extract from Weekly Intelligence Summary, ATC, 16 June 1947. *Project Blue Book, 1947-1969,* National Archives, T1206, NARA, Roll 0002, July 1947.

4. NICAP. (undated). The Harmon Field Photo Case, 10 July 1947. http://www. nicap.org/reports/470710harmon_report2.htm

5. Ibid.

6. 1 October 1958, Caledon East. *Project Blue Book, 1947-1969*, National Archives, T1206, NARA, Roll 0034.

7. Spot Intelligence Report, Flying discs, Yarmouth Harbour, Nova Scotia, 1830 Hours, 17 July 1952. *Project Blue Book, 1947-1969*, National Archives, T1206, NARA, Roll 0012, July 1952.

Chapter 14

1. Ufology Research. (undated). *The Canadian UFO Survey*. http://www. canadianuforeport.com/

INDEX

~

Y

www.ingramcontent.com/pod-product-compliance
Lightning Source LLC
Chambersburg PA
CBHW031043110426
42740CB00048B/796